THE Witch's Magical HANDBOOK

GAVIN FROST, Ph.D., D.D.
AND YVONNE FROST, D.D.

REWARD
BOOKS

REWARD BOOKS
An imprint of Prentice Hall Press
A member of Penguin Putnam Inc.
375 Hudson Street
New York, New York 10014
www.penguinputnam.com

Library of Congress Cataloging-in-Publication Data

Frost, Gavin.
    The witch's magical handbook / by Gavin Frost and Yvonne Frost.
        p.   cm.
    ISBN 0-7352-0200-1
        1. Witchcraft.   I. Frost, Yvonne.   II. Title.

BF1566.F84 2000
133.4'3—dc21   00-039025

Printed in the United States of America

20   19   18   17   16   15   14   13   12 11   10

ISBN 0-7352-0200-1

Dedication

To all the children.

I AM JUST A CHILD

My name is Chea' Paz, which means Grandfather of Peace. The name was given to me by the Indians of my land, and I hold this name with pride. In my many years of existence I have never felt more like a child than I do now. This new world which I have embarked on has made me feel like an alien in my own land. The many years of my studies before entering the School of Wicca seem like just a drop of rain now. I have only completed the Basic Witchcraft course, but the outside reading and the studies I have done have opened the door even more for me. As a grown man I look in the mirror and all I see is a child of the Creator who is looking and praying to the God and Goddess for guidance through the new and enchanted world. I feel that even when I reach the young age of 95, I will still be just a child. For even now I wish on a falling star, chase a leaf in the wind and "believe in Witches!"

So from this child to all, Blessed be the Children.

Chea' Paz
The previous Poet Laureate of Mexico

About the Cover

Nirvana, represented by the purple and white background, is difficult to attain, often hidden behind the darkness of our own temporal lives.

The triple circle surrounding *The* represents a Witch's temple, forever remembered in the lines of Samuel Taylor Coleridge:

> *Weave a Circle round him thrice,*
> *And close your eyes in holy dread;*
> *For he on honey-dew hath fed,*
> *And drunk the milk of Paradise.*

The circles also represent three levels of awareness as we enter any temple. The outermost circle keeps back the Abyss of the world. The second circle represents the Plane of Our Understanding. The innermost represents the Spiritual Plane.

The Pentagram represents the spiritual truths of the Witch's alternative spirituality, fully explained in Chapter XIII of this book, "The Witch's Spiritual Path."

The green of the typeface represents new life, new beginnings, and springtime; for through the information herein your life will be renewed and will grow afresh.

OTHER BOOKS BY THE SAME AUTHORS

Title	Published	Publisher
Astral Travel	1982	Granada
U.S.A. Edition	1986	Weiser
Portuguese Edition	1992	Editora Siciliano
Romanian Edition	1998	Teora
Spanish Edition	1992	Humanitas
Italian Edition	1991	Mediterranee
Good Witch's Bible	1991	Godolphin House
Good Witch's Guide to Life	1991	Godolphin House
Helping Yourself with Astromancy	1980	Parker Publishing
Magic Power of Witchcraft	1976	Parker Publishing
German Edition	1978	Hexenbuches
Modern Witch's Guide to Beauty, Vigor, and Vitality	1978	Progress Books
The Mariner's Manual	1988	Cornell Maritime Press
Meta-Psychometry	1978	Parker Publishing
Power Secrets from a Sorcerer's Private Magnum Arcanum	1980	Parker Publishing
The Prophet's Bible	1991	Weiser
Tantric Yoga	1989	Weiser
Indian Edition	1994	Motilal Banarsidass
Portuguese Edition	1995	Bertrand Brasil
Who Speaks for the Witch?	1991	Godolphin House
Wiccan Census	1991	Godolphin House
Witchcraft: the Way to Serenity	1968	Godolphin House
The Witch's Bible	1972	Nash
Magic Power of White Witchcraft	1999	Reward Books
Witch's Grimoire of Ancient Omens, Portents, Talismans, Amulets, and Charms	1979	Parker Publishing
Witch Words	1993	Godolphin House
Your Sun Sign Cookbook	1996	Godolphin House
She Died by Candlelight	1998	Godolphin House
The Dead Frog Is Mine	1996	Godolphin House

About the Authors

Gavin and Yvonne have lived by and taught the principles of Witchcraft for a total of more than 80 years. In that time they have formally taught more than 10,000 students, and have mailed more than five million responses to querents around the world. From their own experiences and from the experiences of students, they have written some 22 books, some of which have been translated into five languages.

They have that rare ability to simplify complex ideas, as you will see when you read this book.

In 1968 they founded the Church and School of Wicca in an effort to correct widespread misinformation about the Craft. Attacked because of fear in the Christian community, they have successfully defended their spiritual path and have seen it declared a legitimate religion in federal appeals court.

They recently revised their controversial *The Witch's Bible* into *Good Witch's Bible* and the best-selling *The Magic Power of Witchcraft* into *The Magic Power of White Witchcraft*.

Gavin has worked with mystics and with leaders of alternative religions in most countries of the western world, from Aborigines in Australia to Zulus in Africa. He was initiated as a Witch in 1951, and is one of the few western Witches to wear the old-fashioned spirit-through-fire scar on his wrist.

Yvonne, too, is an initiated Witch (1968) and is an accomplished healer, having healed many people and animals. In Missouri she healed a calf under the gaze of a reporter and a cameraman. (The calf never revealed its religious affiliation.) She is a past member of International Mensa, the association for persons having unusually high IQs.

These two forever-young elders of the pagan/Wiccan community have done thousands of hours of presentations through radio, TV, and lectures, in their effort to right past wrongs done to Witches and to educate non-Wiccans about this alternative spirituality. Shows they have done range from Donahue and Imus to the more serious Larry King, as well as Pat Robertson's 700 Club.

Table of Contents

INTRODUCTION. xvii

Chapter 1

The Witch's Magical Life   1

WHAT WITCHES DO   /   1

MAGIC IS REAL   /   4

CHARACTERISTICS OF THE FORCE   /   6

THE WEB OF THE WYRD   /   8

RENATA'S WHITE CADILLAC   /   9

MIND KEYS   /   10

EXAMPLES OF PSYCHIC HEALING   /   11

VISUALIZE YOUR FUTURE   /   11

MAKE A COMPLETE PICTURE   /   12

AVOID UNWELCOME SURPRISES   /   12

BEVY AND THE COFFEE KING   /   13

IDENTIFY YOUR MAGICAL OPTIONS   /   14

BECOME A SELF-ACTUALIZING WITCH   /   14

YOUR TEN-STEP ACHIEVEMENT CHART   /   16

YOUR URGENT NECESSITY   /   17

ALISON AND HER UNWANTED BUDDY   /   18

YOU'LL GET WHAT YOU NEED   /   19

SPELL-CASTING 101   /   20

JEROME GETS HIS HOUSE   /   22

FLESHING OUT YOUR SPELL   /   24

Chapter II

Operating the Web of the Wyrd 25

The Web of the Wyrd Is Real / 25

Twelve Examples of the Web in Operation / 25

Empowering the Web of the Wyrd / 31

Spell-Work 201 / 32

Gladys Calls the Dog Catcher / 33

The Language of Spells / 34

Edwin Used the Wrong Picture / 37

More Is Better / 38

Mind Keys or Triggers for Seven Intents / 39

The Patient Died / 45

Hermes Trismegistus / 46

Wally D and the Native Americans / 47

What Went Wrong / 48

Circles Within Circles / 48

Don't Pick at It / 49

The Sorceress' Cat / 50

Summary / 50

Chapter III

Spell-Work 301 53

Two Plus Two Sometimes Equals Ten / 53

Fireworks and Spells / 54

Gustave Made It Happen / 55

The Human/Earth Dynamo Effect (HEDE) / 56

Stone God/esses or "Mascots" / 58

The Ancient God/esses / 59

Gemstones and Crystals / 60

Roberta Saves Her Grandbaby / 61

The Powers in Metals and Woods / 62

Your Guide to the Powers of Crystals, Metals, and Woods / 63

THE COSMOS / 63

GEOLOGICAL FAULTS / 64

RUNNING WATER / 65

DON GETS FRUSTRATED / 66

YOUR TEN-STEP SPELLING GUIDE / 67

DON'S SPELL / 70

THE NURSES WERE AMUSED / 71

FIXING A SPELL / 71

YOUR TABLE OF MIND TRIGGERS FOR REVERSING INTENTS / 72

SENATOR HELMS AND THE POSTAL RESTRICTIONS / 74

PSYCHIC EMPOWERMENT / 75

TUNING, TIMING, AND TRANSMITTING / 76

Chapter IV

Solo, Duet, or Small Chamber Group   77

VIVE LA DIFFÉRENCE! / 77

WHEN ONE PLUS TEN EQUALS ZERO / 80

DIADIC HEDE / 80

NAOMI GETS OUT OF THE HOSPITAL / 82

NO SEX, PLEASE. WE'RE RAISING POWER / 82

THE CONDOM COMPACT / 83

THE USEFUL DIET / 83

THE FAST / 84

THE ENDORPHIN CONNECTION / 85

MELISSA FEEDS THE DUCKS / 86

LEARN AND PROGRESS / 88

YOUR MAGICAL COMPANION / 88

SYLVIA NO LONGER WEEPS / 89

LOVE SPELL—INTENTS / 91

LOVE SPELLS—ETHICS AND CARE / 91

THE UNIVERSAL TRUTH—IT'S ALL THE SAME STUFF / 92

AMANDA, JAKE, DEBBIE, AND JOHN OVERCOME DEPRESSION / 94

SUMMARY / 96

Chapter V

The Science Behind a Witch's Healing Miracles 97

SCIENCE AGREES WITH THE WITCHES / 97

THE MAGIC BULLET / 99

TREATING THE CAUSE, NOT THE SYMPTOMS / 100

EILEEN BREAKS BOTH ARMS AND SAVES HER MARRIAGE / 101

WITCH, HEAL THYSELF / 102

GINNY CURES HER SKIN CANCER / 104

THE STRESS-BALANCING ACT / 105

RECOGNIZING STRESS MALADJUSTMENT / 106

THE OVERSTRESSED DANCE TEACHER / 108

HAVE YOU TRIED THE NEW DRUG FOR DEPRESSION YET? / 109

IT'S NOT YOUR BODY'S FAULT / 109

ACCUMULATED STRESS / 110

GEORGINE SAVES BETTY'S LIFE AND HER JOB / 111

GEORGINE'S ADVICE ABOUT REDUCING STRESS / 112

PROACTIVE VERSUS REACTIVE / 116

RAGLAND'S SIGN / 117

STRESSORS IN YOUR LIFE / 117

AVOIDANCE THERAPY / 119

SUMMARY / 120

Chapter VI

The Witch's Healing Grimoire 121

WITCHCRAFT AND ALTERNATIVE MEDICINE / 121

HERBS AND THEIR EFFECTS / 122

YOUR SHORT LEXICON OF USEFUL HERBS / 123

EDMUND AND SOO LO'S PRESCRIPTION / 126

PSYCHIC HEALING / 127

THE AURA AND ENERGY FLOW / 128

THE WITCH SAVES GLEN / *128*

MAGICALLY REPLACING LOST ENERGY / *129*

MAKING A MEDICINE BAG TODAY / *130*

CHARGING YOUR TALISMAN, MEDICINE BAG, OR HERBAL
  PREPARATION / *134*

MAKING A MODERN MEDICINE BAG / *136*

PREPARING YOUR OWN WITCH'S POTIONS / *137*

DEATH, THE ULTIMATE HEALER / *142*

SUMMARY / *144*

Chapter VII

The Witch's Defragmented Soul   145

THE SELFISH WITCH / *145*

A FRAGMENTED SPIRIT / *145*

HOW YOU LOSE SOUL PIECES / *147*

MILDRED ALMOST DIES / *148*

WHO OWNS YOU? / *149*

YOUR FIVE-STEP SYSTEM FOR RETRIEVAL OF SOUL PIECES / *150*

AYESHA AND HER FLOWER GARDEN / *152*

PSYCHIC VAMPIRES ARE REAL / *153*

TINA AND THE ACCIDENT / *154*

THE BALANCE AMONG SELFISHNESS, KINDNESS, AND LOVE / *155*

THE "SELFISH" WITCH? / *156*

CO-DEPENDENCE, POSITIVE AND NEGATIVE / *157*

GETTING YOUR SOUL BACK TOGETHER / *158*

GROWTH AND KARMA / *159*

THE TWO-HAMBURGER PROBLEM / *160*

Chapter VIII

How a Witch Recharges Herself   163

UNLIMITED ENERGY CAN BE YOURS / *163*

SOURCES OF PSYCHIC POWER / *164*

CRYSTAL POWER / *164*

GRETA AVOIDS SUICIDE / *165*

YOUR OWN CRYSTAL POWER BANK / *166*

RENEWING YOUR LIFE FORCE / *168*

GWEN AND THE PRODUCE MANAGER / *168*

USING YOUR PENDULUM / *169*

POWER FROM THE EARTH / *170*

ELLA AND HER HERBS / *170*

WINDOW BOXES AND GARDENS / *172*

DORIS SAVES HER $50,000-A-YEAR JOB / *173*

FAMILIARS / *174*

GLORIA JEAN'S FAMILIARS SAVED HER LIFE / *175*

CHOOSING YOUR FAMILIAR / *176*

EARTH SERENITY / *176*

A WITCH'S MORNING EXERCISE / *177*

LIVING ON THE HILL / *179*

HEARTH GOD/ESSES / *180*

EDNA AND HO TEI / *181*

MAKING YOUR OWN HEARTH GOD/ESS / *182*

CONCLUSION / *184*

Chapter IX

The Domain of the Witch 185

YOUR HOME'S FORCES / *185*

WALLS HAVE FEELINGS, TOO / *185*

DONNA'S $100,000 HOME-IMPROVEMENT PLAN / *187*

DONNA'S FIX-IT-UP METHODS / *188*

LET THE WALLS SPEAK / *189*

BALANCING THE FORCES IN A ROOM / *190*

YOUR CIRCLE OF BALANCE / *190*

BEN AND THE FRIENDLY SPIRIT / *194*

CONTACTING SPIRIT PRESENCES / *194*

PREPARING FOR YOUR MAGICAL LIFE / *195*

MACK AND WENDY RECLAIM AN OLD HOUSE / 196

YOUR OWN MAGICAL ROOM / 198

DECIDING ON YOUR PRIORITIES / 199

JANICE HAPPILY QUITS HER JOB / 199

THE GAEA CONNECTION / 200

SUMMARY / 202

Chapter X
Foretelling Your Future 203

THE WITCH'S MAGICAL GUIDANCE / 203

MOTHER SHIPTON AND THE CARDINAL / 204

YOUR AUTOSCOPE: GATEWAY TO PROPHECY / 205

ZENOBIA QUITS / 206

IN YOUR OWN HEAD / 207

OMENS AND PORTENTS IN YOUR LIFE / 208

YOUR GUIDE TO INTUITIVE FEELINGS / 209

MEN, WOMEN, AND DANGER / 210

PHYLLIS AND THE HIT MAN / 211

THE IGNORED "NO" AND FORCED TEAMING / 212

DON'T LAUGH IT OFF / 213

THE SMELL OF FEAR / 214

EXPANDING YOUR BRAIN'S INTUITIVE CAPABILITY / 214

VIOLENCE IN THE WORK PLACE / 216

THE MARRIAGE SWITCH / 217

SUMMARY / 220

Chapter XI
A Witch's Spells 221

THE ETHICS OF WORKING SPELLS / 221

WHY USE SPELLS? / 221

A SPELL FOR COMPANIONSHIP / 222

A Spell for Wealth / *223*

A Spell for Healing / *224*

A Spell for Personal Protection / *225*

A House-Cleansing Spell / *227*

A Spell for Serenity / *229*

A Spell for Removal of Enemies / *229*

A Spell for Heightened Awareness / *230*

A Spell for Acceptance of the Future / *231*

A Spell for Reality / *232*

A Spell for Self-Sealing / *233*

A Spell for the Psychic Cleaning of Tools / *234*

A Spell for the Psychic Charging of Tools / *235*

Summary / *236*

Chapter XII

Your Fulfilled Life 237

Do You Truly Want to Be President? / *237*

The President Gets Demoted / *238*

The Endless Search / *239*

Scoring Your Balance / *241*

Your Action List Today / *245*

Jerry Saves His SUV and His Family / *246*

Mammon and the Advertisers / *249*

The Conspiracy / *250*

V, as in Victim and Vacation / *251*

Existing, Living, Flourishing / *253*

Your Spirit / *253*

Moon Puppy and Patricia / *254*

Progressive Reincarnation / *257*

Summary / *261*

Chapter XIII
The Witch's Spiritual Path   263

THE SHADOW AT THE CENTER OF YOUR UNIVERSE   /   263

ELAINE CURES HER INSOMNIA   /   264

THE BASIC TRUTHS OF WICCA   /   266

THE ULTIMATE DEITY   /   267

TIME OUT FOR THEORY   /   268

ADAM GETS HIS CHILDREN   /   269

YOUR PIECE OF THE DEITY   /   271

POWER THROUGH KNOWLEDGE   /   272

THE LAW OF ATTRACTION   /   274

HARMONY AND SERENITY   /   274

CHANGING YOUR LIFE   /   275

WHERE ARE YOU?   /   278

MAYBE YOU'RE YOU   /   279

Appendix I
Your Easy Guide to Channeling   283

TIME FOR "I"   /   283

DAYDREAMING   /   285

THE POWER OF DREAMS   /   285

DREAM STATES   /   286

INTERPRETING DREAMS   /   287

CHANNELING   /   288

PROTECTION   /   289

FIRST STEPS IN OUTWARD CHANNELING   /   290

FIRST CHANNELING   /   293

FOLLOW UP   /   297

GETTING IT WORKING   /   *299*

RESULTS   /   *301*

Appendix 2

Legal Implications of Joining a Witch Group   303

A NONPROFIT CORPORATION DOES NOT A CHURCH MAKE   /   *304*

RECOGNITION OF THE CHURCH OF WICCA   /   *305*

HEALING AND THE AMA   /   *306*

WARNING   /   *306*

SUMMARY—COVER YOUR A**   /   *307*

INDEX   /   *309*

Introduction

IS LIFE PASSING YOU BY?

This is the ultimate self-help book. With its aid you can reach your full potential. This is the only book of its sort that relies on the work of real Witches who have, over the past thirty years, taught literally tens of thousands of people to develop their powers and thus to improve their lives.

Ask yourself:

Have you reached your full potential?

Is the life you live the one you imagined?

Are you fullfilling your dreams?

If you answer any of these questions no or NO, you need our help.

Witchcraft! The very word conjures visions of occult powers and secret rites. When we say "Witch," the vision becomes one of the traditional Witch with her cat and cauldron. The Witch and her powers are not to be feared. She[1] is the healer, the reader of dreams, the maker and foreteller of the future.

Magic can be defined as the changing of future events by ritual procedures that use the *Force.* The Force is that energy that is known to Chinese as *chi,* to Hindus as *prana,* to Germans as *vril.* It was popularized for all time as *The Force* in *Star Wars.* Because it is a natural force stemming from our bodies, scientists call it *bioplasmic energy.* Over the millennia Witches and others have learned to control, focus, and use it. This book will let you take advantage of their research and experience the power and use of the Force for yourself.

---

[1] We use "she" because 80 percent of those burned as Witches were female. Today American practitioners of the Craft are about 60 percent female, 40 percent male.

Magic and other powers can easily be yours. They are not "occult" (a word meaning literally *hidden*); indeed, each is susceptible to rational explanation.

WHAT WITCHCRAFT MAGIC CAN DO FOR YOU TODAY

Since the dawn of humankind, occult power has both mystified and frightened men. In bygone times, those who evinced such power were burned at the stake as Witches. No one can really say how many people were burned, or hanged, or otherwise tortured and killed. They died because of their known powers—powers that scared those in authority, those who felt threatened by this magical power . . . but that's another story.[2]

The Witch's powers can now be yours. With them you can:

1. Achieve serenity.
2. Predict the future.
3. Gain more than material wealth.
4. Heal yourself and others.
5. Gain any information you need through channeling.
6. Create your own love spells.
7. Tune in to Nature.
8. Protect yourself from unwanted psychic and physical attacks.

We will stop here with these eight promises, but we will leave you with one more promise:

Your Life Will Change Dramatically for the Better
When You Use Magic Witch Power.

There are many other things that you can do with the powers: gain money, gain lovers, or give yourself an edge in the race of life. Some of these ideas may sound negative; throughout the book we will describe techniques that empower you to do both positive and negative things—but be warned that there is an overriding univer-

---

2 Gavin and Yvonne Frost, *Who Speaks for the Witch? The Wiccan Holocaust* (Hinton, WV: Godolphin House, 1996).

sal Law of Attraction: *Your negative thoughts attract negative energies to yourself. Positive acts automatically improve your life, so that your whole outlook becomes happier and more positive.*

Mentally step back a moment to think about such real-world forces as electricity and gravity. Electricity is neither good nor bad; its good or bad qualities come to it with the intent of the user. If you plug in to accomplish a negative intent, the electricity becomes negative. If you plug in to accomplish a positive intent, the electricity becomes positive. Gravity may influence your scale to tell you you're overweight, but without gravity the bathwater would not stay in the tub.

So we leave it to you to decide how to use the powers. Remember always that the Witch's powers are the powers inherent in the planet itself, in the Mother Earth that makes possible the life in us all. The powers of Mother Earth and Mother Nature are the most inexorable that exist. We all know what happens when we try to thwart Mother Nature. We dam one of her rivers, and terrible floods ensue. We pollute her oceans and violate the protective mantle at her poles, and the heating effects cause El Niño with its terrible storms and planet-wide disasters. The powers you will be dealing with are immense.

The Witch's powers are not gender-specific; that is, males can learn them, too. Female magic has a different flavor or mindset than that of the male. She *asks* rather than *demands.* She is often content with longer-term solutions to her needs. Her magic is keyed to the quiet of the night and to the cycle of the moon and the seasons, rather than to the brightness of day and the cycle of the sun. We tend to think of female magic as powers of water and the earth, and male magic as powers of air and fire. Either gender can do both sorts of Witchcraft. Some readers may be more drawn to the traditional male style of working that demands and threatens. This handbook delineates both sorts of magical/Witchcraft procedures.

THE ROAD LESS TRAVELED

When you go on a journey, whether you travel country roads or scenic highways, you need a good road map. This book is a road map to a less-traveled road. Every so often along the way you will need to ask advice of people who have traveled the road before you. We are such people: We have been traveling this road for more than fifty years. In the past thirty years we have helped and advised more than fifty thousand travelers.

Currently most people travel as if they're on a busy interstate. They see only the road itself and the cities and tracks around them. They travel tensely with one eye on the time and the other on the speedometer. Only very occasionally do they stop to look at the scenery. Why don't you try a road less traveled? You will need to pause occasionally for reflection—to decide perhaps which branch to take of the fork that confronts you. Appendix 1 outlines a channeling technique through which thousands of our students have obtained guidance.

Do you just jump from one project to another? Does one day of your life just follow another without a break and without change, without pattern or overarching purpose? Do you have time in your busy schedule for reflective thinking, to look at the map of your life's journey? To decide where you are heading? Without an ultimate goal, and without a map for the journey, you may aimlessly wander around back roads forever, going down cul-de-sacs and dead ends, having to retrace many steps and make sudden uninformed decisions.

There is a better way. You don't have to wait for the next time something comes off the spool or for the next unwelcome surprise. With reflective thinking, you can take a "What if?" approach. "What if my significant other were to leave?" "What if I get sick?" "What if the car breaks down?" and a thousand other "What ifs?" Instead of reacting to circumstances and letting *life* run *you,* you can become proactive. You can plan ahead so that when the unexpected occurs you have already considered it and have thought through a solution(s) or at least some realistic options. Being self-actualizing and proactive is a Witch's way. She employs many techniques for looking at the future and reflectively thinking to gain serenity today.

In this book you will learn some of those techniques. You will learn how to get back in tune with the natural cycles of Nature and how to become proactive, with special emphasis on

1. Lowering your stress level; and
2. Improving your health; and then
3. Magically improving your lifestyle.

The road less traveled is an interesting and rewarding road. It is not like traveling along a freeway, rushing headlong past the signposts that could lead to interesting experiences. You will learn to make a conscious decision about which opportunities are worth exploring and which are not on your journey's map. Occasionally you may use magic and travel a piece of the freeway to gain a goal more quickly; but in general you will find that you enjoy the journey along an alternative road as much as you savor the goal.

YOUR MAGICAL MOMENTS

Many people have sudden brilliant flashes or magical moments that make changes in their lives. They may suddenly show that your preacher is more concerned with money than with the spiritual well-being of his flock. There may be a sudden realization that you absolutely hate the job you're doing or that working for a large faceless corporation is consuming and deadening your soul. People—especially those in the public eye—are talking about their *epiphanies,* as these sudden flashes are called, these sudden new awarenesses. You can hardly pick up a newspaper without reading that some famous person is giving up a career or retiring early, or abandoning news broadcasts or a thousand other changes in lifestyle that have come about through a new awareness that has entered their lives. Gavin gave up the gold credit cards and the comfortable life of a sales executive to teach Witchcraft. Yes, of course it was very hard at first. Without food stamps, we wouldn't have eaten. Without his large executive wardrobe, he would have worn rags.

Such experiences are part of the epiphany: going through the down time to reach fulfillment. Epiphanies come in different sizes to different people. You can have lots of little ones or big brilliant flashes (as in Gavin's case) that cause an abrupt, violent change of lifestyle. In this book we will try to guide you through a series of small epiphanies. This will create the climate for gradual changes in your attitude to life, to the world, and to spirituality, so that you will gain serenity and a new *joie de vivre* that will make your life worthwhile.

When you were young, the world looked new. Anything seemed possible. A life of exploration and discovery lay before you. Today, has life become dull and dreary? The epiphanies this book will guide you through will bring back those youthful feelings to you. Think honestly with us for a moment. Are you truly content? Will you be satisfied if the rest of your lifetime turns out to be much like what you have lived so far? Or do you have that universal longing, that hunger, for something timeless—something that has meaning, something that will endure? In the small hours of the night, does that little voice ever whisper, "I have all this, but it's not what I want or deserve"?

YOU CAN SHIFT THE UNIVERSAL BALANCE

In the film *Star Wars* a planet was destroyed and the effect was felt throughout the galaxy. Popular wisdom tells us that when a butterfly dies in Malaysia, the future of the world is affected. Many powerful Witches refuse to do any magic because they have witnessed the far-reaching effects they can have. We think this attitude may be too arbitrary, that it is better to do *something*—with knowledge and with intent—than just to let things drift along. You need only look around you to see how far out of control this nation has gotten. Through magic you can have a positive effect on the society that surrounds you, and that positive effect will flow outward from your center to affect the whole world. You, too, can disturb the balance. You, too, can improve your life and thus the world.

Blessed be all those who seek and try.

Gavin and Yvonne
Hinton, West Virginia

The Witch's Magical Life

WHAT WITCHES DO

If you were to follow a Witch around for a day, you would find that more than 90 percent of her life is not that different from your own. It is the other 10 percent that you might find unusual. That is the time when she does magical and mundane procedures that make her more in tune with the universe; procedures that help her gain the things she needs, and that let her lead a more serene life.

We can categorize the things that a Witch does under several headings.

1. *Studies her Environment.* In a Witch's house you will find many books, both old and new. Through them she understands as much as she can of economics, sociology, ecology, and working with her mother Gaea, the Earth.

2. *Predicts the Future.* She may use a deck of tarot cards, a pendulum, or the traditional crystal ball. She believes that if she cannot foretell future events, there is little point in doing a spell to change them. That would be like playing Blind Man's Bluff.

3. *Directs the Force.* She uses her own inborn energy, and energy from outside sources (the Force), to aid in many different areas of life. Typically those areas include healing and changing the future. As you read through this book, you will learn that further sources of energy include:

   a. energy from ancient god-forms, stored in the god-forms by the prayers of thousands of worshipers;

   b. energy she has stored in her own special favorite deities or *psychostores*[1];

   c. natural energies from rocks, stones, and specific locations on the surface of the earth;

   d. energy from the movements and alignments of heavenly bodies.

4. *Attains Altered States of Consciousness.* Through techniques she has learned, she enters altered states of consciousness to:

   a. obtain information that is otherwise not available to her;

   b. astrally visit other people, places, and times;

   c. release trapped spirits ("ghosts") from the earth plane and help them progress;

   d. help in soul retrieval so that people who have had traumatic experiences can become whole again.

   The altered-state part of her work falls under the heading of *channeling*. The information she receives may come privately in her own mind while she sits quietly in meditation; or it may come through as a voice speaking to a listener, as it did in the work of Edgar Cayce. Many people call the astral-travel part of the work (that Witches have done for centuries) *shamanic journeying*.

5. *Spirituality.* The Witch's belief system comprises a whole alternative spirituality in what we now call the religion of Wicca.[2]

---

[1] See G. & Y. Frost, *Meta-Psychometry* (Hinton, WV: Godolphin House, 1997).

[2] The religion of The Craft—Witchcraft—developed and articulated by the authors, earned federal recognition in 1972. See Appendix 2.

As you work through this book, you will catch glimpses of the spiritual belief structure. One of the most significant and important parts is a total belief in reincarnation. The Witch recognizes that she has lived on this plane of existence in every conceivable shell (or physical body). She can go back into her own past lives to understand such things as the properties of a specific herb or what it really means to be a cat. Thus she often surrounds herself with animals, especially those animals that are damaged in one way or another. Do not be surprised to find that she has three-legged dogs and one-eyed cats in her home, or that she talks to animals, plants, and trees.

These five aspects of a Witch's magical life can be summarized as shown in Figure I-1. This book concentrates on the magical aspect of her work, remembering that it is but one of the bases about which her whole life revolves and not the whole story. Notice that at the center of Figure I-1 is the Deity. That is the *Ultimate Deity*, the god above all gods. She realizes that there is *something* at the center, which may be unnameable but is still a reality. Her life is a balanced whole; it is not fragmented.

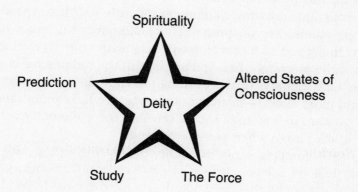

FIGURE I–1
Aspects of a Witch's Magical Life

MAGIC IS REAL

In many of our lectures, especially to student audiences, we ask attendees to do the "hands-across-palm" experiment.[3] They point the fingers of one hand at the palm of the other (without touching) and gently move the pointing hand past the palm of the other. Most people—especially if they are relaxed—can feel a slight breeze or definite change of temperature as the energy from the fingertips hits the palm of the motionless hand. For many students this is their first magical moment or epiphany: Suddenly what we are saying becomes real. This is the energy that the Witch uses in her work. It is in every living thing, and is in itself no more "good" or "evil" than our two favorite examples, electricity and gravity.

You can prove to yourself in other ways that psychic energy or the Force really exists. One popular means is a small device known as the *Crookes Radiometer*. Professor Crookes invented it during his term as president of the British Psychical Research Society. You can often find radiometers in children's toy stores or science stores, and they are available at a scientific level from Edmund Scientific.[4] The radiometer resembles a little paddle wheel inside an evacuated (vacuum) light bulb. The vanes or paddles are white or silver on one face and black on the reverse. When energy hits them, they revolve inside the bulb.

Set up the radiometer and a flashlight as shown in Figure I-2, adjusting the flashlight until the vanes rotate very slowly. Then point your fingers at the radiometer. Silently *will* it to speed up or to stop, whichever you prefer. The radiometer will react to your intent; the speed of its turning will vary with your level of energy. Early in the morning when you are bright, the radiometer will react almost immediately. In the evening after a long day's work, it will respond more slowly—or may not change. We have found, too, that when you are in a state of sexual tension, the radiometer will react more quickly than when you are relaxed.

If a radiometer is not available, try putting a ping-pong (table tennis) ball on a level surface of glass or other smooth, polished material, then cupping your hand around the ball. Depending on

---

[3] See G. & Y. Frost, *Magic Power of White Witchcraft* (Paramus, NJ: Reward Books, 1999).

[4] Edmund Scientific, 101 E. Gloucester Place, Barrington NJ 08007-1380.

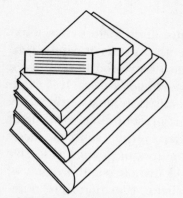

Adjust Flashlight until
Vanes Turn Slowly

Radiometer

Point Fingers of
Dominant Hand
at Radiometer

FIGURE I-2
Radiometer Experiment

your intent, your hand will either attract or repel the ball.[5] This is more challenging than the radiometer; but many people can do it when they are "up," especially if they try patiently and really get the feel of the thing. Work in short sessions: If the mind gets bored with the effort, it will shut down and make no response at all. Then only in special circumstances, where you need to demonstrate this possibility, will it be able to do it again. We often say that once you've convinced yourself of your force, the mind regards the playing of parlor tricks as unworthy.

These simple experiments change people's lives. They suddenly realize that knowledge of the Force born in them has been a carefully guarded secret, and that they have been denied their birthright.

In one instance Yvonne addressed a graduating class of Lutheran ministers and had them do the hands-across-palm experiment. Five of the men promptly gave up their vocation. One followed her home to learn more about the Craft.

---

[5] A video, *The Reality of Magic*, of Gavin demonstrating these experiments is available through Godolphin House, P.O. Box 297-BK, Hinton, WV 25951-0297; or through the web at www.wicca.org.

CHARACTERISTICS OF THE FORCE

Psychic power, the Force, has some unusual characteristics. First and foremost, it is *bioplasmic energy*; in other words, it can be generated most easily from people. It can also be stored in inanimate objects that one might call *mascots* or *hearth god/esses.*[6] It is available as well from certain classes of minerals (foremost of these are crystals), and from the cosmos itself. It is present along earth fault lines, near flowing water, and from many other sources. Many Witches seek out one or more of these *places of power,* as Carlos Castaneda calls them. Some authors build a whole occult system on their one epiphanic discovery, little realizing that there are other places of power—and that all are well known.

A competent Witch examines her environment for sources of this all-important Force because she can easily deplete her own energy in magical work and she needs places where she can recharge herself or call upon more energy to do the task at hand.

One characteristic of the Force that seems to be little understood is that it is *tuneable.* Just as you tune an old-fashioned radio to get the station you want, so you tune the Force to do the task you want it to do. Imagine if you like that instead of the radio tuning in various stations, it tunes in various *intents.* Figure I-3 shows a psychic radio and transmitter. At one end of the dial there might be *Love,* at the other, *Attack*; and as you go along the dial you may find such options as *Healing, Luck,* and other intents that may help you in a spell to fulfill your dream.

To tune her radio to a specific intent, a Witch uses what one might call *mind keys.* Written records dating back as far as two millennia reveal the systems that various magical workers have used to tune the Force for various intents. In groundbreaking work, Yvonne cross-correlated these old sources and constructed a *table of correspondences.* In a typical table the mind keys for a spell to gain wealth might be as shown in Table I-1.

---

[6] *God/ess* denotes a demi-god such as Buddha, lower than the Ultimate Deity which is genderless.

Your Psychic Radio
Transmits and Receives

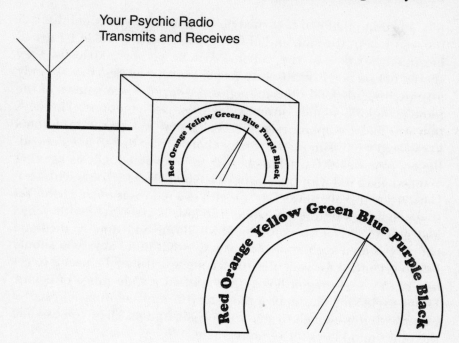

FIGURE I–3
Your Psychic Radio and Transmitter

Intent: WEALTH

Sight	Taste	Smell	Touch	Sound	Timing	HEDE[7]
Color	Flavor	Scent	Feeling	Chant	Moon	Speed of Chant/ Dance
Gold	Port Wine	Saffron	Velvet	Gay-ah	New	Slow

TABLE I–1
Mind Triggers for Gaining Wealth

---

[7] Human/Earth Dynamo Effect (see Chapter III).

In addition, if you're turned on by astrology, you could think of the sign Leo in the sun, and of fire. Tables such as Table I-1 are of inestimable value to the capable Witch; yet paradoxically they should not be taken as absolute gospel for your work. They are only a guide; they depend on thinking of the various frequencies of the force as colors, sounds, aromas, feelings, and emotions. The keys that *you* feel are appropriate for wealth may not be the traditional keys—and what is more, they may change from day to day depending on your wealth associations and on your mood. Let us say that you associate red with the curing of a blood disease. You might associate red with Valentine's Day, or with the red roses of true love. Yet if you look at a traditional table, true love is associated with Venus and green. Therefore you should sit down and quietly meditate before you do a spell, to decide exactly what mind keys you should use to get tuned for *your* desired frequency. It may be useful to get one of those 64-crayon boxes that contain a wide range of colors. Simply selecting the appropriate crayon and coloring a piece of paper with it is enough to give you a basic tuning. Then you can add the other mind keys for reinforcement.

We do not know exactly why, but timing of spells is critical for greatest effectiveness. It seems that your highest emotional output peaks with the phases of the moon. At full moon and new moon, when ocean tides are highest, your output is at its maximum. You can also reinforce and strengthen it by spinning in a circle as described fully in Chapter III. With such a combination of factors you are creating the *Human/Earth Dynamo Effect* (HEDE).

THE WEB OF THE WYRD

In convincing your own mind that what Witches do is real and effective and practical, the next step you may want to take is a little experiment that we have our students do. We have them send to a good friend, in the middle of the night, a powerful mind-picture of red roses. Ninety percent of students report that when they try, they succeed—that the target person has a dream in which roses figure prominently or that the target wakes with the strong desire to buy red roses. We believe that this works by what is loosely called a *telepathic link*. Earlier you formed some kind of psychic link to the target person. Along the link you send the intent of dreaming about or wanting red roses. Various experiments show that the link is not limited to one single other person. If you expand your experimental work you will find that you can send the same picture to many friends all at once.

Because of this and similar research, Witches believe that all living things are interconnected by psychic links. There is a great psychic internet. All you have to do to influence someone is to know their right "address"—in this case a psychic link—and use the appropriate mind keys to tune your transmitter to the right intent. When you send that message out on the psychic internet, it strengthens the psychic link between you and the target. Capable occultists who can actually see these links will tell you that the link glows with the message and (carrying on with the metaphor) the link will change color with the intent.

RENATA'S WHITE CADILLAC

Renata M lives now in the deep South and is pursuing a new career as the manager of a telemarketing firm. For many years she headed the psychology department of a major medical university in the northeast. Her epiphany occurred when she found that so much of the healing lore she gained through her African-American heritage still worked in a modern hospital—for instance, that laying on hands almost halved the time needed for a fractured bone to heal. Abruptly disenchanted with modern allopathic medicine, she gave up her respected and well-paid position and moved to Georgia to be nearer her family. For a short time she was relatively strapped financially.

Her old faithful Cadillac chose precisely that time to expire. She patched it together, but knew that replacing it was only a matter of time. She visited several Cadillac dealers and in one showroom she saw a vintage white Cadillac convertible with (would you believe?) powder-blue upholstery.

She knew that car was destined to be hers, and she took steps to acquire it. She visualized the car in her future, and through channeling she outlined the path she needed to take to get it. First, of course, she had to stop the car being sold to someone else; so effectively she hexed the car as it sat there in the showroom. Every time she went to the dealership to get a new part for her old clunker, she renewed the hex. A couple of times salespeople came over when they saw her standing near it and told her what a good deal she could get on it because no one wanted it.

In parallel with the hex on the car, she started looking for a new job. She was way over-qualified for most of the work on offer. Finally she found a position as a mid-level manager designing tele-marketing sales pitches. Her old classroom voice came in handy and she soon became "the voice" of the firm. The company prospered and Renata got her life into fair order—except that she still didn't have her Cadillac. On the day after Christmas 1991 her heart sank at the empty spot on the showroom floor where her car had stood for so long. When her office reopened on the 27th, the Cadillac was parked in her boss' spot. "You bought my Cadillac?" she demanded incredulously.

"Damn thing! I bought it for my wife—and she won't drive it! Until I unload it she's got my Beemer. What do you mean, 'your' Cadillac?"

"I've wanted that car since the first day I saw it." The emotion in her voice must have been obvious.

"Okay, I'll do you a deal. You take the Caddy in lieu of this year's bonus, and we'll call it square."

Renata knew that the value of the Cadillac was many times that of any possible bonus, so she readily agreed and drove home that evening in her white Cadillac.

MIND KEYS

You can see that Renata did two things:

1. She hexed the Cadillac by thinking thoughts of an accident at it.

2. She put a psychic link between herself and the Cadillac, trying to draw it to her and to get it actually in her future.

People have different ways of "visualizing" emotion. Most of us see colors and immediately associate them with emotions; e.g., red for rage, green for love, brown for depression. *Seeing* is not the only sense. You also have *smell,* in which you might think of a sharp, acrid orange for rage, or lavender for motherly love. Similarly you have *hearing*. You might hear a blast of trumpets for rage and a pleasant Viennese waltz for love. In tables of mind keys, sounds have largely been reduced to various chants—fast, slow, staccato, and so on—to suit the various intents. Further, there is *taste*. Something could taste really awful for rage or very pleasant for love (maybe chocolate). Also there is *touch* (in occult terms, *tactition*). Something really rough and gravelly could equate to rage, whereas something smooth and velvety would be more loving. Almost all the senses have their equivalent healing therapies. Two that are currently popular are color and aromatherapy.[8]

The more of your senses you can trigger with mind keys, the more effective will be the pulse of energy you send along the psychic internet. In Renata's case, she could actually put her hands on the Cadillac in the showroom and will the energy directly into it. This is exactly the same procedure that a spiritual healer might do when she lays hands on afflicted people to heal them.

EXAMPLES OF PSYCHIC HEALING

Our files contain thousands of cases of psychic healing. They range from our daughter (then four years old) laying hands on a visitor's heel and curing his torn Achilles' tendon, to Yvonne's making a growth on a cow go away before the skeptical eye of a journalist. The laying on of hands is effective; it works; and it is easily demonstrated. Many hospitals now have "touching nurses" in the wards especially for broken bones. They lay hands on the broken limbs—and lo and behold, the bones knit in about half the usual time.

VISUALIZE YOUR FUTURE

Dream your dream. Weave your spell.
What's ahead will turn out well.

You can improve your own future by visualizing what you want and then visualizing the steps toward your goal. Visualization is an amazingly powerful tool, and we hear about its results in the most

---

[8] An instructional videotape, *Photochromotherapy*, fully explores the effect of color in magical work and healing. Contact Godolphin House, P.O. Box 297-BK, Hinton, WV 25951-0297 or at www.wicca.org.

unexpected places. Scott Adams,[9] creator of the popular *Dilbert* comic strip, describes how he visualized himself getting a score of exactly 94 percent on a critical examination that he thought he might be lucky to get 50 percent on. His final score? 94 percent. Inventors from Edison on down have continually used visualization to solve problems in their work. What Renata did was visualize that white Cadillac in her future and herself driving and enjoying it in Georgia. Further, of course, standing in the showroom, she imbued it with negative thoughts. She actually used the memory of a crash that she had witnessed. That was enough to turn other customers away from the car.

You can do it, too. All you have to do is sit down and decide what is the top-priority item or person that you want in your life now. If your visual memory is not the best, then attach a suitable photograph or sketch of your target to your bathroom mirror. Remember that the affirmation is not that you *want* the target, but that the target *is yours*. If you affirm the thought, "I want money," guess what? You will continue to *want* money. Have you ever heard a small child scream, "Mine!" when someone takes something away from him? That's your affirmation, paired with the visualization, that will bring the item into your life.

MAKE A COMPLETE PICTURE

Our coven has its own history and lore. Part of the lore is an incident we have told many times. Some years ago the women decided the coven needed more men. They did a ritual to bring men in, and immediately we were inundated with applications from men—gay men. Delightful and friendly and sincere though they were, this was not precisely what the women had intended.

AVOID UNWELCOME SURPRISES

This points up the importance of exact visualization. Get all the details right; leave no part of your intent undefined. If your goal is a new lover, your visualization should include personality as well as

---

[9] Scott Adams, *The Dilbert Future* (New York: HarperCollins, 1997).

tight buns. Just a pretty smile or an attractive shaving lotion probably will not be enough. That delightful-looking person may be completely incompatible with your own personality, even to the extent of liking line dancing rather than ballroom, or an equivalent mismatch.

Your work on visualization should engage all your senses. Beyond the image you use as a focusing tool (whether it is one you create or one you choose from a range of options), you need the scent, the feel, the sound, and the flavor (if you will) of the desired object. You may say, "Well, what does a new car taste like?" It matters not what it tastes like to us; its flavor matters only to you. It is *your* visualization. From this point of view perhaps it is not correct to use the word *visualization*; thinking of it as a *construction* may work better for you.

When your construction is complete, imagine it in the future, coming down the river of time into your grasp. The more energy you put into this construction and into its arrival in your life, the more likely will be the result.

Magic works in future time. You can't suddenly materialize something "Poof!" in your immediate space. If you did, it would mean a sudden displacement of matter, the equivalent of a bomb. Always bring things in over time.

BEVY AND THE COFFEE KING

Bevy J is a skilled, gifted occultist living in the Midwest. Several years ago she accepted a challenge from a friend who dealt in commodities futures. He told her, "I dare you to make me rich!" Now she knew that he played the commodities markets, so during her next channeling session she visualized a page of futures options. The one that jumped out at her was coffee; sensibly, she advised the friend to buy coffee futures. At the same time she began actively to visualize the price of coffee going sky-high. She would take some grains of coffee in one hand and a piece of gold jewelry in the other, and visualize the price of coffee going as high as the price of gold.

Coffee prices began to rise. Soon her friend had the opportunity to roll over his options into yet more options, and so it went on for several weeks. He was growing very uneasy that the price would suddenly drop; for if it did, he would lose a fortune. Through her channeling and her visualization, Bevy insisted that he roll over and buy more and more options. Finally one day in her channeling she saw a mountain of coffee beans glissading down a cliff. She opened her eyes, picked up the phone, and told him, "Sell—now!" He did. When the dust settled, he had made literally millions of dollars in the market. Out of gratitude he bought Bevy a comfortable ranch-style home in a fashionable suburb of their city.

IDENTIFY YOUR MAGICAL OPTIONS

When you decide on an objective, through channeling you can make some decisions about the specific path to achieving the objective. As you go into your channeling session, have before you a piece of paper with a precise question written on it. Remind yourself of the question just before you set your timer.[10] During the session you will usually receive guidance (in whichever way your awareness operates) to the answer. Sometimes the answer comes in a song, sometimes by smelling a friend's cigarette. It's not always a picture. If you make up a little visual aid that shows several different paths to your goal, then guidance can easily show you which path is best to follow. In a simple example (diagrammed in Figure I-4), the problem is lack of money. The next line shows possible ways of getting money into your wallet. The top line shows the consequences of each path. On the far right are some blank boxes. They let your mind fill in blanks of yet another path(s) that you had not thought of. Before you construct such a diagram, it is helpful to write down the next two or three goals that you would really like to achieve.

BECOME A SELF-ACTUALIZING WITCH

In your present life situation it may look as if making new goals is futile, but that's a catch-22 dilemma. If you don't make new goals, you will be stuck forever in your present situation. When you begin to think about new goals, then you can start thinking of ways to achieve them that will get you out of your present *reactive* state. A reactive state is one in which you go on drearily from day to day

---

[10] Appendix 1 contains precise directions for channeling.

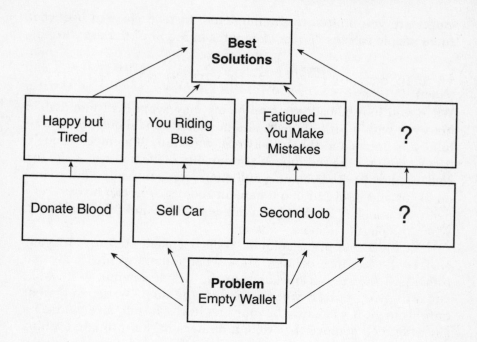

FIGURE I–4
Diagramming Your Questions

only responding to situations as they arise; the car breaks down, you get it fixed. You have a fight with the boss; you either fix it or quit. A controlled, *self-actualizing* response or lifestyle is far better. Think ahead. Maybe if you took the car in for maintenance more often, it wouldn't break down—or maybe you need a new car. Now plot your path, and with the aid of channeling, *get* that new car. This is the self-actualizing approach that Witches use. Are you just like a plankton drifting in the ocean at the mercy of every current and breeze, waiting around until something pushes you? Or are you instead someone who has a goal in mind? You may not swim hard in that direction, but at least you keep moving toward that goal, not drifting aimlessly but always moving purposefully.

When you read these words you may feel that Witches are just like any other counselors. They all say, "Develop a budget. Plan your future." Yes, it is true that we are saying something similar. But instead of planning a future all by yourself, you have the help of all the universal knowledge available when you begin to channel information from those on the other side of the "Invisible Barrier." No longer are you limited to the mundane. Instead you can use what some people call the "Great Computer in the Sky" to help you.

YOUR TEN-STEP ACHIEVEMENT CHART

When you look ahead, your problems may seem insurmountable; however, with a little thought and guidance, you should be able to fulfill any dream and achieve any goal you want. Remember, though, that sometimes the sacrifice in your quality of life may not make the goal worthwhile. To become a millionaire, do you really want to live on beans and Kool-Aid in a tenement room so you can invest every penny you make? So decide on one goal today and fill in Table I-2. When the path is unclear—channel.

In the Description column, spell out each step toward your goal. In the Sacrifice column, show what you are willing to give up to achieve the step in question. In the Result column, write what you will give yourself when you gain the step. Write, too, what improvement it will cause in your life. In the Result, give yourself a gift when you achieve that step; a dinner out, an intimate evening with someone special, the thing you will most enjoy. In human beings gene survival and hunger are the strongest motivators.

OVERALL GOAL _____

STEP	DESCRIPTION	SACRIFICE	RESULT
1			
2			
3			
4			
5			
6			
7			
8			
9			
10			

TABLE I–2
Steps to Your Goal

YOUR URGENT NECESSITY

In defining your goals and the steps to achieving them, do not fall into the trap Jimmy Buffett calls *overkill*.[11] He warns that if you "run too fast and shove too hard, you'll be pushing up the daisies in the old boneyard." Let your goals be things you really need, not those an advertiser wants to convince you to buy. American big business practices a clearly cynical exploitation of gullible consumers (conditioning you to be one up on the Joneses). New products, especially in electronics, are constantly being developed overseas and not marketed in the United States. Only after the American market is saturated with a product will a new and better one be offered. VHS video gets replaced with DVD. Audio goes from 1/4-inch tape spools to eight-track to 1/4-inch cassettes to compact disks . . . the examples are endless.

In fact, examples of such abuse are apparent every day of the week. Right now people are buying SUVs (so-called sport-utility vehicles) for some $30,000 to $50,000 to replace their perfectly functional, perfectly adequate smaller cars. *Consumer Reports* points out that not one in ten buyers ever takes the vehicle off road and only about ten percent of them ever expect even to use the vehicle in four-wheel drive. Now we see advertisers claiming *safety* concerns as justification for the SUVs—and to be a good parent, you must elevate your children's position in a rear seat so they can see out the window. "Buy our SUV or feel inadequate as a parent. Don't be guilty of rearing an underprivileged child." This actually increases the danger to your child if a window shatters in an accident.

In doing spell work there is probably nothing more important than the *real need* you have to be doing the work. Lots of people do general healings or a spell for money or love without that all-important urgent need for it to succeed. The healing is directed toward someone whom they don't really know, so the importance is less, even though the case may sound worthwhile. With regard to working for money, they probably have been living and eating fairly comfortably. They aren't starving, they're fully clothed, and the car still runs (though perhaps not so well as it might). And maybe there is a necessity for a little money—but there is no urgent necessity for it to happen right now. So you don't have a permanent friend or a comfortable significant other? Why do you really need one this

---

[11] Jimmy Buffett, *Banana Wind* (MCA CD MCAD 11451, 1996).

minute? Wouldn't next week be soon enough? When you are actually planning your spell, make sure to base it on a true urgent necessity, not just some vague wish.

ALISON AND HER UNWANTED BUDDY

Alison studied sociology at North Carolina State University in Raleigh. In common with many of her friends and peer group, she began investigating the "occult." Regrettably, people who are newly come to the field anoint themselves instant experts and sit right down to write another book on the subject. They have had their epiphany through finding some facet of alternative thinking, and want to share it with everyone right away.

Alison decided that she would like an occult buddy, and that a giant rabbit would be fun. She went through all the steps in the one book that she had read, and she got it right. When her spell was complete, she could indeed see a giant rabbit in the corner of her dorm room. She was flying high. All the rest of that day the rabbit followed her around. One of her friends could also see it and envied her success. Everything was fine until Alison went to bed that night. Her simulacrum (an image or likeness) got into bed with her and quickly set about doing what rabbits are famous for.

This was not at all what Alison had had in mind, and now she faced a problem: how to get rid of her unwanted buddy. The first thing she did was get up and get dressed again. She carefully read the book from which she had obtained the spell for making the rabbit, but nothing told her how to get rid of it. She was like the little girl in the Brothers Grimm fairy tale who didn't know simply to affirm, "Little pot, stop!" She stayed up all that night, not daring to go to bed. By the next night she was really distraught, both from lack of sleep and from the fact that the rabbit seemed to be growing more solid and real with every passing hour. She decided she would try going to bed and not thinking about the rabbit, and see what happened. Of course that's a near-impossible task. Have you ever tried to not think about anything? Do it now. Don't think about hubcaps for the next ten seconds. Not too easy, is it?

Anyway, Alison was soon out of bed again and dressed. She was clearly out of her depth and caught dangerously in the undertow of her amateur effort. By now she was very worried indeed. She decided to go to a party given by one of her friends, the one who had seen the rabbit, and see whether the distraction would decrease the rabbit's strength.

Her friend urged Alison to call us. That caused another problem, because our phone is unlisted, and this was before the days of our website. Fortunately one of the young people at the party knew where we lived (at that time it was very close to the university campus), so all of them trooped down to see us.

We had never quite had this problem presented to us in this way before. We knew for sure that the more Alison brooded on the rabbit, the more strength it would gain, and that the normal banishing procedures used for spiritual matters would not work because the rabbit was a direct manifestation of her own mind. We decided to try cutting off her thoughts by enclosing her in protective rings, anklets, and headbands. Such protective devices work in two directions: They can be designed to protect you from the thoughts of others, and to stop your thoughts from escaping your immediate vicinity.

As soon as she put the protective devices onto her body, the rabbit began to fade until only Alison could see it; a few minutes later it completely disappeared. We didn't know how long she would have to wear headbands, rings, and anklets, so we told her just to try it. After a couple of days she came back and told us that she could take her protection off and the rabbit did not reappear.

YOU'LL GET WHAT YOU NEED

If you exactly follow the steps in any spell, and if your intent is positive, normally you will get a positive result. That result may surprise you, since it may not be exactly what you asked for. It may be something more, something different, or something entirely unexpected. When such a thing occurs, step back mentally and take a broader view. You may realize that the spell has produced for you exactly what you needed. Perhaps your subconscious (the larger part of your awareness) has been at work and knows better than your conscious mind what you really need.

If a spell is to have an effect, you must *do* it. There is an old story about Aaron, who prayed for twenty years to Jehovah, "Oh, Lord, let me win the lottery!" One day a sunbeam shone down from the clouds and a mighty voice thundered, "AARON, BUY A TICK-ET." That's exactly how spells work. If you don't take the positive steps, collect the materials you need, and do the procedure, you can be sure that very little will happen. Even the simplest visualization must be focused. At the very least, you must get a photograph or some other *psychic link* to the object you are working toward.

As we go forward in this book you will find that in order to tune spells and make them really effective, you need various props. None of the props we will name are difficult to obtain, but obtaining them may take time and a few dollars. Remember: The more effort and the more intensity you put into your work, the more likely it is to succeed. After thirty years of shared work on this effort, we are convinced that the high intensity of a single worker can overcome the thought forms of thousands of people who are putting out such vague, amorphous thoughts as, "Gosh, I kind of wish Horse X would win the Derby."

SPELL-CASTING 101

Just as Alison found an unwelcome buddy in her bed, so you can get things that you do not necessarily want. Be careful in planning out your spells; neither leave gaps inadvertently in your wish list nor leave ill-defined areas. If you do, you will surely get something weird. These results are usually not so difficult to control as Alison's rabbit was, but sometimes things can go very wrong. You should be particularly wary of taking part in spell casting done by people who may be experienced but are clearly flakes.

The steps of a proper, effective spell—and their sequence—are well known to serious workers. They are easy to understand and to follow. Just make sure you do all the right steps in the right order, and you will get positive results.

Are you confused by the word *spell?* A spell is simply a procedure written down so you can follow each step without error. It is comparable to a recipe for a cake or the things you do when you get up in the morning. You take a shower, dress, have breakfast, brush your teeth, go to work . . . whatever your life consists of: You do defined acts in a certain sequence.

Accurate definition of the urgent necessity is critical. That definition must be clear and complete, free of ambiguities and gaps.

The next thing will be a psychic link to the target. This can be a photograph, a personal accessory such as a handkerchief that has been used and not cleaned, or anything else that will bring your mind directly into contact with the target and focus your entire attention on it. The third item on your checklist must be the method you will use to raise and send energy. In succeeding chapters we will give you various schemes for doing this and for enhancing your power. For now let us say we are going to use just your own inborn energy. And lastly, you need some closing statement of intent—a resolution. This can be as simple as a yell, "My power!" or "My car!" or "Heal!"

You will need to work at an appropriate time. If your target is a living person, it is usually best to work when that person is asleep. There is a widespread tradition, therefore, of working at or near midnight. If your work is targeted on an inanimate object, consider how that object will come into your life. Normally it will be through the agency of living people. Someone will give it to you, someone will make a mistake and send it to you, or some other similar thing will happen. A Cadillac isn't going to drive itself out of the showroom and pull up in your driveway. Instead, an intermediary agent will play a part in getting the desired target to you. Thus, again, it is best to do your spell when such people are open to psychic suggestions. That is obviously not in the middle of a busy day of work or socializing, so midnight seems to be an appropriate time. If your target is not open at the time you work, the energy you send out may reflect back to you; however, you want to be sure that no residual energy lingers around you. Therefore, as a final resolution of your spell, it is traditional to add some phrase such as "Guides and Elder Ones, I release any remaining energy to you. Do with it as you will." Such an affirmation lets Them know that you're finished now and want to leave the astral arena tidy, without loose ends.

Here is a list, then, of the steps in your spell-casting procedure.

1. Define your urgent necessity.
2. Establish a psychic link.
3. Decide the source of the energy you will use.
4. Choose a time.
5. Choose an affirmation.

Figure I-5 shows these five magical pentagrammic parts.

FIGURE I-5
Your Pentagram of Spell-Casting

JEROME GETS HIS HOUSE

Jerome F lives in downtown San Francisco in a beautiful traffic-stopping Painted Lady[12] that he acquired many years ago before his part of town was fashionable, almost before the term *painted lady* was invented. He could see the beauty beneath the decay, and fell in love with the house at a time when it had gotten beyond the fixer-upper stage and looked like a hobbyist's horror. He visualized it; he photographed it; he even took a stone from its tiny yard; so he had adequate psychic links to it. Then he meditated for a whole week on possible ways to acquire the house. All he could get through meditation was impressions of himself in class—and the classroom was not like those he had known in college. Instead it looked more like a conference room. And everywhere he looked he could see the number 21. Soon he realized that the message told him to study with Century 21 Realty for a salesman's license.

This seemed far too mundane to be a magical solution to his desire for that house, but he had nothing better going. He did a spell in which the urgent necessity was the house. The next time he walked by it, a Century 21 sign on the property announced that it was for sale. He knew then that his guidance had been correct. That

---

[12] *Painted ladies* is a generic term for beautiful old gingerbread houses restored and painted up colorfully to look wonderful. San Francisco is full of them—a sightseer's delight.

day he signed up for their next course, and at the same time asked about the house. The office staff told him that it was a real dog—a nonstarter—because it needed so much work. Of course the conference room behind Century 21's offices resembled the one he had seen in meditation. As he reported there for one class session, an elderly lady had come to the office to voice her discontent, insisting that her house should have sold by now. As she turned to leave, Jerome asked her whether her house was the one he was interested in. No, he didn't tell her he had a personal interest. Instead he invited her to coffee around the corner and offered to take her home. He told her that until the house got some really serious repairs, it would never sell. He offered to do a major part of the work himself, provided she took it off the market until they both agreed it was ready to show. By the time they parted, they had agreed that he would work on the house but would defer presenting a bill until the house sold.

It turned into a very good deal for them both. Lucinda was getting more feeble, and Jerome often helped her in such simple things as grocery shopping. Gradually his equity in the house grew to several thousand dollars. One day he decided it was time to try to talk her into selling the house to him. He redid his spell with more emphasis on his own purchasing. The very next day Lucinda asked him whether he wanted to buy the house, since he had put so much loving work into it. He agreed, but said frankly that he was not confident about getting a loan. She agreed to carry the mortgage for him. Lucinda moved into a retirement home, but didn't really like it. When she saw her former dwelling looking so stunning, she asked Jerome to set her off apartment space on one floor in return for a substantial reduction on the mortgage payment. The terms of their arrangement stipulated that she dwell on the sunny side of the house and have access to the back garden. He readily agreed, and Lucinda happily moved into a ground-floor flat that he carved out for her.

An added bonus for Jerome was that he now knew a great deal about the old houses of San Francisco and he had passed the exam for his salesman's license. He set himself up as a specialist in the old houses and in helping people with their renovation plans. Very soon he had a small group of artisans doing the actual work. Today, between sales commissions and the income from his small specialized renovation firm, he is comfortably well off and thinking of running for city council.

How big a part did magic play in Jerome's effort? Well, some; but hard work also played a major role. He got up on his hind legs, took definitive steps such as meditating, and enrolled in the class that meditation led him to. He realized that when the guides give guidance, but their channeler disregards it, the guides will soon begin to feel, "Why should we bother?" So he followed their suggestions with all his might.

FLESHING OUT YOUR SPELL

As you continue through this book you will learn Witches' secrets for improving and strengthening the work they do. This chapter is a brief introduction to the magical world of Witchcraft. In later chapters we will flesh out the spell casting so you will be more successful. At the same time we will round out the picture by helping you understand the spiritual side of the magic.

There is no need to delay your work. Yes, you don't know everything about spell casting, but we don't either—and we've been doing it for a very long time.

We have already reminded you that if you do nothing, nothing will result. Your life will continue directionless and will be nothing but a hassle. You should *enjoy,* and you should not have to work endless hours to gain that enjoyment.

Be like a Witch. Think reflectively to make your life self-actualizing. Don't drift like a plankton. Rejoice.

Operating the Web of the Wyrd

THE WEB OF THE WYRD IS REAL

If you have had doubts about the reality of the messages that can travel along the telepathic links of the psychic internet, read these testaments. Most of them deal with major events—the milestones of the psychic world—the accident, death, and healing experiences. These accounts are only a representative few chosen from thousands of such statements in our files. Reading them, one is forced to the conclusion that telepathy, healing, and prediction are real phenomena, and that the web exists.

TWELVE EXAMPLES OF THE WEB IN OPERATION

37BP[1]

A long time ago I was on a date with my fiancee and for no apparent reason, I decided to take her home early. I could offer her no explanation. Instead of taking the long route to her house as I always did, I went the short way which runs by the hospital. When

---

[1] All students of the School of Wicca receive code numbers to protect their identity. Unfortunately even today, centuries after the Burning Times, this is a practical necessity. The files are available for review by certified researchers.

I neared the hospital, I pulled in and parked my truck (naturally my date was upset). She asked what I thought I was doing and I replied that I had the feeling that her sister was here and needed help. We went in and found out her sister was in labor with complications. No one else knew anything about her condition. An unusual fact is the labor was premature and she lives several counties away. Also I parked my truck next to her brand new car that no one had at that time even seen.

Her mom was very upset about the whole affair and accused me of dabbling in the occult. Now it has been about eight years and I have not had a close girlfriend since, but I have had several unusual encounters with the "unknown," although I rarely mention this or other incidents to anyone.

27CP

Music has always "played" a major role in my life. Yesterday, it just might have saved it. I was extremely depressed over the events that had happened over the last four months in my life. I had been in a car accident, leaving me disabled, and had totaled my car. My engagement broke up. My father had an operation. Three very close friends moved or died. Other "friends" have "all of a sudden" found "other things to do" with their time than to be with me. I guess people's attitudes changed when I wasn't "normal" anymore. Such a shame. Anyway, I just wanted to die. I didn't want to live with me any more.

I prayed to my Guides to show me what to do, to die (end it all) or to live again. After my prayer, I spent some time in silence. I started to cry and walked over to a table where my stereo was. I looked at the stereo for a minute, then turned it on. What happened next was a total shock, literally! I felt a tingle go in my hand, up my arm and then shock me! My stereo fell silent for 10 seconds before I could put in a tape or record, out of the speakers, came the songs "Don't Give Up On Us," "Never Gonna Give You Up," and "There's No Easy Way Out." I couldn't move, literally, as if being "held" there to listen. I felt arms around me, as an embrace and a reassurance that my life was going to turn out fine. After the third song was over, the presence I had felt was gone.

I believe my prayers were answered. I guess I'll be around for a long time! Let the music play!

36NV

When I was 15 years old, I believe I had my first psychic experience. My mother was preparing the evening meal one day. Suddenly, she dropped her pots and pans and began to cry. My room was adjacent to the kitchen, so I went to investigate the problem. To my surprise, my mother was standing near the stove with her hand over her mouth and looking toward the front door. I turned to see what she was looking at and got the shock of my life. In the doorway was a tall glowing figure, somewhat human-shaped and surrounded by white glowing light. The figure didn't move, but it seemed to convey the word "peace" in my mind and my mother's. I walked over to the glowing figure and reached out to touch it. The word "peace" entered my mind again. I felt deep inside that I knew this figure somehow. While I was next to it I felt warm and cold at the same time and my feelings were serene; I didn't feel scared. As I reached out, the figure disappeared. At this period of time, before the figure appeared, my mother and I were quarreling bitterly, and causing other relatives to take sides. Several weeks after seeing the figure, I was looking through the family photo album and came across a picture of my grandfather who died while I was still a baby. As I looked at the picture of him, the feelings I had had while I was next to the figure happened again, along with the warm and cold sensation. This led me to believe that the figure was my grandfather, and he was telling us to be at peace with one another, and to quit the quarreling. Ever since that day, my mother and I get along really well. Every once in a while we will have a disagreement, but it is always settled peacefully.

34QX

Some 24 years ago I was working as a waitress in a little coffee shop in Santa Monica. We had a large number of regulars. When they came in, most would say hello or wave and I would put their orders in. One morning a man came in. I got his usual coffee, apple pie with a slice of cheese, and water with a slice of lemon. When I put his order in front of him, he looked at me rather funny and all of the color drained from his face. He asked how did I know what he wanted, especially the lemon in his water. I smiled and said, "George, you always have the same thing." Then he asked me how I knew his name. Before I could answer, he said he had just arrived from the east coast. He said he had never been in Santa Monica before. After that he never returned to the coffee shop.

34PWE

For three consecutive nights I dreamed that my grandmother had died and that she was buried in a light purple dress. I do not recall any other thing of my dream. I remember my mother being very upset when I told her of my dreams. One winter afternoon we received a telegram saying that my grandmother had passed away during her sleep. I remember my mother crying and wondering how I could have known it.

The years passed and when I was a teenager an older cousin came to visit us. She lives in the same city where my grandma used to live. There was nothing in common between us until by chance we talked about when grandma died. She proudly pointed out that grandma was buried in a dress that she (my cousin) had made in sewing class. I inquired about it, and my cousin told me it was a "light purple dress." This knowledge of her death and the way she was to be dressed for the burial before the actual death is something that has always perplexed me.

39YW

One night, a few years ago, I was awakened from a sound sleep by a violent coughing attack. My first thought was "Daddy, I smell smoke!" I quickly checked my apartment for fire. As I went from room to room, my coughing subsided and the smoky smell began to fade. But that one thought stayed in my mind, and I felt a strong sense of panic. Heedless of the time, I went to the phone and called my dad, who lived approximately seventy-five miles from me at that time. It took me several minutes to convince him to check for fire just to "ease my mind," as he put it. Finally, I got him to agree and to call me back. In approximately forty-five minutes, he called. Due to a fault in the construction, as we later learned, the bottom of the fireplace in the den had fallen out, dropping embers and smoldering ashes onto the furniture and carpet below in the recreation room. There was no intense fire, but a considerable amount of smoke. Damage was minimal, but could have had severe results, had he not agreed to my urgent request.

21RL

The night before I was due to board an airplane to attend my father's funeral in San Diego, I had a vision of people with me on the plane and flowers. I woke up, told my husband, and decided to change planes. After a delay of an hour at the airport, I boarded another plane and flew to San Diego. Upon landing there, I learned the other plane had crashed, killing all on board.

40BC

Last month I was riding with an acquaintance, her daughter, and mine. I turned to look at the girls in the back seat and abruptly said, "Put your seatbelts on. We're going in a ditch." Without question they both did as told. The driver glanced at me and asked, "What?" Then an angry silence. Several miles down the road we skidded on an apparently ice-free dip in the road and ended up "you-know-where." At this point the woman was furious with me, insisting I had subliminally influenced her actions. We all got out and walked over the rise to stop in stunned disbelief. There jackknifed in the road was a tractor-trailer. If we had come over that hill at our speed we would have slammed into the truck. Our car lying in the ditch warned other oncoming vehicles to slow, avoiding any accidents.

45JN

I have a friend whose mother suddenly became very ill. She was rushed to the hospital in severe, doubling-over pain. The doctors were convinced that her cancer had returned (after a twelve-year absence) and that she had a blockage of some sort in her bladder (which produced the severe pain). I told Carla that her mother would be okay and to try to relax and take it easy herself. She had worked herself into a frenzy. The next day I set to work. I was lying in the sun (I do some of my best meditation sessions this way) nude and just concentrating on the sun's rays on my skin. I tried a sort of astral projection where I could see the cancer and imagined a white aura balancing with red. Little by little the white became less dominant and more balanced. I used the sun's rays as a healing agent. The whole time I could see Carla's mother sitting in her kitchen chair as we all did only the week before sipping ice tea on a hot day. She seemed in perfect health.

I used that scene and went back to it. I could see us all there and concentrated on her healthy state. Then I went to the blockage. I could see it! I thought hard on it and made it burst through. That color was yellow. I actually saw it burst. I felt as though I pushed it through somehow. All of the sudden a nice light yellow and light blue and then light green feeling swept over me and I felt this incredible peace. Then I remembered where I was and just smiled. I felt good. That evening I visited Carla and she had the most incredible news! What the doctors thought was cancer had somehow vanished (for reasons they couldn't explain) and the blockage had burst through. She had a bit of infection from it, but nothing that couldn't be treated with antibiotics. She was going to be just fine and could go home in a couple of days. And everyone thought she was going to die. It really worked and I felt so happy and relieved for them.

44VB

I kept seeing my younger son Jason in a yellow car overturning on a curve on a mountain. I envisioned this same thing four times in two weeks. Naturally owning a yellow car at the time, I never let him drive it out of town, because we live in a valley and the only way out of town is over mountains. He came by one afternoon after school. He and a friend were going up to a park in the mountains about twenty-five miles from home. I asked him to take his ski jacket because of snow on the higher elevations. My son drove his friend's car to the park; his friend drove home. When Jason started to get into the car on the way home, he said later he heard my voice telling him to put his jacket on. He said my voice was so clear to him, as though I were there.

Halfway down the mountain the wheels locked, the car rolled twenty-seven times and skidded several hundred feet on the passenger side with Jason's arm underneath. He had a concussion, bruises and a bruised elbow and pavement burns on his right hand. They were wearing seatbelts. When the boys left my home I did not know it was a yellow VW Thing.

You can imagine how I felt when I walked behind the tow truck and looked at that yellow Thing.

40PM

I was in the mountains alone with the children. I was lying in the sun in the buff when I suddenly felt danger around my five-year-old daughter. I looked for her and found her at the creek surrounded by three wolves. I didn't have the shotgun. Without thinking what I was doing I sent out a thought to the wolves warning them and telling them to leave without harming her and I wouldn't harm them. The wolves slowly left but kept looking back. My baby was so frightened she couldn't speak for a while but otherwise she was unharmed. It's not normal behavior for wild wolves to leave prey they have trapped.

41YJ

My sister, who was younger than I and only thirty years of age, was going to have a hysterectomy. No cancer, just an ovarian tumor so we were not too worried about her. Two weeks before surgery I traveled 300 miles to see her and to make plans to be with her kids when she went into the hospital. Something came up and I couldn't be there. On Monday before she went into the hospital on Wednesday, I started to get very nervous and worried; I kept hearing this voice telling me she was going to die the day she had surgery. It kept getting stronger and stronger and it said to write her and tell her you love her. I didn't know what to do. I was afraid they would think I was insane if I asked them to delay surgery. On Thursday, I walked the floor waiting for them to call after surgery. At 5 P.M. they called and said she was doing great and was back in her room. I was so very happy and that night I went to bed early for my first good night of sleep in a week. At 11:30 P.M. her husband called and woke me up and said she was dead, a blood vessel had burst in her brain. You can imagine after that I almost had a nervous breakdown because I keep wondering what if I had gotten the surgery delayed, would she still have died?

EMPOWERING THE WEB OF THE WYRD

Any time you put out thoughts, especially those that are emotionally loaded, they go out along your web links. The stronger the thought and the stronger the link, the stronger the impact of the thought on the connected person. Thus your links to your significant other or to your children are probably very, very strong. And if, for instance, you have a traumatic experience, then if any of the receivers are in a quiet mood, they will get the full impact of your thoughts. The human mother knows when her daughter has been in a traffic accident.

When you are working a spell, you need the strongest possible psychic link to the target and the best possible mind triggers to your intent.

SPELL-WORK 201

Despite what you have heard all your life, magic is not always the solution to every problem. Before they commit to the intricate procedure and the effort involved in casting a spell, Witches make a carefully considered decision on the alternatives available. One alternative to magic is that four-letter word *work*. Another alternative is channeling—a receptive, listening mode, not the clamor of magic. (Prayer equals asking. Channeling equals listening for guidance.)

There are two kinds of spell, corresponding to the two directions in which the mind can reach:

1. a *spiritual* upward-reaching spell that affirms your desire to live in harmony with the will of the Guides[2] and Elder Ones (as best you can perceive it);

2. a horizontal, *secular* spell to affect future events.[3]

Think about these two directions and the reasons for each until you can clearly distinguish between them; then decide which sort applies to your purpose. Yes, even in truly spiritual activities, a little magic creeps in if you do healing work; but the two activities can be—perhaps should be—quite separate. The secular, temporal, paycheck world has little to do with spiritual growth, beyond functioning as a classroom.

---

[2] Guides are discarnate entities whom you will contact during channeling. They have chosen to teach those of us still "alive" in earth-plane shells.

[3] We are simplifying, as usual. As with everything else, the "two-types-of" polarizing paradigm, either/or, may not fit your experience. Often it's not either/or; it's both—and more. Of course, *horizontal* and *vertical* are also oversimplifications.

GLADYS CALLS THE DOG CATCHER

Gladys Frost, Gavin's late mother, lived in a condominium in Lee-on-Solent, England. Her sister-in-law and best friend, Wynne, lived close by in a beach cottage. Though English people traditionally lavish affection on their dogs, somehow many dogs got dumped in Wynne's front yard. She was too kind-hearted to take them to the veterinarian to be put to sleep, so she was always looking for homes for dogs. Eventually one day Gladys visited Wynne and saw that the situation was out of hand. There were three large dogs in the front yard, one of them an obviously disturbed black Labrador. Now Gladys liked dogs herself, and she made overtures to the black Lab because they are well known to be intelligent, courteous dogs. But this dog wasn't, and it bit her. She was really scared, fearing that the dog had rabies. They called the local veterinarian. He caught the dog, put it to sleep, and examined its brain tissue. He was able to assure Gladys that the dog was not sick. Nevertheless, Galdys insisted on rabies shots for herself and Wynne. This was a very big step indeed in the lives of two senior women living in tranquil retirement.

After all this, Wynne decided that she should take steps to discourage the dog-dumping. She did a little spell that she hoped would discourage dogs from wandering onto her property. Yet the next time Gladys visited, there were *five* dogs vying for territory on Wynne's miniscule front lawn. Furious, Gladys charged into the house and called the RSPA (Royal Society for the Protection of Animals). When she got no reaction from them, she followed up with a call to the city dog catcher. He promptly came out and took the dogs to the pound. The next time Gladys visited Wynne, there were no dogs.

Wynne needed a while to overcome her pique at Gladys's taking matters into her own hands. When she was stable, she confided that news of Gladys's action had been broadcast about the neighborhood. Now nobody would risk dumping dogs anywhere near Wynne's cottage.

Why did Wynne's spell not work? It was not focused on a single person or dog. Without a defined target, there is little chance a spell will be effective. In contrast, it was real-world steps that got the job done.

THE LANGUAGE OF SPELLS

Language used in spells is meant to express an emotional intent. It does not matter what words are actually used, provided that they express a high emotional level and a carefully defined intent. Do not be surprised if your Guide gets involved, showing or telling you a better way to do something. Some groups favor the use of old languages and archaic terminology. When they understand the emotion behind the words, that will work well for them, for they have put a great deal of effort into research and understanding of the words. But when participants just parrot incomprehensible phrases or read from a script to live out some fantasy, the spell fails.

When Solomon called down power, he used Hebrew names that we now regard as archaic; when he wrote on his pentacles, he used Hebrew letters. Solomon was a Hebrew. When Hebrew was replaced by Latin as the language of scholars, Solomon's words were translated into Latin because that's what learned people could read and write. The translation made Solomon's work effective for those who could read and understand Latin. Today we use plain English if that is our native language.

We do not yet understand well the mechanics of communication, but records show many examples of (for instance) people under hypnosis being controlled by instructions in languages they had no knowledge of. In other words, somehow the mind translates messages into actions even though the words "ought" to be meaningless. In the same way, animals will respond to commands in many different languages even when the words sound different.

We believe this happens because commands, especially psychic commands, are expressed not in actual words, but in emotionally coded signals that trigger reactions in the deepest recesses of our minds. Thus, in doing magical work, you must transmit the emotionally coded signal, not some words that have little or no meaning in your reality. If you transmit gibberish, gibberish is what the receiver gets. When a person who speaks only English attempts to transmit thoughts in ancient Hebrew, he lowers his chances of establishing contact for two reasons:

1. He doesn't key his mind correctly.
2. The receiver is unable to understand the transmission.

Contrast that with the example above where the *words* spoken to someone under hypnosis were in a language strange to that person, but where the *thought* transmitted was in English—the individual's native language.

It is also obvious that the repetition of a meaningless magical name is useless:

Stand. Face east. In a loud voice repeat sixteen times, ‎יהוה‎.

Instructions like this are common in magical texts. The pronunciation of the word is lost; the nearest we can come is "JHVH" or, in chanting, "Elelu."

Similarly you might find instructions like,

Kneel in a perfect circle. With the blade of your athame between your teeth, your wand in your right hand, and your white-handled sword in the left, think: "Tetragrammaton."

Tetragrammaton literally means *four-letter word*. In occult circles it is taken to cover all the spellings of the names of God. Unfortunately, in the world at large a *four-letter word* has a somewhat different connotation. Witches prefer to think of the word *God* or *Goddess,* believing this thought results in better two-way understanding. It is easy to change the language of an incantation to your local language, though you need to retain the significance and the emotion of the original words.

Ancient ways are often useful guides, but in psychic work it has been our experience that we don't know enough about them to make them fully effective. So let us establish some guidelines for verses suitable for Craft work in today's world, as summarized in Figure II-1.

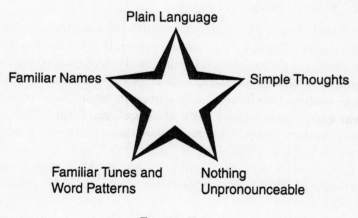

FIGURE II–1
Your Pentagram of Successful Spell-Casting

What works?

1. Plain language;
2. simple thoughts;
3. familiar names;
4. no unknown, unpronounceable alphabet or runes; and
5. familiar tunes and word patterns.

In the past, number 5 above has meant that Witches were accused of performing black masses and other sacrileges when they used well known hymn tunes. The reasoning behind our use of Christian format is obvious: Most Witches in the English-speaking and English-thinking groups once attended Christian churches regularly and thus are familiar with the emotions engendered by a given set of tunes and words. The person or group whom you are trying to influence—even if they are out of the body—are most likely to have lived in a Christian matrix. Success stems from the familiarity and comfort of a familiar format.

In the Craft this process is called *stealing back,* and we do it frequently. Of course *stealing back* refers to the fact that early Catholic spells and feast days were copied almost entirely by Catholics from earlier Wiccan practice! The church has now so lost the significance and requirements of the spells and feasts that they have become nearly meaningless in their present usage; but they still work marvelously when restored to their original context.

YOUR PSYCHIC LINK

In most spell-work, one step may consist of directly influencing a specific person. To aim the Force accurately, you need a psychic link to that person. In medieval times, nail clippings and hair served as popular psychic links. Hence, there is a great amount of folklore about disposing of body wastes. The most powerful negative spell we have ever seen calls for the hand of a dead murderer.[4] This is from the early modern historical period; occultists still regard it with skittish awe. The "hand of glory" or "dead hand" was popular among thieves, who perceived it as an aid in their work. It must have been the ultimate psychic link to negativity.

---

[4] The "Hand of Glory." The user cut off the hand of a criminal and drew the sinews taut so it could clutch a candle made from the body fat of the same corpse.

Today the most common link is a photograph of the target person. A photo combined with a little of the body fluids (saliva, blood, urine, or semen) forms a most powerful link.

The psychic link can be regarded as the bank account number or e-mail address of the target. The more information you can put into the psychic link to strengthen it, the more accurately the force that you send out will hit the target. A partial account number will not work so well as if you have all the digits.

Some links contain their own forces and thus may ruin an otherwise good spell. In this category we put such things as a used handkerchief or the girlfriend's pantyhose. If you are doing a spell to heighten a lusty relationship, the pantyhose might be very appropriate; but a dirty hanky might turn the whole thing off.

EDWIN USED THE WRONG PICTURE

Edwin L is a Hollywood stunt man who lives in downtown Los Angeles. He is growing a little old now for the more athletic stunts; he contents himself mostly with car stunts and with coordinating other stunts. Through all this he comes in contact with many stars and starlets. For many years he took advantage of every starlet who thought he might "know someone."

Ed was a happy man until he met Candice. Perhaps because she rejected him, perhaps because he was fed up with easy conquests and one-night stands, lightning (as the French say) struck. He fell for her. Despite his best, most suave efforts, he couldn't get anywhere with her. Being an amateur Witch, he decided to do a spell. One night he broke into her locker at the studio and "borrowed" a pair of her shoes and a publicity photo. To charge them, he put them under his bed while he made passionate love to yet another starlet. Once that one had departed, he did a spell for companionship and love. At the height of the spell he dumped the shoes into hot water and burned the picture. Early the following morning he returned the shoes to her locker, then went on to the cafeteria for breakfast until she reported in.

She still wanted nothing to do with him. He knew that spells take time, so he waited patiently for results. He was somewhat dismayed that other starlets around the lot seemed to be following Candice's lead in spurning him. This contrasted all the more sharply with approaches and broad hints from Jean, one of the senior secretaries. Everywhere he went, Jean seemed to be waiting for him. She was not unattractive, but she was old—almost as old as he was, for pity's sake!

After a week of Jean's pressure, especially since by now he was hard up for companionship, Ed agreed to Jean's invitation to a dinner date. When he called to pick her up, she answered the door in her bathrobe. She invited him in and asked him to help her dress. Since she was nude under the robe and the bed was right there, Ed's response was immediate. Only afterward did he have time to notice a green candle burning on a side table with his picture near it. When Jean was coherent again, she told him she was a Witch and about a week ago she'd suddenly felt a violent passionate urge for him. Ed congratulated her on her spell-work, and then rather shamefacedly told of his own failure.

Jean laughed so hard she almost burst. When she returned from the bathroom, still laughing, she told Edwin, "My daughter Candice asked me if I had taken her picture of me. She couldn't figure out where it had gone."

"Did you look like her when—?" Edwin was in trouble.

"When I was younger, yes. She's the very image of me at that age. You spelled *me* into your life, you idiot. Now what are we going to do?"

Well, they never got to dinner that night. As matters developed, Edwin found how deeply this woman of his age shared his interest in the occult, and realized that she was far more interesting and knowledgeable than any of the pretty nymphets he had so cheerfully slept with.

In the month before they married, they both undid their spells—but they could detect no difference in the passion they shared. At the last contact we had with them, they were still very enthusiastically married (or in Witch terms, *handfasted*).

MORE IS BETTER

When you decide to do an attracting spell, remember that it is a caging spell and thus has negative connotations. In Edwin and Jean's case it did no harm, and they undid it before they finally handfasted. Women should be especially careful when doing spells of this type. Men often have less control of their sexual urges than women, and if Jean had decided at the last moment to call a halt, things might have turned very ugly. It is often said that women have no need of "Playboy" magazine, since all they have to say to that hunk at the appropriate moment is—"strip!"

It is clear to us that Edwin didn't look closely at the photo he "adopted," and it turned out that the shoes he took belonged to the studio and many women had worn them.

If you are doing a spell for a specific person, get as many links and as varied as you can: the more, the better. If you are doing a spell to bring an unknown into your life, write down as many characteristics as you can think of. In this case, avoid using an actual picture of a living person. Instead, be as descriptive as you can. Many experienced Witches feel that a single-spaced typewritten page is not excessive.

In doing spell-work, remember to take one step at a time. No matter what your final goal, break down the process into the steps of Chapter I. There is still validity in the old saying,

The gods help those who help themselves.

Doing a spell is one thing; putting yourself in the path of people whom the spell will attract is a second essential step. ("Buy a ticket, Aaron!") Look at the profession(s) and the hobbies you've specified. If you want a doctor, get trained to become a nurse or an EMT (emergency medical technician). If you want a dancer, take dance lessons. It's easy. From your description there will be obvious things you should do and places you should go, instead of just haphazardly going to the meat-market of a singles bar. Focusing your mundane and your magical life gets better results than magic alone. Sitting at home moaning, "I want . . ." as you telescope into your own fat before the idiot box—that just doesn't work. Become self-actualizing. Get up and do it!

MIND KEYS OR TRIGGERS FOR SEVEN INTENTS

There are thousands of things you might want to work toward, of course: far too many for us to list them all. Instead, we have condensed the options to just seven, based on the old principle that most people are largely interested in the basics.

Beyond these two areas of interest, the five we've added summarize the requests we constantly get for help. Notice that these are generalized intents. In later chapters we will expand on the general topic for such things as healing specific diseases. *Attack* may look like an unconventional title for an intent. It really applies to any time you anticipate going into a demanding situation such as asking for a raise, getting the auto mechanic to do your will, or any time when you really need to be assertive.

COLOR

In many ancient temples people who sought healing sat in sunbeams shining through colored windows. The famous rose window of Chartres Cathedral is one well known example of the practice. These days, large corporations and restaurants spend exorbitant amounts of money on getting room colors right. The "hurry-up-and-eat" reds of the fast-food franchises are matched in industry, where think-tank rooms (also in red) accelerate brainstorming sessions intended to solve problems.

The colors in your life affect you: the cheerfulness of sunny yellow, the wealth that purple indicates, the fear stimulated by red-splotched black. Hence, it is only sensible to use color as one of the most powerful mind triggers.

FLAVOR

Just as with color, flavor triggers your emotions. Bitter tastes correlate with loss, and sweet with love and home comforts. We all know the emotional connotations of taste; for instance, the taste of fear.

AROMA

Is aromatherapy one of the new discoveries of the later 20th and early 21st centuries? We have news: It's been around for centuries. The other night as we approached a restaurant, we caught one of those awful cooked rotten meat smells from the kitchen. We dined down the block!

TOUCH

Just as the other sensory inputs do, touch triggers your mind. Imagine you are in the dark and touch something cold and greasy— or alternately, some warm soft skin. Immediately, your mind is either repelled or attracted. Thus, touch can engender any emotion you can imagine.

CHANTS

Before the dawn of recorded history, people used chants to tune their minds to specific intents and to raise energy. Some of the haunting Gregorian chants are nothing more than energy-raising devices designed to help the monastery or church in which they were performed.

Many Witches and occultists seem to think that the Hindu *aum* is the only chant available; not so. The Hindu system alone specifies an appropriate chant for each deity, and each chant has its individual speed and pitch. The Table of Seven Intents (Table II-1) provides basic chants for the intents. The HEDE column defining the speed of the whirl also gives its timing. For slow HEDE, the chant is slow and the pitch should be a low, resonant hum—to a musician, *largo.* From the Pitch column you can see that the pitch, the speed, and also the style of the chant change. It can be *staccato;* it can be *resonant.* It can be *wailing.* All of these subtleties affect the type of energy you send out.

DRUMMING

If you are fortunate enough to have a keen drummer working with you, she should drum at the same rate as the HEDE is being transmitted or the chant is being done. Her style of drumming should change to fit the style of the chant; that is, she should use a large bass drum for the low chants, and a small high-pitched drum or even hollow wooden blocks for the staccato chants. Interestingly, in Korean shamanic work (which can be documented to over 2,000 years ago), five to seven percussionists play a wide range of instruments to raise power and to attain altered states of consciousness.

TIMING

In Table II-1, Timing focuses on the moon and its phases. It is well known that all animate beings are affected by the moon's gravitational pull. For millennia farmers have planted those plants that grow upward in a waxing moon (within three days of a new moon) and root crops by the light of the waning moon (within three days of a full moon).

| INTENT | SIGHT | TASTE | SMELL | TOUCH | CHANT | CHANT | CHANT | TIMING |
DESIRE	COLOR	FLAVOR	SCENT	FEELING	SOUND	PITCH/STYLE	SPEED	MOON
Wealth	Gold	Burgundy	Saffron	Velvet	Gay-ah	Low, Resonant Hum Largo	Slow	New
Love	Emerald Green	Port Wine	Orange Blossom	Making Love	Yah-weh	Medium Flowing Legato	Medium/ Slow	New
Serenity	Light Blue	Flounder	Lavender	Gelatin	A-um	Low, Resonant Hum Largo	Very Slow	Any
General Healing	Grass-Green	Salt	Rose	Baby Skin	Aye-oh	Very High Wailing Spirituoso	Very Fast	Full
Attack	Red	Chili	Tobacco	Burlap	Ele-lu	High Sharp Staccato	Fast	Full
Luck	Dark Blue	Oatmeal and Brown Sugar	Narcissus	Cuddling	Aye-oh-em	High Sharp Staccato	Fast	New
Protection	Yellow	Butter	Night-Scented Stock	Waxed Wood	Homm	Medium Flowing Legato	Medium	New

TABLE II–1
Mind Triggers for Seven Intents

In ancient times and still today religious festivals are scheduled by a moon calendar. Though the Crucifixion must have happened on a fixed calendar date, the Christian church calculates it by the moon. "Easter Sunday is the first Sunday after the full moon which happens upon or next-after the twenty-first day of March." Witches understand that the great holidays or sabbats were all tied to a moon calendar, one we still use. Cowans[5] mock the great Craft festival of Samhain, which is celebrated on the night of the full moon nearest November 1. Yet that same feast appears on modern calendars as Hallowe'en or as All Souls' Eve. The big difference is that cowans celebrate Hallowe'en arbitrarily on the same calendar day every year without considering the phase of the moon.

To maximize lunar energies, you will work when the moon is overhead: preferably close to its zenith. This means midnight at full moon when you want things to decrease, and noon at new moon when you want things to grow. Such timing may seem to contradict the tenet that you should work while your target person is asleep. Thus you have to give some thought to wording your spells precisely to accomplish the appropriate action at the correct phase of the moon. Some examples:

Increase my wealth	new moon
Decrease my debt	full moon
Heal Aunt Josephine (shrink her tumor)	full moon
Heal Aunt Josephine (increase her vitality)	new moon

Your favorite astrologer may try to convince you that you should do your spell in the appropriate sign of the zodiac. Yes, it is true that spells done in the right sign work a little better. Be sure your astrologer realizes that you want the moon in the right sign at the time you're working.

The conventional table of zodiac birthdates gives dates when the dawn sun is in a given sign. In general, the moon at midnight or noon is four signs off from the sun sign. As Figure II-2 shows, as the Earth rotates, the subject is in each sign for two hours.

---

[5] Cowan: one not of the Craft. Just as Scots Highlanders have *sassenachs*, Greeks have *barbarians,* and Jews have *gentiles,* so Witches have *cowans.*

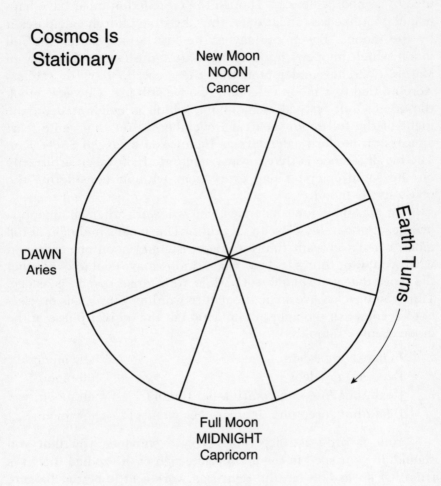

FIGURE II–2
Sun Signs in Moon Time

The figure shows that if, for instance, Aries (March 21–April 22) is the dawn sign (sun sign), then this means that Cancer (June 21–July 22) is the sign of the new moon at noon and Capricorn (December 21–January 21) is the sign at midnight. To get the correct dawn sign for your spell, look at Table II-2.

NEW MOON RITUALS FOR GROWTH		FULL MOON SPELLS FOR DIMINISHING	
Required Sign	**Dawn Sign**	**Required Sign**	**Dawn Sign**
Aries	Capricorn	Aries	Cancer
Taurus	Aquarius	Taurus	Leo
Gemini	Pisces	Gemini	Virgo
Cancer	Aries	Cancer	Libra
Leo	Taurus	Leo	Scorpio
Virgo	Gemini	Virgo	Sagittarius
Libra	Cancer	Libra	Capricorn
Scorpio	Leo	Scorpio	Aquarius
Sagittarius	Virgo	Sagittarius	Pisces
Capricorn	Libra	Capricorn	Aries
Aquarius	Scorpio	Aquarius	Taurus
Pisces	Sagittarius	Pisces	Gemini

TABLE II–2
Required Sign and Dawn Sign

THE PATIENT DIED

Otis R was elderly and infirm. His granddaughter Belinda despaired for his life. A neophyte Witch, she had tried various herbal remedies to no avail. She was very fond of her Grandpa and wanted to do all she could for him, and her mother and an elderly aunt encouraged her efforts. Belinda "knew" she couldn't do a spell because the timing was not right. An astrologer friend had convinced her that she must wait for the correct astrological sign to come around. While she was dutifully waiting, her Grandpa passed away. Whether or not Belinda's spell would have saved him is moot now—but that did not diminish her guilt for not having tried. Only when she became more knowledgeable in the underlying principles of progressive reincarnation did she realize that her spell could have been done at any time and might have prolonged his life; but it could also have caused his spirit to degrade through being kept in an earth-plane shell after its learning in this level of existence had been completed.

Later Belinda was able to channel her Grandpa. That finally removed all her negative feelings, since he sounded more happy where he was than he had been in his earth-plane shell.

HERMES TRISMEGISTUS

The ancient sage Hermes Trismegistus (thrice-master) wrote down a law that has persisted to this day. It says that anything you send out will be returned to you threefold. It has been known since earliest times that psychic links are a two-way communication system. When you tune yourself to a patient's illness, you open yourself up to getting that illness.

You have around you a protective electromagnetic field that occultists call an *aura*. Many people can see the aura as a colored field; others hear it; still others can "feel" it. Its effects can be photographed in a process known as *Kirilian photography*. When someone is sick, the aura changes and shows the illness; the psychic link to that person also changes to match the aura. Using color as an example, a dull red aura and psychic link indicate a blood disease such as AIDS. To communicate along that link in your healing, you will tune to dull red—but now a two-way street is open. You can receive not only the patient's problem but also any other dull red emanations.

Hermes Trismegistus's threefold axiom may be a little arbitrary; we doubt that it is subject to proof by experiment. But energy does often return to you at least doubled; and if the feedback starts, it can be returned to you at almost any level—maybe twentyfold. Who knows?

With all this in mind, it is clear that when you send something out, you must be very careful about

1. putting up a reflecting shield;

2. minimizing the time you spend in "dull red";

3. getting rid of any residual energy immediately, once the spell is completed; and

4. retuning yourself so that anything reflected will be nullified.

Doing these things is relatively easy.

WALLY D AND THE NATIVE AMERICANS

Wally D lives in St. Laurent, a suburb of Montreal. When we knew him some years ago, he was working toward his doctorate in sociology. His major field of interest was the healing "folklore" of the large Native American Algonquian population in the St. Laurent area. He had recently married, and so had Gavin. The two young couples lived in adjacent apartments and became friends, often sharing meals and occasionally going places together. Two or three weeks in succession, Wally and Deena had to break supper engagements because Wally was sick. "I've caught something from my Algonquian informants," he said when we met him in the hall. When he recovered, the dinner dates resumed; still Wally kept on getting rather peculiar illnesses. Deena was very concerned. "He's getting it from the Indians!" she fretted.

Gavin took Wally out and asked him, man-to-man, what was all this with the Native Americans. Was Wally getting overly friendly with some of the relaxed Algonquian maidens? Wally told him that his sociology work was very interesting and rewarding because they had been doing some psychic healing circles, and they had actually let him not just observe but participate. Gavin, too, had several friends among the Algonquians, and he suspected that something was amiss in the healing circles. He talked with one of the lower chiefs and learned that yes, indeed, Wally was a powerful transmitter and they had used him in several circles. "Did you protect him? Did he get grounded out afterward?"

"Well, you know, he's a bit uptight, like most of you white boys, so he doesn't relax properly afterward. Still, he's married, so that should be all right."

Gavin knew then that Wally was not using the quickest standard method of grounding and changing psychic frequencies, which is having sex.[6] Thus until he grounded out, Wally was still open to the healing frequency they had been using; and this in turn left him vulnerable to the illnesses they had been working to heal.

---

[6] He could have used other methods of grounding, such as working in his window-box garden or taking a cold shower.

Finally we persuaded Deena that she needed to accompany Wally to the circles, and to make sure that after each one he was grounded and his frequency changed back to that of his life in the mundane world.

WHAT WENT WRONG

As you have learned, the Web of the Wyrd results in two-way streets. Wally's story illustrates what can happen when someone comes into the "occult" not knowing the possible consequences of leaving those doors open after a working. The Algonquians were working within a circle, and they were skilled enough to minimize the time spent on any intent. Those two facts alone constitute a protective shield. However, when Wally left the circle, he was still excited and "up," still very much open to the psychic connections that workers made within the circle. He did not, as we say, ground out that excess—but most important, he did not retune himself away from the frequency of the healing.

Thus, in constructing a spell, you need to consider the closing parts as carefully as you do your actual power-raising and tuning steps.

CIRCLES WITHIN CIRCLES

The Witch's circle is her temple. It serves two purposes: It forms a protective field in which to work; and it forms a container for the raised energy until she directs it to its target. For each ceremony she constructs the circle anew so that

1. The emotions from the previous circle do not affect the new ceremony;

2. the worker(s) will remember the Sacred Measure and the symbols; and

3. no physical evidence remains between times that anyone is practicing the Craft.

Currently it is not a burning offense to practice a federally recognized religion, so some Witches permanently mark the floor of their ritual space with the accurately dimensioned circles. Then for the actual circle they cover the permanent circles with sulfur, salt, or copper sulfate.[7]

With regard to casting of circles, size is everything. Traditionally a coven casts a circle 11 feet in diameter and a single worker a circle 5 feet in diameter. Gavin learned long ago that all ancient monuments, from Stonehenge to the Rollright Stones, were built to a measure called the *megalithic yard* of 2.72 English feet, and that the yard varied with latitude. Honoring those facts, the directors of the School of Wicca decided to have neophyte Witch students cast circles to that measure. Some 50,000 circles later, findings proved conclusively that the Ancients were right. Today we recommend a coven circle of 10.88 feet in diameter and a solitary circle of 5.44 feet. This is the outer defensive and containing circle. It marks the plane where a *sphere of protection* intersects with the ground. The sphere goes into the air over you and into the ground under you; its equator coincides with the ground.

Findings from student work show something else as well: Only those circles made of electrically conducting materials will work. Typical effective materials are:

1. Damp sea salt
2. Copper wire 1/4" diameter
3. Charcoal
4. Copper sulfate
5. Burnt sulfur

Another way to put up a reflective shield is to surround yourself with outward-facing mirrors. For centuries mirrors have served to reflect and dissipate energy. The cheap, thin plastic mirrors available in home-improvement stores won't work; you need good plateglass mirrors, ideally with a mercury-silvered surface.

DON'T PICK AT IT

Once you've done a spell, it's natural to wonder whether you did it right and to worry about what effect it had. Every time you do this, though, you tune yourself back down to the frequencies of the spell

---

[7] We do not suggest consumption of this product in anyway. It is to be used in circle.

itself—and of course *that* opens you up again to the illness you were supposed to be curing. It is easy to construct a spell in which you tune yourself, build a chant, clap your hands or clap out a candle, and send the energy out, all in maybe less than thirty seconds. The mistake many individuals (and groups) make is to discuss it and let their thoughts dwell on it afterward. Forget it. Either it will work or it won't, and you'll learn soon enough whether it did. Dwelling on it will dilute its effect and will leave you open to illness or harm.

THE SORCERESS' CAT

Many old woodcuts of Witches show a cat accompanying the Witch. That cat's fur is swelled out as it would be if the cat were hooked up to a source of high-voltage electricity. Every individual hair sticks stiffly out. The woodcut shows the stereotypical *familiar*, supposedly the Witch's satanic helper. In fact, the cat is serving here as the grounding device for her excess energy.

Today you don't need a cat. You can get rid of excess energy if you kneel on the cool earth and put your palms and forehead flat down, or you might take a bath, or have sex. Whichever means you choose, do it as soon as possible after you complete the spell. If you choose sex as your means, you will gain the added advantage of adjusting your endorphins so that you can channel.

If none of these procedures is an option but you still need to retune yourself, drink a glass of very cold water with the juice of a lemon added. Listen to some upbeat music, or dance a few steps of something lively such as swing or samba. Any or all of these choices will move your mind away from the ritual and into other, more "up" spaces, and you will get back into the normal flow of your life without difficulty.

SUMMARY

The Web of the Wyrd explains many "occult" phenomena. Not the least of these is the two-way, bi-directional nature of psychic links. We also know that the links grow weak over long distances, although Russian research has proven that they work over at least 3,000 miles and American work demonstrates that they work through many hundreds of feet of ocean water. Workers long believed that the links did not work across oceans, and it is true that they are weakened in trying to work from, say, the United States to Europe; but they still work.

Spells are relatively easy to construct and, if constructed with care, work amazingly well with no risk to the worker.

Spell-Work
301

TWO PLUS TWO SOMETIMES EQUALS TEN

What can you do when your spell has failed or been only partly successful? First, a check of the spell is in order. Make sure that the steps are in sequence and that the psychic links and mind keys are appropriate. Often, though, the problem lies not with the spell but with the energy you put into it. If you did it when you were down or depressed, you should recharge yourself before a second attempt. It may also be that you need to put more energy into the spell to overcome other forces, such as the negativity of the patient, or of those surrounding the patient.

There are many sources of the Force. As Figure III-1 shows, you can add one or more of them to your spell-working. Following is a partial list of these sources:

1. Yourself and HEDE;
2. Stone god/esses or "mascots";
3. The ancient god/esses;
4. Naturally occurring elements such as crystals, metals, and wood;
5. The cosmos itself;
6. Running water;
7. Geological faults; and
8. A group of friends.

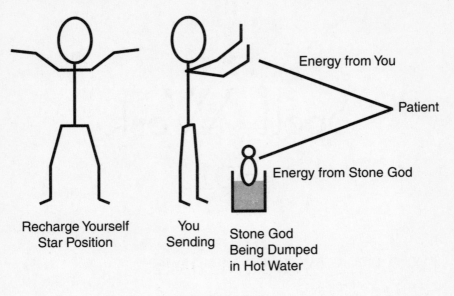

Recharge Yourself
Star Position

You
Sending

Stone God
Being Dumped
in Hot Water

Energy from You

Patient

Energy from Stone God

FIGURE III–1
Using Energy from Hearth God/esses

FIREWORKS AND SPELLS

You may already have learned that when you do such things as feel your own energy or control a Crookes Radiometer, or move a table-tennis ball across a table, you have to be "up." You have to be excited and genuinely involved in the process. To get the most out of a spell you must be involved, "turned on," and excited about your goal. It's no good just to hope languidly for something to happen. You have to really *want it,* and you have to put that need out in a very positive, forceful way. We think of this approach as being explosive, just like a firecracker going off. In fact a friend of ours fires a gun at the height of a spell, and he does seem to have a very high rate of success. You don't need a gun or a firecracker, though. A loud yell, a solid clap of the hands, the burning of a picture, will all work, just as long as you get involved with the spell, not caring about your personal image. If the spell is to succeed you may have to make a fool of yourself. Which do you care more about—your image in the eyes of associates or the success of your working?

GUSTAVE MADE IT HAPPEN

Gustave S lived in the little town of Geiselgasteig just south of Munich (Muenchen), in the German state of Bavaria. Geiselgasteig is well known as home to a large segment of Germany's thriving film industry.

Gustave had written a rather offbeat play about *zauberers* (sorcerers) in Bavaria. The play contained a great deal of unusual information that he had channeled about the real relationship of Adolph Hitler's Nazi party with sorcerers. He also interviewed several elderly men and women who personally experienced, and clearly remembered, what really happened during the Nazi regime. He felt a strong and enduring desire to show vividly that the Nazis were not half so much into the occult as many commentators had supposed. He also wanted to show that the German occult community felt a lifelong distaste for Nazi aims and behaviors. In the play he had naturally included a threatened heroine, an evil Nazi villain, and a good sorcerer. It was a good story, but not politically acceptable in Hitler's home ground of Bavaria, even fifty years after the whole thing had so painfully resolved itself.

Gustave's informants wanted the story told. Yet the more he pushed, the more resistant his bosses seemed. Finally he realized that the studio was assigning him less and less work. Maintaining his upscale lifestyle living in the upmarket community of Geiselgasteig was becoming difficult. With the encouragement of his informants, he put together a spell. He thought the spell would imbue his manuscript with so much energy that the company president would want to read it—and turn it into a film.

Gustave was an excellent, skilled designer and caster of spells. He did all the right things. At the height of the spell he even slammed the manuscript into the candle that served as his focusing point. Then he sent the manuscript off to the president of the studio and confidently waited for a phone call.

That call did not come, though a couple of lower-level people in the studio told him they thought the story was first-rate. When Gustave asked around, he learned that the manuscript had never reached the president's desk; a secretary had shuffled it off to a "reader."

He rethought the situation and decided that this time he would go directly for the president. Instead of empowering the manuscript, he would put the desire into the president to read the manuscript. He designed another spell, and this time went all out. He got more friends around him to play-act the heroine being attacked by the Nazi villain and saved by sorcery. The keys he used were wealth and prosperity for the president of the studio. Fortunately he had made several copies of the manuscript. At the height of the spell, he blew up one copy with a charge of black powder.

Gustave's spell succeeded. The movie itself, though well received by critics, was not immediately a wild success. It turned out to be a cult classic, not a runaway box-office hit.

THE HUMAN/EARTH DYNAMO EFFECT (HEDE)

For centuries observers wondered about the great effectiveness of Sufi spell-work, particularly the successes attributed to "whirling dervishes." We believe that there is a rational, understandable explanation for such success. Gavin brought together the worlds of radiation physics and occult research. The Force seems to be some kind of electrical waveform transmitted at an extra-low frequency (ELF) with as yet undefined phase coding. Living entities (and some inanimate objects) have electrical fields. When you, acting as a little electrical field or magnet, spin in the Earth's giant magnetic field, just like a dynamo you produce a high amount of the Force tuned to the speed of the spin (or *whirl,* as we prefer to call it). Figure III-2 shows this effect.

You turn yourself into a minute electromagnetic machine. In effect you can make yourself into a powerfully pulsing magnet. And when that magnet moves in the Earth's cosmo-magnetic field, you amplify your powers. The fastest and easiest way to generate additional power, therefore, is to pivot around yourself in a fast spin, as Figure III-2 illustrates. This technique has been practiced for centuries. It is still current among whirling dervishes and "Turners," a religious sect in England and the United States. In the Craft we call it the Human/Earth Dynamo Effect or *HEDE.* The idea is that you direct and modulate some of the Gaea-magnetic force with your own power.

In the Northern Hemisphere, to build up a positive field, you spin clockwise or, as Native Americans say, sunwise. The Craft word

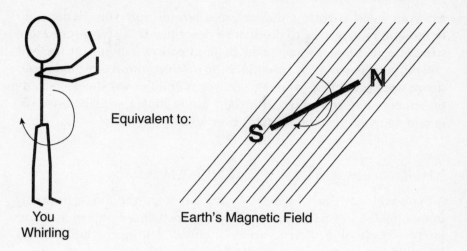

Equivalent to:

You
Whirling

Earth's Magnetic Field

FIGURE III–2
Generating HEDE

for this is *deosil.* Typically, you could spin deosil chanting the correct chant and building your power to a peak, then explosively release it to trigger the electromagnetic force.

To generate negative energy, you spin counterclockwise or *widdershins* in the Northern Hemisphere (contrary to the sun's movement). This is especially useful when you wish to diminish magic or to counter an attack placed against you.

You can spin at different rates, from a very slow rotation to a high-speed whirl. Table III-1 (on page 63) suggests the rate of spin for various intents you may have.

Some people have not learned to spin on their vertical axis.

1. To spin sunwise (*deosil,* or clockwise in the Northern Hemisphere): Imagine the ball of your right foot fastened to the floor.

2. Leave the right foot stationary while you spin on the ball (behind the toes) of that foot, using the left foot to push yourself around.

In spinning *widdershins,* you spin on the ball of your left foot while you use your right foot to push yourself around. In either case, tilt your head slightly backward and stretch out your arms. The technique is far easier to do than to describe. This step is precisely what is called for in square dancing and contra dancing, at the call "Swing your partner." It resembles the motion your feet would make if you were propelling yourself along on a child's two-wheeled scooter, except that you move in a tight circle, not a straight line. We encourage you to stand up right now and try it.

STONE GOD/ESSES OR "MASCOTS"

As you will learn in Chapter VI, you can store the Force in inanimate objects. In their work Witches use specialized objects to store energy. Such objects are variously called demi-gods, stone gods, hearth gods, or mascots. As in all other matters, of course, these objects can represent either gender (or none) so a more correct (if cumbersome) description might be *stone god/esses.*

You can get or make your own stone god/esses, and when you're feeling optimistic you can charge one of them with laughter and happy force. Then, in doing a spell, you can dump the stone god/esses into boiling water to release the happy energy, directing it toward someone who might need it.

What if you come home one day in a red rage? You can dump that energy, too, into a stone god. For such energy you might choose a figure of a raging bull (Taurus). Then when you need it, you can "withdraw" the red energy (for example) to help cure a blood disease.

Whatever mood you're in, if you want to save some of the energy, all you need to do is dump it into a rough stone set aside for the purpose. (Objects with irregular conformation or rough surfaces store energy more readily than those that are polished.) Of course little stone statuettes of deities are ideal for purposes of storage. When you hold the stone god/ess in your hands as you "deposit" energy in it, some people may assume you are praying to a deity.[1] Besides storing the energy for later use, the practice gets you back in balance: It frees you of the "mood" you're in.

---

[1] It may be better not to burden such people with too much knowledge; work where they can't see you.

When you have a set of stone gods for various intents, you can keep them together on an altar so that their energies balance each other out, or you can lock them in a heavy steel box to contain the energies.

THE ANCIENT GOD/ESSES

For millennia, certain god/esses have been worshiped and prayed to. Some have so many requests that their force is not just depleted, it's like a black hole of negative energy that can suck you dry. Force is still available from many of the ancient god/esses. You need only invite that energy in to help you with your work. Some Witches speak of this as *drawing down the moon*.[2] Essentially it is what members of Santeria do when they call in the Orishas; they allow an ancient deity to possess their body and run it around.

To call on ancient god/esses is inherently a dangerous procedure.

1. You don't know the name by which earlier peoples called the deity.[3]

2. You don't know what specific prayer force remains in the deity today.

Further, if the deity force *enters* the worker/supplicant, it may stay—preferring to remain in a physical state on the earth plane rather than existing in a nonphysical astral void. The literature contains countless case histories of possessions and illness caused when a worker called a deity into him-/herself. The current approach is to call the god/ess into a statuette in a circle separate from the one in which you are working. In Germany this is called a *vril-eck,* that is, a *power corner.* Gavin personally witnessed one such attempted summoning of Mars into a statuette, which promptly exploded. When the dust settled, only fine grains of powder remained. The summoning (invoking) had clearly worked, but the force answering was too large and powerful to be contained in the statuette.

Figure III-3 shows a relatively safe way to call an ancient god/ess.

---

[2] Margot Adler, *Drawing Down the Moon* (New York: Viking Penguin, 1997).

[3] Right. Okay, pronounce *Isis* for us in the ancient Egyptian dialect of the times.

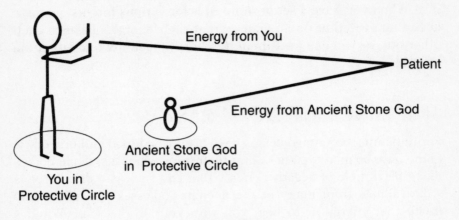

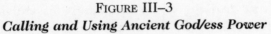

FIGURE III–3
Calling and Using Ancient God/ess Power

GEMSTONES AND CRYSTALS

Long before crystals and gemstones became fashionable, Wiccans collected and used them. We use them as an adjunct to our work in healing, meditation, scrying (crystal gazing), and other activities. Shamans have known the powers of gemstones and crystals for hundreds of years. Stones can help to change attitudes, to heal, to increase psychic abilities, and much more.

You can carry more than one type of stone at a time; they do not cancel each other out. Carry your stones in a pocket, a bra cup, or a pouch fastened to your belt. If you want to absorb energy, wear or carry the stone on your left side. If you want to transmit the stone's vibration, wear or carry it on your right side. Wearing stones will affect your aura and your links in the Web of the Wyrd, according to the nature of the stones. For example, emerald has a very loving vibration. To attract this to yourself, carry an emerald in your left pocket. To increase the loving vibration in your interaction with others, carry an emerald in your right pocket. This is particularly good for people who tend to be gruff or abrupt with others.

When purchasing a stone in person, buy the one that you are attracted to, avoiding, if possible, polished stones. If you are right handed, hold it in your left hand.[4] If it feels good to you, it is meant for you and will work for you.

Exposing crystals and stones to sunlight is an excellent way to energize them. However, before you energize a stone, especially a new one or one you have just used, you will want to remove any negative energy from it. Place your stones in a nonmetallic container filled with water (distilled or from a spring or a well) and a pinch of salt (sea, kosher, or rock salt). Put the container in the refrigerator for a day, then take the stone out and place it on a sunny ledge for a day. Repeat this procedure for three days.

Opals should soak for not longer than ten minutes at any time because they absorb water. After you soak an opal, place it in the sun to help it dry out. After using a stone or crystal, you should give it a ten-minute soak as described above. This will cleanse it and let it work better for you.

Our Native American friends tell us that each stone has its own spirit; hence you can talk to it and request it to help you in specific ways. Manmade crystals are spiritually dead, so use them only for decoration. Natural crystals are what you want to use in your working. For absolute maximum accuracy in directing the Force, use a crystal with a whole, intact point, not a broken point. Broken points give a shotgun blast of energy; energy from a whole point resembles a laser beam in its intensity and focus.

When working on any medical situation, consult a physician first. The interpretations below represent opinions only; they serve as supplement to, not replacement for, medical advice.

ROBERTA SAVES HER GRANDBABY

Roberta is a student of ours living in Houston, Texas. Her own words describe the experience that taught her of the power of crystals:

> Red and green lights flashing, bells ringing, monitors, tubes, wires, patches, needles, IV's; equipment galore with dials, knobs, and more flashing lights

---

[4] Your dominant hand is your main transmitter of energy, and your secondary hand is your receiving hand. If you are truly right-handed (not just bullied into being right-handed long ago because it was more convenient for some adult), your right hand is dominant. If you hold a stone in your dominant hand, you will tend to impress your feelings on it instead of receiving its energy.

and ringing bells. Houston Space Center? No! This is the inner core area of the Neo-Natal ICU where my first grandchild has lived in his "isolated incubator condo" since his premature birth shortly after the "witching hour" on January 19, 1990.

His parents and we have been standing by with bated breath as Nikki (Nikolas) fired up first one system, then another, inching up his gradual progress. Oxygen is still the primary concern; for although he was essentially breathing on his own, it is necessary to respirate him periodically throughout the day until this could be weaned.

The time element? Indefinite! Daughter and I discussed utilizing a stone to help Nikki. I suggested the crystal as the "balanced ultimate" containing the entire spectrum both of color and the mineral kingdom itself, while amplifying whatever quality might be needed. Sunday afternoon, February 11, Bonnie presented the crystal to her son. His little hand enclosed the gem with a sense of knowing. He settled down and just held it for the longest while before dozing off when he finally loosened his grip. His Mom washed it, returned it to its little bag and taped it to the inside of his condo. Shortly after midnight, less than twelve hours later, Nikki was taken off the oxygen and has not required it again.

Every day since, Bonnie gives Nikki a crystal and the same process is repeated; only now, he remains awake and alert. When he is finished with his gem (or when the crystal is finished with its transmission?), his little hand opens. On Valentine's Day, Nikki was promoted—less than three days after being given the first crystal. He is now on room air, still in his condo, but one step closer to coming home. The magic of the crystal continues, constantly revealing itself to us through our creative use of its numerous powers. Its only limit is our own imagination.

THE POWERS IN METALS AND WOODS

Apart from crystals, many natural elements—metals and woods— hold inherent power. Rough pieces of metal ore and rough pieces of wood work better than smooth pieces, especially the metals. Yes, a beautiful locket can enhance the idea of love, both by its shape and because it is composed of a valuable metal. For casting spells, though, you need the metal to be unrefined, in its rough state. Wood chips should be used as an axe might have broken them away from the parent tree. If you are starting with a smooth piece of wood or metal, you can rough up its surface with a file.

YOUR GUIDE TO THE POWERS OF CRYSTALS, METALS, AND WOODS

Table III-1 shows typical crystals (or semi-precious stones), woods, and metals you can use for seven intents. Remember, they can charge you, yourself, as well as put energy out to affect others.

INTENT/ DESIRE	CRYSTAL	MINERAL	WOOD	HEDE SPEED OF WHIRL
Wealth	Gold	Gold	Teak	Slow
Love	Rose Quartz	Platinum	Heather	Medium/Slow
Serenity	Emerald	Silver	Willow	Very Slow
General Healing	Fire Opal	Copper	Olive/Rowan	Very Fast
Attack	Bloodstone	Iron	Ash	Fast
Luck	Rutilated Quartz	Tin	Locust	Fast
Protection	Black Tourmaline	Steel	Yew	Medium

TABLE III–1
Natural Sources of Energy for Seven Intents

These are the same intents shown in Table II-1. Now you can expand your spell-work to include sending out natural energy of the appropriate vibration. Moreover, you can make a piece of jewelry containing the appropriate stone, metal, and wood, to be worn by the target of the spell.

THE COSMOS

Energy continuously flows to Earth, mainly from the sun but also from other parts of the cosmos. Planets affect this energy flow; this is why astrology works. When you stand with your feet in contact with the earth, the energy flows through you and into the earth. This flow is strongest when you stand with head tilted slightly back, hands out with palms up, and with bare feet on grass or bare soil. You can actually feel that flow as it passes through you. Just before a ritual, it is wise to stand and recharge yourself in this way. Some people make up a little script to go with the recharging, taking a form something like this:

Stand now and feel the presence of the Cosmos.
Feel the earth our Mother under your feet.
Visualize your feet as rooted in the earth.
Like a tree take the energy into your hands (leaves).

You use what your body needs, and let the rest flow through you into the Mother.

Stand up and try this for 30 seconds now. Let your mind dwell on the thought of things growing and the energy flow. You can automatically recharge yourself—any time, anywhere.

In traditional folklore Witches worked on mountaintops. Today we strive to do the same. Our experiments show quite clearly that more power is indeed available on the tops of mountains than in valleys. The Ancients knew this very well. During the building of Beijing, the capital of China, thousands of coolies went to work to build a hill on which to site the royal palace. Working in an elevated area—even if it is only on the top floor or the roof of an apartment building—is preferable to working in the basement.

GEOLOGICAL FAULTS

Places of power (as Carlos Castaneda calls them) occur at geological faults in the landmass. There are many reasons for California's prosperity; among them must be included the fact that the San Andreas Fault runs very close to the coast and all the highly successful cities sit west of the Fault. East of the Fault the land is much more thinly populated, though it serves well for agriculture. In England the land is crisscrossed with ancient marked lines—*ley lines.* These are artificial faults, intentionally created by human will. Anyone can detect the flow of psychic energy along them with such mundane instruments as a pendulum. When you stand on a ley line, the pendulum reacts to thoughts flowing along the ley. When you move even a couple of feet away from the line, the pendulum remains still. Roads, railway lines, power lines, and many other manmade changes to the natural environment work in exactly the same way as a geological fault. The Ancients ordained that a Witch should work at a crossroads; that is, the intersection of two psychic lines of force. On the same principle, be sure to bury the peelings (if you will) from your spell-work at a crossroads so that the energy flows away from them along the psychic lines instead of remaining near you. When Europeans built the first railroads in China, they were required to build in curves so that bad *chi* would not have straight lines to follow.

You can construct for yourself small artificial ley lines. Collect rocks foreign to your locale, and place them equidistant on lines radiating out from the center of your work space toward each cardinal point. If you align two rocks in line in each direction, you can immediately feel the difference at the center of the ritual space. The ideal spacing of the rocks goes back to traditional circle dimensions. Multiples of 10.88 feet (4 megalithic yards) seem to work best.

RUNNING WATER

Any water in motion, even waves rippling on the shoreline, produces energy. We do not yet fully understand the mechanism; it seems related to the fact that waves curl back on themselves and that river currents create little counter-eddies along each bank. These currents are a series of mini-whirlpools that spin either clockwise or counterclockwise. Imagine a river as shown in Figure III-4. On one bank the eddies move clockwise and on the other, counterclockwise. If you stand near the bank with the clockwise eddies while you do a spell of increase, the energy from the river reinforces your own energy. You can work on the opposite bank to do a spell of decrease.

River energy extends quite a distance back from the actual river and affects people living in towns on riverbanks. You yourself can probably think of positive and negative towns. A simple example might be St. Louis, Missouri. It directly faces East St. Louis, Illinois, on the counterclockwise bank with its widdershins eddy. East St. Louis appears run down, and St. Louis itself thrives on the clockwise (deosil) eddy. Exceptions exist to this guideline, but other factors come into play to explain them. Another river may join the main stream, or an underground river or channel may counter the usual psychic currents.

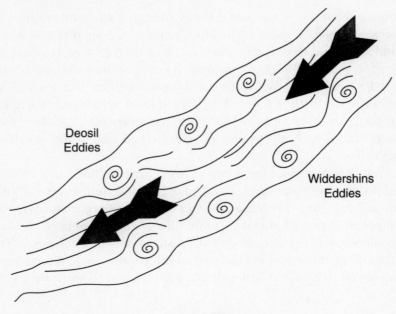

Deosil
Eddies

Widdershins
Eddies

FIGURE III–4
Rivers and Eddies

DON GETS FRUSTRATED

Don G was a taxi driver in Lubbock, Texas. He had earned a master's degree in fine arts from Texas A & M, but after graduation the only job he could get was a low-paying teacher's position. He decided that driving a taxi paid better. Of course he wanted to pay off his student loan and improve his lot in life, so he started tutoring on the side. As so often happens in the real world, he fell in love with one of his students, a young lady in her sophomore year at college. Tessa didn't seem ready to commit to any serious relationship, but Don wanted to settle down right now. He decided he would do a spell. Because he had studied ethics, he rejected all the traditional love spells[5] as being much too "caging."[6] Instead he felt he should do a

---

[5] An instructional videotape *Love Spells* from the School of Wicca considers this subject in detail. It is available through Godolphin House, P.O. Box 297-BK, Hinton, WV 25951-0297.

[6] *Caging spells* are those where another's autonomy is violated by making them virtually slaves of the spellcaster.

spell that would encourage Tessa to want to settle down and raise children. Now this was quite a difficult undertaking, and eventually he contacted us. He asked about the best mind triggers and other aspects of the spell he wanted to work. We referred him to some of our earlier books, and more or less forgot about him.

About a month later he showed up on our doorstep,[7] thoroughly frustrated and confused. "I have to have this, this, this, this, and this, and I have to do that, that, that, and that—but there's only me, 'cause I can't get Tessa to take part in it and I really don't know what comes first."

Against our better judgment we invited him in. Patiently we went through our usual spiel of "Put it in the order that appeals to you most and that makes sense to you. Do the best you can. Don't be a slave. Be inventive."

"Yes, but—"

"Yes, but what?"

"You're supposed to be the experts! You tell *me* what to do!"

"Okay, Don . . . but if you don't like it, change it."

"No! No! No! I want you to lay it out the best way possible and then I'll do it."

Lots of people demand that same step-by-step "expert" layout. All our explanations about why they should design it and do it for themselves don't seem to fit people who have grown up through the American educational system. Or perhaps computer-literate individuals want procedures that work just like a computer: Point the mouse, click on "start" to close down the computer, and walk away.[8] The Craft and magical work are not video games. We cannot offer total help to you; in the final analysis only *you* can help you.

In the end we gave Don his rigid outline—again, against all our better judgment. We have not heard Tessa's views on the subject, but the couple still lived together when we last heard from them.

YOUR TEN-STEP SPELLING GUIDE

When you have put together the steps to your goal and are ready to do the spell-work, you need to prioritize your variables in each indi-

---

[7] A practice we relentlessly discourage.

[8] Yes, that's the way Windows 95/98 works.

vidual effort. Belinda could have worked a spell at almost any time, either to increase her Grandpa's vitality or to decrease his suffering. Her feelings of guilt were not necessary. Once we ourselves worked out how long it would be until all the astrological and earth conditions were perfect for a particular spell. The best conditions would occur 380 years in the future. We had to hope that we would all have died and been reincarnated by that time. Figure III-5 shows the steps that lead up to and follow your spell. The spell itself involves the set up, the sequence, and the work:

A. Set up the space.

B. Decide on the sequence and the methods you will use to build and release the force.

Chanting   Stone god
Dancing   Ancient god force
Drumming

C. Complete the work.

Far too many spells go off ill-prepared; then people wonder why the results are erratic and off-target. In deciding your priorities, answer these questions:

How many psychic links do you need?
How many mind triggers do you need?
What is the appropriate near-term timing? Should you wait?
Can you work indoors, or does it have to be outdoors?
What is the weather likely to be at the time you have selected?

Never overlook the important steps *after* the spell:

1. The closing down as described in Chapter II

2. The follow-up

In the follow-up you may find that something unexpected has happened. When you meditate on that result, you may realize that it was actually a better outcome than the one you had first intended. This shows you are not alone in doing your work. Your Guide or perhaps even other spirits have interceded.

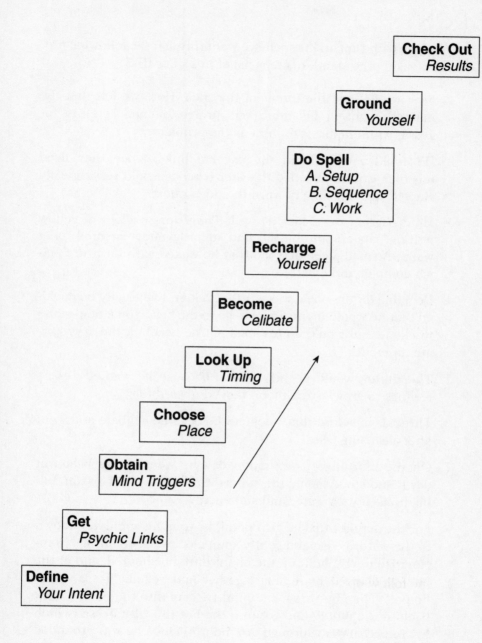

FIGURE III–5
Your Spell-Casting Flow Chart

DON'S SPELL

In working with Don on his spell, we went through the following procedures, using the standard steps listed in Figure III-5.

1. First we defined the *intent* of the spell. Here we felt that the main thought in his mind was protection and serenity for Tessa, with emphasis on him as the protector.

2. He could easily obtain the psychic links, since they lived together, and he decided that her topcoat would serve ideally since it had a feeling of warmth and comfort.

3. Mind triggers were easy as well. They were a sheet of yellow writing paper, some butter, and some lavender-scented toilet water. A small piece of wood that he waxed with furniture polish completed the list.

4. Deciding on the place was a little trickier. Eventually he decided that he would invite Tessa to go to the beach on a new-moon weekend and would do his spell on the beach at the appropriate moment.

5. The timing would be new moon, because he wanted Tessa's feelings to grow as the moon moved toward full.

6. Three days before that weekend he became celibate and went on a cleansing fast.

7. On the morning of new-moon day he went to the beach at dawn and stood facing the sun as it rose over the horizon, filling himself with water and sun energy.

8. For the actual ritual at high noon, he took his mind keys down to the water's edge and gently spun clockwise, chanting "Hom-Hom-Hom." He built up the chant until he shouted, and at the end he clapped his hands together and yelled, "Tessa, come home!" Then he threw his mind triggers into the ocean, went back to the motel, and got into the hot tub with Tessa (which led to bed and a thorough grounding). Once he was grounded and Tessa had fallen asleep, he sat and channeled. The many impressions of home scenes and warm comfortable hot meals assured him that his spell had been successful.

THE NURSES WERE AMUSED

After a side-on collision in traffic, Ned W found himself in traction in a Florida hospital, in pretty rough shape. His coven decided to send him some healing energy. Being relatively new in the work, they agreed to do an *aum* chant and send love energy.

It worked. With his leg suspended from a ceiling pulley, and both arms in casts out to his sides, poor Ned got sexually excited. He couldn't get rid of this feeling. When it came to bathroom time, the nurses were first amused and then genuinely concerned. He simply could not pass water. To relieve his bladder pressure, they had to use a catheter; and in his physical state even this was quite difficult. Finally one of the night nurses took pity on him and quietly, as you might say, adjusted his endorphins.

Of course the following night the coven planned to do it again. Fortunately that day one of the ladies from the coven told him what they were doing and he instantly put two and two together. They redefined their helpful efforts.

FIXING A SPELL

In discussing intents, we have talked so far about general intents, including an all-purpose healing spell. Such a spell works well to raise energy levels and to strengthen the body's immune system in a generalized way. When you work on specific illnesses, you need to tune your output to send the energy that will do the most good, not something that will cause useless side effects. Sending sexually loaded "love" energy to someone who is ill is wasteful and mainly useless.

The first thing Ned's coven had to do was reverse the spell they had cast. Their psychic link had been a picture of Ned in virile good health, stripped to the waist chopping wood while his wife, Nelda, watched from the background in a skyclad state. The coven had used an emerald-green mind trigger and a very long, drawn-out *a-um* chant. It happened that it was close to new moon, yet they had done the spell in the evening, since that was when most people could attend.

Clearly there was confusion in the work and in the energy they sent. The biggest problem was the picture of Nelda skyclad; that must have affected some of the members. Further, the use of emerald green, not the hospital's calmer green, didn't help. In reversing their work, they used a photo of Ned asleep in a deck chair, a very fast *mu-a* chant with a widdershins dance, and an amber mind key. After completing this spell in the early morning, they waited until midnight to do another healing spell. This time they used a more appropriate set of mind keys and a picture of a healthy-looking Ned leaning on an undamaged car.

Their work was successful on both counts. Ned was able to regain control of his functions, and he healed rapidly.

YOUR TABLE OF MIND TRIGGERS FOR REVERSING INTENTS

Yvonne causes much amusement in our lectures when she tells young women, "If you think someone has put a love spell on you and you don't want to be love-spelled, get one of their old shoes and urinate into it." This irreverent degrading of a person and putting something yellow into a psychic link is simple and effective, if politically incorrect.

When you are thinking of reversing a spell you have worked, do not try to do everything backward as some authors recommend. Instead, reverse the mind triggers by using their opposites to neutralize them.

Use the opposite emotional triggers, such as the opposite color from a color wheel.

Use a different psychic link.

Do the spell at the reverse phase of the moon (fourteen days from your first working).

Reverse the chants; for example, *a-um* to *mu-a*.

Table III-2 shows these reversals for five previous intents. We have not included *causing illness* to replace *health* or *causing unrest* instead of *serenity.* These are too negative. Of course you can do them—if you don't mind facing the consequences implied by the Law of Attraction, because inevitably what you send out will be attracted back to you.

Intent	Color	Metal	Wood	Feeling	Chant	Moon	Speed/Whirl/Chant
Confusion	Orange	Brass	Chess Board	Pincushion	Mu-Ah	New	Very Fast
Hate	Rose-Red	Broken Cast Iron	Ash	Sharp Knife	Weh-Yah	New	Fast
Vulnerability	Purple	Aluminum	Balsa	Thin Rubber Sheet	M-Moh	New	Slow
Bad Luck	Yellow/orange	Copper	Fir	Broken Glass	Me-Ho-Eya	New	Fast
Poverty	Blue	Lead	Basswood	Burlap	Ha-Yag	Full	Slow

TABLE III–2

Mind Triggers for Reversing Five Intents

SENATOR HELMS AND THE POSTAL RESTRICTIONS

In 1985 Jesse Helms decided that all "fringe" religions with non-profit mailing privileges should lose those privileges. He and his staff constructed Amendment 705 to Senate Bill 3036 to make such churches ineligible for the better postal rates. Because this would have affected the operations of the Church and School of Wicca in a massive way, we immediately went to Washington and started lobbying for the amendment to be dropped. Larry King invited us on his talk show to discuss the subject. Within four or five days (and, we must say, with help from the Christian Right), the amendment was shelved.

A group of pagans and Witches in the western states started agitating to have the amendment dropped—days after it had already been shelved. They caused so much furor that Congressman Walker decided this was a hot-button issue and took the amendment back off the shelf; he submitted a modified version in House Bill 3389.

The pagans and Witches on the west coast were busy empowering Congress over a dead issue.

In a similar way, more recently, a Christian fundamentalist learned that Witches on an army base were practicing their (federally recognized) religion at a federal facility. Senator Bob Barr of Georgia and others discussed with the media the possibility of writing a bill to outlaw such activities in the military. Barr quickly found that this was not acceptable to the Pentagon. After a couple of demonstrations in Washington and some letters from his own constituents, he quietly dropped the idea. Months later the Internet was still aflame with discussion on how to make sure that religious freedom was extended to the military. What this did was keep the issue before the public for much longer than was necessary. The prolonged hoopla empowered it so much that it became a plank in Bush's platform in his bid for the presidency.

These empowerments are national affairs. In a minor way the media do it all the time: "At Joe's Fish Stall the fish smell bad"—and Joe's Fish Stall gets more business. "Didn't even know we had a fresh fish stall in town," is a typical comment from the man in the street.

You do the same thing, too. The boss has you on the carpet for something you consider was unfair. You go around complaining to all your friends about what the boss did. You're not helping your-self—you're empowering the boss! You're strengthening his image as an ogre and a martinet, so people pay more attention to his every word.

PSYCHIC EMPOWERMENT

These examples from the mundane world illustrate the principle of *empowerment.* The principle works at the psychic level as well as the mundane. We believe that the psychic link is tuneable to thoughts just as your output is tuneable. Let's use color imagery for this illustration.

A little anger runs along part of the Web to you and turns it red. Because of that anger you get angry and send back *more* anger. This brightens the link, making it even redder than before. The "enemy" receives more anger from you—and sends back yet more anger. The self-reinforcing feedback loop is getting out of control. Such thoughts only strengthen the psychic link between you and your enemy.

I'm sure you've heard the Christian platitude that urges, "Love your enemy." Here you see why it works. Instead of returning anger, if you return love, the feedback loop isn't enhanced; in fact since love is on the opposite side of the thought spectrum from anger, it is neutralized and ideally balanced out of existence. If an exact bal-ance could be found, the whole link would become dull and fragile. Thus returning the opposite will often get better results even than using a mirror spell or a mirror box, which returns the same energy it receives. If you can train yourself simply to avoid speaking and thinking of the "enemy" except in pleasant terms, you will further weaken the link. The trick is to kill the link. Sending too much love will reinforce the link with love; conversely, too much hate strength-ens the link with hate—so try for a balance.

If you decide on a psychic attack, remember that your outgo-ing pulse may be reflected back along the link that you yourself have built, and harm you.

Suppose you didn't vent to co-workers about your boss, but when you went home you continued to think negative thoughts about him. We are sure you can see that you are giving him a stronger link so that he can more easily control you.

TUNING, TIMING, AND TRANSMITTING

This chapter has been all about getting it right—tuning your outgoing pulse of energy to go to the right objective and to do what you expect. Amorphous love spells and putting out general pulses to "help the earth" simply don't work. They are a waste of energy. If you want to help the earth, choose someone in government and change their mind on a bill that's pending in Congress; or do something equally definitive. Several of us worked together a couple of years ago on the President's head during the ecological conference in Brazil, and indeed his final speech surprised many of his aides in Washington. He did not totally change his mind from black to white, but he moved significantly further toward the ecologists' viewpoint than he had been before. Yet even the day before that speech the media had thought he would not have the guts to take such a stand. Did we affect him? We think so.

You too can affect people in power. Remember the saying, "They put their pants on one leg at a time, too"—unless it's a skirt. Ah well.

Many people, even those working in Witchcraft, either seem skeptical or don't really understand what they are doing. The skeptical ones don't think it's going to work anyway, so it doesn't matter much what they do or don't do; with such an attitude, the effort may sink without a trace. It's the ill-informed ones who are dangerous.

In this chapter you have learned a total system of tuning yourself to gain the best results for various magical intents. At first glance it may all seem extremely complex; however, as you work with it and use it, you will find that it becomes second nature to you to think of such things as, "The moon will be full a week from Tuesday. I need to get X to do my spell" when X is the thing that will trigger your own mind. At presentations we may ask such questions as, "What gets you most tuned in to anger?" The answers range from "A mosquito buzzing in the bedroom" to "A little over-bred piss-and-tremble dog peeing in my lap." Use the mind triggers that suit you, those you can easily get and handle. Do not make your spell-work a chore. It should be enjoyable, with both effort and result exactly what you want them to be.

Solo, Duet, or Small Chamber Group

VIVE LA DIFFÉRENCE

To this point we have addressed the single practitioner. Now we move on to the (even more interesting) situation of two or more people working together. Observers have long known that in doing a given spell, two people of opposite gender working together are capable of raising more energy than two people of the same gender.[1]

About twenty years ago Dr. Loy Stone (then president of the Church of Wicca) investigated the magnetic fields surrounding living organisms. He encased the organism (or in humans just the head) in a very large coil of super-fine wire; then he connected the output of the coil to a galvanometer. He found that most males would deflect the galvanometer one way, and most females would deflect it in the opposite direction.

Knowing what you know from Chapter III about the Human/Earth Dynamo Effect (HEDE), you can see that if people have opposite magnetic polarities, then working together would be like connecting two batteries in series; whereas people with the same polarity working together would resemble two batteries in parallel. In other words, you will get double the voltage out of the batteries in series compared with what you will get from the batteries in parallel, as shown in Figure IV-1.

---

[1] Here, *opposite gender* is not precisely what we mean. We mean two people between whom sexual attraction is present, or could be. Thus, when we talk about gender we mean gender of the spirit, not the physical genitalia; we have known many same-gender couples to raise just as much energy as any heterosexual couple.

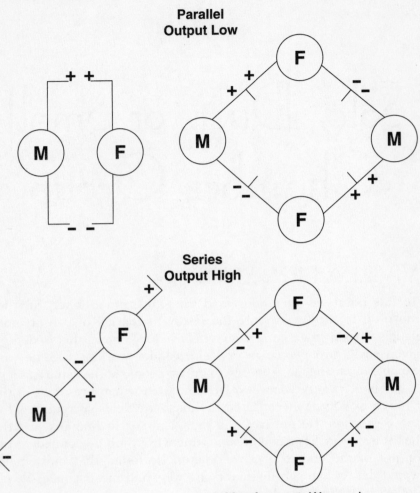

**Parallel
Output Low**

**Series
Output High**

Men face out, Women in.

M = Male F = Female When in series, they face in opposite directions.
M+ = LH. M- = RH. F+ =RH. F- = LH. + and - indicate magnetic polarity.

FIGURE IV–1
Series Gives Maximum Force

To feel that energy for yourself, do a modified hands-across-palm experiment. Stand facing another person. Put your right hand with fingers parallel, palm down, over his left hand. Then place your left hand with palm up under his right hand with palm down. You will feel either a flow of strong energy or very little energy. The surge occurs, of course, when your co-worker is of the same gender or if the person is of the opposite gender but the hands are crossed. Figure IV-2 shows this experiment. When you work with a mixed-gender group, your balance improves if you have an equal number of opposite polarities. In the old texts, the men always faced outward from the center and the women inward. You can see from Figure IV-2 how such an arrangement strengthens the Force. Remember: Holding hands is a no-no. The Force is polarized parallel to the fingers—and with the fingers crossed as in holding hands, the power switches off.

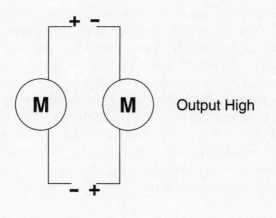

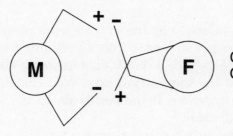

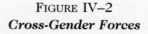

FIGURE IV–2
Cross-Gender Forces

WHEN ONE PLUS TEN EQUALS ZERO

If you yourself can send out a pulse of power, then two people should be able to send out twice as much. The more people, you might think, the more power. Regrettably if workers feel reservations about a specific spell they are involved in, they function as a power drain, not as a contributor.

You may read that one skeptic in the group ruins the procedure. This is absolutely true. We compare it to having three or four good cells in a car battery and one dead cell. If you have any automotive experience, you know that the one dead cell makes the battery useless. The purpose of spell-work is to make sure that everyone is tuned to exactly the same frequency when they send out the Force. No spell, however, can guarantee that everyone wants to send out their energy to support the group's purpose. In fact, occasionally you will find someone is actually a force-vampire and sucks the group's entire output to keep for their own purposes. This is often the case, unfortunately, with a powerful group leader, or charismatic minister, especially one who fears he is losing control of the group. He steals the energy so that he can be more powerful.

Some scholars postulate that pre-Christian shamans realized they could gather power from a group. If the shaman offered all that power to a god/ess, (s)he could gain personal credit with that god/ess. Thus the modern priesthood was born. The priest barters the chips (as it were) from his entire congregation with the god/ess for the priest's own aggrandizement.

DIADIC HEDE

You saw earlier that a person spinning in the earth's magnetic field can produce a large output of power. The same thing can happen when a couple dances. Figure IV-3 shows what happens when a couple holds just one hand and spins on a central axis. This means that the hands must hook together. If the hands touch correctly, the power will be at least doubled.[2]

You can turn the members of a group into the rotor of a dynamo: Alternate their fields as in Figure IV-1. Or you can make

---

[2] If this doesn't work for you, each can hold the other's wrist.

your own dynamo by forming two circles of workers and rotating one within the other in opposite directions.

Try some of "ye olde-fashioned folke dancing." Some dances "work" while others fall flat. Looking at these dances through the eyes of a Witch, compare the movements of the dancers and their polarity with what you now know about HEDE. The dances that "work" produce psychic energy! This energy can be seen and felt by capable psychic Witches.

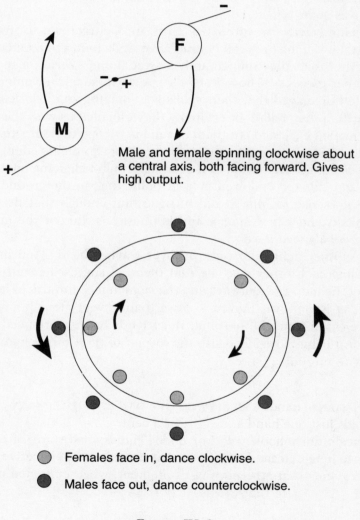

Male and female spinning clockwise about a central axis, both facing forward. Gives high output.

Females face in, dance clockwise.

Males face out, dance counterclockwise.

FIGURE IV–3
Diadic and Group HEDE

NAOMI GETS OUT OF THE HOSPITAL

Naomi S was a healthy widow living in Washington, D.C. Late one night as she made her way to the Metro from the Smithsonian, she was mugged. Not only did the muggers hit her over the head, they also stabbed her. They must have thought she had seen one of their faces, and tried to kill her lest she identify them later. As it turned out, though, she had no memory of it. Yelling "Fire!" as soon as she was attacked probably saved her life because it drew attention to what was going on.[3]

Naomi was in intensive care in Georgetown University Hospital for almost a week before her friends found her. Once they knew the story, they immediately started doing a series of spells to speed her recovery. These were very powerful magical women, and they felt dismayed that their spells were having an effect less dramatic than they had hoped. Finally they e-mailed us with the story. We e-mailed back and got them to send us a copy of their ritual. We could see nothing wrong with it. Channeling two nights later on the spell, Gavin got the vision of a dead light bulb balancing on a knife edge, immediately followed by a lit bulb lying on the ground. This made no sense to him. It did intrigue him enough that he called Naomi's friends. In response to his questions, he got the answer, "We're a balanced coven."

Another light bulb went on over Gavin's head. "You may be canceling each other out," he told them. "I suggest in your dance you let the men face outward and the women face inward." The very next day Naomi was moved to a ward and twenty-four hours later was released from the hospital. Her friends had experienced problems in raising power because the format of their circle had a tendency to minimize power.

NO SEX, PLEASE, WE'RE RAISING POWER

Witches often work *skyclad* or nude. The skyclad state, of course, tends to heighten the excitement that contributes to effective working. it seems that a turn-on of excitement, whether sexual or not,

---

[3] At shouts of "Rape!" or "Help!" bystanders are hesitant to get involved. Workers in public health and safety tell us that "Fire!" will get a better response.

helps power a spell. Another option for a group that uses sex as a power source to increase the excitement is for the group members to be celibate for three days before a spell.

Many neophyte (trainee) Witches mistakenly think that most power comes from a mutual orgasm. Lots of power gets raised at such a time—but only very experienced workers can detach themselves from the moment and send that power out. Thus, having sex in the circle is self-defeating. As we say, once the donkey gets the carrot the motivation disappears.

A couple who are homeostatic and sexually fulfilled may have trouble stopping a Crookes Radiometer from turning. A couple who have been celibate for three days, on the other hand, can stop the radiometer dead in its tracks—or can make it go wild. If you are going to use sexual energy to drive your spell, you should be celibate for two to three days before the working and you should have the promise of a sexual interlude as soon as you complete the working. The promise of fulfillment after a celibate period still drives the force upward and results in successful spell-casting.[4]

When any group uses sex to drive a ritual, all its members should clearly understand that they are allowed—nay, required—to refuse any partner with whom they feel uncomfortable. Any exchange of partners that is not voluntary and joyful will fail to drive the ritual. All workers will have wasted their time and effort. No leader has the right to coerce any Wiccan into having sex with someone they don't like. Such an act constitutes as rape, which is an anathema to members of the Craft.

Similarly, we Wiccans do our utmost to avoid transmission of sexually transmitted diseases (STDs) and to avoid unwanted pregnancy. The coven takes scrupulous precautions before accepting newcomers. Typically, it requires multiple medical tests over time and a waiting period of a year and a day before granting admission to a sexually driven ritual.

THE USEFUL DIET

You may decide that sexual power is too problematic for you. If that is true, you can instead use starvation as the driving force for a spell.

---

[4] For a complete explanation of this phenomenon, see G. and Y. Frost, *Tantric Yoga, the Royal Path* (York Beach, ME: Samuel Weiser, Inc., 1990).

Any time the body is threatened with extinction, apparently the possibility of relief from the situation generates power. "When we've done the spell, we get to eat!" If we fast before a spell-working, and promise ourselves a pleasant meal, we have (if you like) upped the ante on the success of the spell. This system works for a single practitioner and for any sized group. It works best when the people who fast live in close contact with one another for the duration of the fast. Sharing the experience of fasting seems to allow a closer concentration, a better tuning of minds together, than when people fast separately. The same practice applies to group work. In our group we go to a beach motel, fast together, and then work in the motel's meeting room on its top floor.

What you should do now is a series of experiments with a willing friend:

1. Try the duet hands-across-palm experiment right after you both have had a good meal.

2. After 24 hours without food, do the experiment again.

3. After another 24 hours without food, do the experiment again.

4. Go yet a third day and try it again.

You will find that the energy peaks in young people after the second day and with more mature people at the third day. Come on now, try it. You need to do the research.

If you add to this little experiment the mutual promise that you can eat as soon as Step 4 is completed, you will feel a marked increase in the level of energy on that third day. The promise of food raises the level of excitement even in the most aesthetic of us.

THE FAST

When we talk about a fast, we do not mean total starvation; instead we might talk about a purifying diet. Most Witches hold jobs, and the ritual moon cycle often doesn't allow for a spell to be done in the next long weekend. So to keep the body engine fueled, most Witches of our persuasion go on a cleansing fast, eating only homemade bread with pure honey, and drinking only water. You will find that this cleansing fast causes you to feel unwell. This is the normal withdrawal from the drugs and toxins we regularly eat. If you get really sick, consult a regular doctor. He may recommend a fast of fruit and rice instead.

Obviously one under a physician's care should modify the fast in accordance with that physician's guidance.

THE ENDORPHIN CONNECTION

The human body spontaneously produces a natural form of morphine,[5] which scientists call *endorphin* (*endo*—within, + *morphine*). Many situations stimulate such production: simple hugging, dancing, massage, laughing, and singing. All of these produce the beneficial endorphins that have been called the body's "happy pills." The greatest quantity of endorphins comes from orgasms. All this information on endorphins is relatively new. Its significance to those who practice the Craft and magic is this: The guidelines for Wiccan ritual were in place many centuries ago, before researchers had even dreamed of discovering today's concrete, objective information about endorphins. (At least this is true of information available to incarnate beings on the earth-plane level.) Yet from a scientific point of view, Craft rituals are perfectly constructed and would not work with a different construction. Dr. Pert's work[6] corroborates the methods Witches have long been using in apparent ignorance of the physical facts underlying them. The dovetailing of tradition with new knowledge is beautiful to see.

One effect of endorphins on the body is drowsiness and relaxation. If you go into a channeling state with high endorphin levels, the channeling works far better and you are much more likely to be able to get out on an astral trip. Some workers call this getting into an *altered state of consciousness* or *shamanic journeying*. If you want to find out whether the spell you've done will be effective, channeling immediately after its completion can get you that answer. Not only will you learn the degree of effectiveness; you will also learn where you may have made mistakes and perhaps what you should have done differently. Thus, if a Witch's spells are to be effective, she should do the part that raises and releases energy, then get into a relaxed state and channel.

---

[5] See Candace Pert, Ph.D., *Molecules of Emotion* (New York: Scribner, 1997).

[6] Op. cit.

In the state that endorphins induce, you feel too relaxed to produce much psychic energy. Thus, when constructing a complete spell you have two states to consider:

1. the power-raising state of tension and building excitement, and
2. the post-spell state of relaxation.

Between the two stages, many Witches *ground* themselves—sending any excess energy into the Earth Mother Gaea. They simply press their palms to the floor or the earth for a moment and release any surplus force. This is not sufficient to raise the endorphin levels high enough for successful channeling. To raise the levels you could dance something slow and gentle like a waltz, or have a couple of drinks. You may relax to soft music or perhaps take a warm slow bath, or do whatever other relaxing things you like to do. Since most Wiccan rituals involve people of two genders, and most Wiccans are not uptight with body hate, we find that sexual release is the quickest and easiest approach, both to ground and to flood the body with endorphins for successful channeling. This is especially true, of course, if celibacy has been part of the ritual preparation. Cuddling and hugging under these circumstances may produce excitement, not relaxation.

We *do not* recommend using psychedelic substances to achieve altered states of consciousness, because there is evidence that mind-altering substances lead your spirit to unusual parts of the astral. These places in the astral are not always friendly and are often out of your control. We know full well that many people have used them and do use them; but reliance on artificial substances whose long-term effects are not always beneficial is dangerous—as is the fact that these drugs are illegal. To use them would be to break the basic Wiccan guideline of

If it harm none, do what you will.[7]

MELISSA FEEDS THE DUCKS

Melissa and Eddie W were neighbors of ours in Raleigh, North Carolina. Eddie was Indian by birth, and Melissa, a southern California flower child from the sixties. Melissa had gone to India to live on an ashram and had met Eddie there. They had lived happily

---

[7] The *none* includes yourself.

together for several years in the ashram and decided to marry and raise a family. At this point Melissa's father died. He had been widowed earlier, so all his estate went to Melissa on condition that she return to the States and live there for five years. Clearly he assumed that once she got caught up in the materialistic American world she would forget her Indian experience.

On their arrival in the States, Eddie took a low-paying waiter's job and Melissa took up her former secretarial career. Both found themselves overworked and irritable, thoroughly stressed out. When we met them, they were fighting chronically and both had low-grade infections. We actually met them because they made such a racket one night in the condominium next door that they kept us awake. The pity of it was that they didn't *need* to live a life so unpleasant. Her father had left a considerable estate, and the executors were willing to allow her living expenses while she fulfilled his stipulations. But Melissa was stubborn. She would take no part of her inheritance until she completed the five-year requirement and could return to India.

In the States, they became so involved in making a living wage and in adjusting to a "normal" American existence that they lost their way spiritually. We told them, "Take a week off, both of you together. Relax. Go walking. Feed the ducks at the pond."

They had a thousand "Yes, buts." Eddie would lose his job. Melissa would have trouble with hers. They didn't realize that it was their entire future life and health they were gambling with. They didn't make any changes, and pretty soon Eddie didn't seem to be around any more. "He's living with an Indian woman," Melissa tearfully told us. "He says I don't understand him any more. He says he doesn't even like me. And he won't get a better job even though I'm sure he could. He just wants to live off Poppy's money! He's always yelling at me to get some money from the executors."

To get some money from the executors—that's exactly what we, too, encouraged her to do. Eventually she agreed. She gave up her full-time job and part-time teaching, and she did in fact feed the ducks. She became a healthy, well-adjusted, vibrant woman. Whether fortunately or unfortunately, she and Eddie did not reconcile. She very much wanted us to do a "love spell" on her behalf[8] that would bring him back; but we told her that was like caging someone and that for ethical reasons we wouldn't do it.

---

[8] The only spells we do for others are healings of other Church members. We will do readings and help you write your own spell. Only *you* can write a good spell for you.

LEARN AND PROGRESS

Humans are tribal creatures. For millennia we have lived in small groups or villages. The Industrial Revolution broke that pattern; nowadays it's often only two against the world. Torn from his Indian background in a large extended family strongly supportive and mutually sharing, Eddie couldn't appreciate Melissa's attitude. In Eddie's reality all the family resources should be pooled and shared.

Witches try to work as a small group, and some of us aspire to live as a group, realizing the vast saving that such living gives on the mundane level. The group also gives so much mutual support and spiritual comfort in times of trouble that the loss of autonomy involved is well worth the cost.[9]

Melissa and Eddie lived happily in one culture but could not adapt well to another. Living the eastern life in a western culture can be extremely challenging. It is enormously difficult for western people to trade their autonomy for Tantric security; the mystique of John Wayne is still alive and well. Apparently we must all still be independent frontierspeople, absolutely, totally avoiding "co-dependence" if we aspire to live up to the Duke's standard.

When it is not mutually stifling and instead becomes a means to a greater end such as security and comfort, a means through which one can progress into spiritual exploration, co-dependence is not a bad thing. It can become a partnership instead of a toxic host/parasite situation. In fact, it is probably essential for success.

YOUR MAGICAL COMPANION

In any work it is rewarding to have a companion who shares your goals, aims, and belief system. This is doubly true in Witchcraft, especially with regard to raising energy to convert into force that goes out at the peak of a spell-casting. Time and time again we find couples who are totally mismatched in their attitudes toward these concepts. A Witch married to a cowan has to find another companion outside the marriage for circle work. This can cause all sorts of tensions at home, and those tensions reflect badly on the effectiveness of the magical work. Normally, two ordinary people working

---

[9] See Betty Friedan, *Fountain of Age* (New York: Touchstone Books, 1994).

together can put out about twice the energy of the single worker. When those two people tune in to each other, then suddenly the output of energy dramatically increases. Some workers say that it's five times the amount of a single person on a good day. From our experiments, we believe the maximum we can claim is four times the amount. Whatever the amount, it is much more than two people can generate who occasionally see each other in circle. Thus, for serenity in life and for good spell-working, the Witch should be extra cautious and choosy with regard to finding a life companion to whom she commits.

For these reasons the Church of Wicca does not handfast two people who have not lived together for at least a year and a day. That handfasting means a contract relationship, and the maximum that we will write the contract for is five years. An expiration date makes quite a difference in people's mindset.

This is not to say the contract cannot be renewed. It says only that the contract isn't a life sentence inflicted on two people who cannot work together or who grow in different directions.

SYLVIA NO LONGER WEEPS

Sylvia B lives in Fayetteville, North Carolina. Earlier she had lived with her German husband in Washington, D.C., where he had worked for the German embassy. Sylvia's parents had emigrated from Germany while she was still a baby and they were really happy when she chose a German to be her mate. She, too, was happy, because Hans shared her occult interest. It looked as if they had the makings of an excellent handfasting; nevertheless we refused to do the rite of passage for them because they had not met the requirement of living together for a year and a day. They went off and had a normal civil ceremony anyway at the county courthouse. Theoretically that bound them together for life.

Once the knot was tied, Hans became a different man. All the domineering Prusso-German characteristics surfaced. Why this should happen in a relationship of the late twentieth century, nobody could say; but our own opinion is that people do change when that contract is signed—when that great door slams shut and people may subconsciously think, "You're mine now, stuck with me from here on." Some women feel very trapped—or entitled—and some men feel, "Now that she's mine I can do what I like with her and she has to like it or lump it." No, not a bit of this goes on in accessible parts of the mind, but nonetheless it may lurk in some improbable people.

Hans was not especially cruel or downright evil; it was just that where there had been lots of conversation, lots of pleasant dates, there was now silence. Instead of taking Sylvia with him, he went alone to embassy parties and to those given by friends while she sat dutifully at home alone. Sylvia didn't know what to do. But in channeling she kept getting the message, "Dump him." After only three months of married life she felt that it was much too soon to do that. Instead she began to blame herself for the failure of the marriage. She set out on a campaign of doing everything Hans asked her to do and trying desperately to please him. She did a couple of little spells hoping they would stop his drinking and bring some measure of sweetness and light back into her life. After one such spell Hans found the peelings—the burnt candle, his photo, the remains of a circle—and he literally went out of control with her. He didn't actually hit her, but he made so much noise yelling at her that neighbors called the police.

No one pressed charges because there were no charges to press. The next night Hans went out with his friends and got roaring drunk while Sylvia wept at home. She called us and asked whether we would help her do a love spell. As usual, we recommended reference books, but would not help her do a caging spell. When she realized that such a ritual would permanently cage her with a man she was beginning to detest, she decided not to do a love spell at all. Instead she did a love spell for Hans and one of the secretaries at work. Gerda, too, was German-born, and had shown a lot of interest in Hans in Sylvia's presence.

Pretty soon it was plain to everyone that Hans was seeing a lot of Gerda. Sylvia was able to get her divorce and significant alimony and freedom because Hans could not contest the divorce. His infidelity was public knowledge.

The cellular phone company that employed Sylvia offered her a promotion to a managerial position if she would transfer to Fayetteville. She seized the chance and got away from the area where she had felt so much pain. In North Carolina she decided to start her own group, and from within that group of students she found a new significant other. At the present time she has heeded our rules on handfasting and though she has been living with this new man for nearly three years, she still has not decided to tie that knot. Instead they work very well together and have many, many healings to their credit. He works as an EMT at Fayetteville's biggest hospital, where he encounters a constant stream of worthwhile cases they can work on.

LOVE SPELL–INTENTS

"Love" may range from motherly through brotherly to lustful relationships. (This last one is often a combination of intents.) Motherly love may combine with spiritual and friendly love. When you decide you simply must do a love spell, no matter what the consequences, first decide very carefully your real intent. Then look in Table IV-1 for appropriate mind triggers. The mind triggers listed are the traditional ones. If you don't feel comfortable with them, make up your own.

LOVE SPELLS–ETHICS AND CARE

Every week many people contact the School asking us to do love spells. In every single case we refuse—yes, even if they are members of the Church of Wicca. A love spell is a caging ritual. It subverts the free will of the target. It doesn't guarantee the target will like being caged. And ethically it breaks the Witch's prime rule: "If it harm none, do what you will." Love spells often end disastrously because the people involved never seem able to define exactly what they want or why. Maybe a couple of individuals know each other and one of them decides, "This is *it,* and a little magic will bring the relationship to fruition." Most such individuals have fallen in lust, not love. After a few bonks, as the Brits say, they discover they share no common ground—yet now that nonreversible love spell has bound them together.

If you decide to do such a spell, look at the details with care. Let's consider a simple candle spell.

Two people choose candles in appropriate colors. Each worker anoints his/her respective candle with body fluid, perhaps saliva. They choose a third candle from the appropriate table to represent the intent of the spell, and arrange it with the others into a triangle.

INTENT	COLOR	AROMA	FLOWER	CRYSTAL	ANIMAL
Sensual	Turquoise	Orange Blossom	Cactus	Turquoise	Scorpion
Partnership	Green	Myrtle	Rose	Emerald	Swan
Spiritual	Lavender	Water Lily	Thrift	Amethyst	Dolphin
Friendship	Blue	Nutmeg	Asparagus	Sapphire	Centaur

TABLE IV–1
Mind Triggers for Love Spells

At new moon (because this is a growing spell) the workers light all three candles. The spell caster looks into the flames for about five minutes, visualizing the desired outcome. (S)he claps out the candles. At each of the three claps, (s)he yells something equivalent to, "Come to me!" The next day (s)he moves the candles a little closer together and repeats the entire procedure.

This procedure is repeated for perhaps nine days—and now comes the critical part. If the spell is nonreversible, the instruction will say, "Melt the candles together and bury the resulting mass at a crossroad. Or alternatively, let the candles burn out on the last day of the procedure."

These are irreversible acts. After the last day of the procedure, if you retain the candles, you can reverse the work by starting the procedure at full-moon midnight. This time, night after night move the candles apart.

THE UNIVERSAL TRUTH–IT'S ALL THE SAME STUFF

Whether it's the head-woman of a Chilean village doing an apparently incongruous ritual to cure a baby, or a Tantrist or a Wiccan with his or her carefully orchestrated rituals, the universal, underlying truths remain. Survival, whether of genes or of the body, is the drive that is probably the most effective in raising power. Methods of gaining and altering states of consciousness can put you in touch with the psychic internet, which we call the Web of the Wyrd.

Getting western people to dissociate copulation from love and affection, getting them to think of it all as a means to an end, just like fueling up the car, turns out to be very difficult—especially since most people can hardly be described as candidates for a centerfold spread. This is not to say that you should not enjoy the work. Working to raise energy with clenched teeth? You lower your chance of success.

To achieve the follow-up part of the spell, you need to have a good grounding and an emphatic raising of endorphins; so this, too, should be included in the group's thinking.

If any group ritual is to be successful, uniformity of intent and a recognizable format are necessary. All participants must follow the agreed format, from intent, through the actual raising of power, to the aiming of the power at its target. You can easily see the confusion that would arise if they deviated from a common (shared) ritual format.

Why do we use the ancient forms of ritual? They *work!* They make things happen, perhaps because they awaken ancient race memories. Those old memories serve as emotional keys to unlock the power with which we seek to attune ourselves. To repeat the old cliche, "If it works, don't fix it." In some groups it is fashionable to act very laid back about scheduling and format; but successful work takes some knowledge, a little planning, and discipline! One person working with dedication or two people working in unison will be far more effective than a dozen people chanting a phrase made meaningless by parrot-like repetition or recited through gritted teeth because they don't like the leader's phraseology. The ritual will succeed if:

1. the participants are unanimous in their choice of the ritual's intent or objective; and

2. they take specific, proven steps in the traditional format to draw on their own power and to invoke cosmic forces for the purpose of gaining the chosen positive result.

When performed properly, rituals always change the future. If your attempt fails, it is because you omitted a necessary step, or you did something you shouldn't have. Very rarely, a ritual "fails" because other forces are at work. If you want a million dollars but your Guides feel that poverty will teach you more, you won't get the million. If you ask for a healing but the patient dies, perhaps the

Guides, seeing more of the big picture, healed in a way you don't understand.

In the way rituals are currently worked, two things seem to present problems:

1. In today's hurried life, rituals get shorter and shorter, and the amount of preparation done for them grows correspondingly shorter and more hasty.

2. The nation's citizens by and large have forgotten or lost many rituals of earlier times. Only recently have Wiccans begun to reconstruct many such rituals that should be available to bring order to people's lives.

Rituals add new dimensions and significance to life. Think for a moment about a young person going through a puberty ritual. In the Jewish bar/bas mitzvah, they honor the young person and show the new responsibilities; this is far better than simply buying the child something, and letting it go at that. Young people need to be shown the responsibilities inherent in their new status, and need to be honored and tested in a way that is meaningful and memorable in their own terms, in their own reality.

AMANDA, JAKE, DEBBIE, AND JOHN OVERCOME DEPRESSION

These four people met at one of our regular seminars.[10] To their astonishment they found that they had all traveled from Connecticut. All had come for one reason alone: The theme of this gathering was magical methods of overcoming stress and depression.

They planned to form a small group when they returned home—and they did it. At first their interest was keen. The simple fact of finding like-minded people with whom they could feel safe; the excitement of arranging such things as places to hold meetings; getting to know each other on many different levels; and beginning

---

10 Places and dates of Church of Wicca seminars are announced at website http://www.wicca.org.

to work toward their first healing—all this was new and thrilling. So enthralled were they that they almost automatically overcame their individual depression. Also noteworthy was the fact that the four singles were now two couples . . . or rather, in some respects, they were four people in a group marriage. They decided to drive their spells with both sex and fasting.

In two consecutive full-moon circles, they worked successfully for healings. The third circle they graded a partial success; but on the next occasion nothing seemed to happen, and they looked upon it as a failure. Because of that one apparent failure, they began to drift apart.

If they had stepped back to look at the situation as we did when we were asked, it would have been clear that their initial enthusiasm had been an added drive to their rituals. Once the work became old hat, the boost of that extra magical excitement faded away. They never would have recovered it except that one of Amanda's friends was a very well-respected senior nurse in a Hartford hospital. She was a single woman, having lost her husband in an industrial accident at the submarine yards in Groton, Connecticut. His death left Darla with two young children to raise alone. Now she had been diagnosed with both HIV and cancer, and was given only about six months to live.

The group decided that Darla would be the subject of their next healing. Amanda called Gavin to ask his advice, and since it was such an important, meritorious healing, we two decided we would go up and help run the circle. Our presence in the circle encouraged the four workers to be extra attentive in their preparations. Gavin arranged with Amanda to make available photos of Darla and the children for the workers to see.

We are glad to report that the healing was a great success. Darla's cancer went into remission, and she is able to control her HIV with drug therapy. That success was immediate and dramatic, and it reignited the interest of our four Witches in healing and in the power. Since that time they have done many more successful spells; and (perhaps more important) their own depression is only a faint memory.

The feeling of being needed, the feeling that you are doing essential "good" work and are appreciated for it, revitalizes the most depressed spirit.

SUMMARY

This chapter reveals that the spell starts with excitement and ends in serenity. This requires an adjustment of your endorphin levels during the spell. The adjustment can be done in many ways, of which the easiest is sexual release. Current scientific research shows that this is the only possible way for the follow-up astral trip to be fully successful. Thus, the sequence of steps in the spell is of importance, second only to the development of mind keys that are meaningful in your own reality.

Most small groups end up with healing as their prime spell-casting objective. Shifting their focus to this objective, members find that their lives undergo a transformation. Very subtly at first, but then as more healing successes accrue, the group's spiritual attitudes change. The mundane things of everyday life become less and less important, and that pay raise or that new car fades into the background. This path nourishes and satisfies the spirit so fully that the ego takes second place; the sense of doing work that is worth your while is so nourishing that you no longer need to gorge your spirit with big-ticket trinkets.

The Science Behind a Witch's Healing Miracles

SCIENCE AGREES WITH THE WITCHES

It is an age-old belief of Witches that the body heals itself. Thus, the traditional Witch would not only administer potions; she would also be the tribe's psychologist, seeking the *cause* of the dis-ease as well as its cure.

Modern medicine (that is, medicine since perhaps 1975 CE [common era]) has discovered that the body actually heals itself at the cellular level. Every cell in the body has on its surface *receptor* molecules. The body either produces, or obtains from a medication, molecules called *ligands* that mate with the receptors. When the mating occurs, the receptor orders the cell to make changes within itself. It is those changes that result in healing. Interestingly, the cell receptors actually vibrate; thus, it seems that toning and sound can change the receptors' rate of vibration to enhance their capture rate of ligands.

Professor Pert's[1] discovery of the opiate receptors was an essential breakthrough—especially when Professors Hughes and Kosterlitz discovered endorphins (the ligand for the opiate receptor).

---

[1] Candace Pert, Ph.D., *Molecules of Emotion* (New York: Scribner, 1997). See Chapter IV.

The opiate receptor mates with many different opiates. At their mating, the entity experiences a state of bliss. The entity *enjoys* the state of bliss; and, once having known it, will do almost anything to repeat it. This is why addicts steal and rob for drugs. It is why Tantrists strive for a large number of orgasms to force the body to overproduce endorphins. As Professor Pert says:

> A shocking but exciting fact revealed by the opiate-receptor findings was that it didn't matter if you were a lab rat, a First Lady, or a dope addict—everyone had the exact same mechanism in the brain for creating bliss and expanded consciousness.

Notice particularly her mention of "expanded consciousness." Until very recently no self-respecting medical researcher would ever discuss consciousness—not unless he wanted his career to take an abrupt downturn. Consciousness is something that cannot be quantified (and, therefore, according to modern medicine, cannot be acknowledged).

The body produces the ligands necessary to fill the needs of the receptors that keep the cells balanced and happy. Most of this ligand production is under the control of the brain (which by the way also produces and uses ligands for fine-tuning our state of well-being and health). In various circumstances the brain curtails its production of ligands, and the entity gets sick. It may not always be the brain's "fault." After a radical hysterectomy, for instance, a woman cannot produce so much testosterone and estrogen as her body needs to keep it in balance and humming along because the producing sources have been removed. Similarly, a man whose testes have atrophied through some medical procedure cannot produce a balanced amount of testosterone and he becomes irritable.

When young people undergo an artificial curtailment in their production of endorphins through society's denial of all mating dances and sexual activity, they may become unstable, frustrated, and angry. Many turn to drugs as a first line of defense against the artificially imposed barriers. If they can't get drugs, then anger takes over; too often this results in such things as school shooting sprees and in reckless, dangerous driving of vehicles.

THE MAGIC BULLET

For many years the government funded research in an effort to find a magic chemical bullet to prevent addiction to drugs. They sought a feel-good substance to take the place of the "naughty" products. Unfortunately, the body responds to the chemical bullets in the same way it does to the drugs themselves: It wants more and more of them.

Then in France in the 1980s, doctors and psychologists addressed this problem objectively. They started a whole new teaching program in the schools. It advocated an approach they called *outercourse*.[2] Essentially outercourse means having orgasm (working singly or in combination) without intercourse. The national furor was instant and wild, but the doctors persisted. It has worked. The outercourse curriculum is now being taught in many schools outside France, and it has had several dramatic results.

1. Teenage pregnancy is the lowest it has ever been.

2. Grades have risen by an average of 20 percent.

3. Riotous, destructive behavior has disappeared. For example, there is no teen gang warfare.

The magic bullet is called simply outercourse.[3]

What does all this mean to you? It means that when it comes to healing, the body cures itself—as Witches have been saying for centuries.

---

[2] Instruction in outercourse is shared. Originally each senior class is taught; then in following years the seniors teach the juniors under supervision of the school nurse or other qualified professional. Dr. Joycelyn Elders, once Surgeon General, advocated teaching teens masturbation. Exit one Surgeon General.

[3] British Broadcasting Company, February 9, 1999.

TREATING THE CAUSE,
NOT THE SYMPTOMS

The twentieth century was noteworthy for the rise of a mechanistic approach to healing. In such an approach, if something is wrong with a patient, the physician prescribes a powerful drug,[4] performs surgery, or takes some other simple, straightforward physical approach to fixing the problem. In many cases, of course, that makes perfect sense. A physical problem? Find a physical solution. If you have a broken arm, it's only logical to get a cast on it. But very few doctors take the next step and ask not, "How did you break your arm?" but, "*Why* did you break your arm?" The mind and the emotions play no role in such healing work.

A handful of researchers have attacked this question. They find that patients with broken bones share certain attributes. They experience *interruptions* in the "normal" flow of life. Table V-1 shows some examples.

One strict parent and one permissive parent

An interrupted education

Failure to gain a college degree because of the interruption

A person whose general health apart from the broken bone is either normal or better than normal

More than one marriage, but a low number of children per marriage

---

TABLE V–1
Personality Types Who Experience Broken Bones

Some twentieth-century mainstream doctors labeled these conclusions ridiculous and resolutely ignored them. How could being of a particular personality type mean that you will experience a broken bone instead of some other complaint? Gradually, though, in the last decades of the twentieth century holistic healers and wellness doctors have come to realize that there was sense in what Witches of yore had claimed. The illness is the *symptom* of a problem, not its *cause*.

---

[4] In this chapter *drug* is a shorter way of saying *pharmaceutical.* It implies no illegal substance.

We have heard anecdotally of hundreds of cases of doctors who worked around the clock through epidemics without ever getting ill—yet who died within a couple of years of their retirement. Every human carries within him-/herself, or every day is exposed to, an unimaginable host of germs, bacteria, and viruses. Healthy people brush them off—until they need a sickness to make them reassess their lives.

The Witch with her tarot cards and the psychologist with his Rorschach ink-blot tests serve a similar purpose. The tarot, containing more images, seems to us to work better than the ink-blots—but then we're biased. So when you get sick or when somebody near and dear to you needs healing, the very first thing to do after the panic stabilizes and the regular doctor has been called, is to ascertain what in the patient's *situation* may be causing the problem. In our times, stress is blamed for many of these diseases, and following stress we find depression. It is true that stress causes disease—but stress doesn't spontaneously appear. It's the person's *lifestyle* that causes the stress. So the Witch must always look for the underlying hidden causes instead of being satisfied just reflexively to apply our methods, psychic or physical, blindly.

EILEEN BREAKS BOTH ARMS AND SAVES HER MARRIAGE

Eileen McG lives in Vancouver, British Columbia. At the time of this incident she was 29 and had been married for only two years. Her husband, Ewan, was a new immigrant from Wales who was making a successful career in selling condominiums. When she bought one through him, lightning struck.

As a rising executive in a shipping company, Eileen frequently jetted off around the Pacific Rim to visit agents and shippers, while Ewan was a contented and comfortable man, easily selling a then hot product with his laid-back approach. He was proud of Eileen, and supported her bid to break through the glass ceiling in any way he could. She rejected his offers, though—even spurning the rides he would have given her to the airport. Naturally that spurning rankled with him. Surely and steadily he withdrew his support and started looking elsewhere for his endorphin adjustments.

Getting up late one morning, hurrying through her preparations for work, Eileen stepped out of the shower, fell, and broke her arm. She had never been sick before or even near a hospital, so the whole procedure traumatized her. Ewan acted his normal supportive self, and for once she did accept some of that support. Not more than two weeks later, she was back in her high-speed independent mode, driving herself to work and playing hard. Part of her playing was horseback riding. Before her arm was out of the cast, she fell, breaking the other arm and compressing a vertebra.

Now she was truly an invalid. She had to accept help from dozens of different people. Normally she would have hated the situation; but because of the pain in her back, she was blissed out on morphine. She found she liked both the attention and the bliss. She had her epiphany—accepting help wasn't evil or weak. It could be pleasant.

As she hovered in her twilight sleep, she was startled to see her dead old grandmother materialize. The grandmother started, as the Canadians say, to tick her off. Afterward, Eileen told us, it was almost like the Ghost of Christmas Future talking to Scrooge and showing him how it would be. Ewan in bed with another woman, herself alone, a dried-up stick, begging for support on the street; for, as Grandma said, "You'll lose your job too if you don't soften up and accept help."

Eileen took Grandma's advice seriously. Ewan now has twin girls to look after as well as supporting his (still running) wife in her high-powered job.

WITCH, HEAL THYSELF

Many Witches, especially those who lead covens, have successful and fulfilling lives. Yes, they are busy. Yes, they feel stressed. But if they are wise, they do not overstress. They show a tendency to ignore the "regular" doctor (the allopathic medical doctor)—that is, to ignore the guy with the mechanistic approach.

The tendency can be dangerous. When you buy a new car, it is only sensible to follow the recommended schedule of maintenance, and to be fairly scrupulous about doing such things as changing the oil. As the car ages it needs more maintenance. In the throw-away society of the western world, when the car's maintenance bills get very high you probably throw it away and buy a new one. It surprises many students of the School of Wicca when we require them to have a medical exam before we initiate them. A few of them have actually gone so far as to turn down initiation because they didn't want to have a physical. Maybe they felt afraid underneath that the physician would find something wrong. How far can you afford to go down that road of denial and madness? Or perhaps we should say, "What's wrong with this picture?"

The worry you cause yourself when you think something may be wrong with your body probably *makes* that thing wrong with you. If your thoughts obsessively turn to, say, your pancreas, and you invest time worrying about pancreatic matters, what else can your pancreas *do* but go wrong? In psychic terms, if you think you have an illness, you move your tuning dial to the frequency where all the attributes of that illness can come into you. Someone who sees your auric protective field would tell you, "The color of your aura is now tuned to the disease you're thinking about."

The only way you can overcome this is to know that you don't have that disease. That's why you must go to a regular doctor (an RD), have your checkup, and if something is wrong with your system, get it fixed; but additionally make sure that you do the next step. That is, talk with a capable psychic or with an intimate about factors in your life that prompt you to *need* that disease. If you had it, what unwelcome aspect of your life could you evade?

A stage hypnotist with his repertory of tricks perfectly demonstrates the body's ability. The hypnotist touches a subject with a pencil, telling him, "This is a red-hot poker." The subject flinches, and before your eyes a blister appears at the site of the touch. The hypnotist says, "Oh, oops, it wasn't a poker at all. Look. It's just a pencil." The blister goes away! This is a healing. Again, no special drugs, no unusual surgery, no incantations were required to remove the burn. The mind did it.

Around the globe, humans consume an amazingly varied range of foods. We know full well that the French diet is full of all those things we're not supposed to have: heavy creams, sauces, buttered steaks, and showpiece desserts. We know, too, it contains one thing that we should have: at least one glass daily of red wine. In 1999 the oldest human known was a French woman; documentation showed her to be 126. She smoked regularly, drank regularly—and had all her faculties until her final few days. She certainly didn't go by the food pyramid or any other "official" guidelines. With this in mind it is interesting that the United States is worldwide fifth in life expectancy and even our much vaunted medical establishment admits that their record on infant mortality is abysmal.

Your attitude to life and to living factors as highly as the diet you consume and the doctor you visit. Professor Dean Ornish, M.D.,[5] writes, "We found that most people who were eligible for surgery were able to avoid it by changing their lifestyle." His research clearly shows that using his combination of diet, meditation, and support-group therapy not only made the surgery unnecessary; it also repaired the damaged organs . . . just like the blister going away.

GINNY CURES HER SKIN CANCER

Ginny Y was a lovely lady, high priestess of an active coven in Philadelphia. She was also a home health-care nurse who traveled thousands of miles annually around the Philadelphia area to visit her patients. As happens in the normal growth stages of a coven's existence, Ginny was replaced by another high priestess. Within a year, government cutbacks in the health sector meant that she was laid off from her home-care job. At first she kept very busy catching up on all the tasks she had postponed because of her earlier busy schedule. When she began to relax she noticed a sore, rashy area on the back of her left hand. She took it to her doctor. He said she had skin cancer, and that she should have the skin peeled and grafted. This promised to be a very expensive procedure. Since she now had no health coverage at all, she decided to try fixing it herself.

The first thing she did was start using a salve made from aloe vera. That certainly removed the itching and eased the discomfort. She knew it was a coverup, though, that she was just buying time, and that underneath the salve the skin was still damaged.

Now her new high priestess gave her a tarot reading. In response to her question, "What should I do about my skin cancer?" the cards told her, "Move south and get a new job." She and the priestess discussed all this back and forth; Ginny realized that just maybe her skin cancer was a symptom of her need for friendship

---

[5] Dean Ornish, M.D., *Dr. Dean Ornish's Program for Reversing Heart Disease* (New York: Ballantine, 1992).

and attention. She came to see that, as much as she enjoyed her new life as a retiree, she was actually very lonely and understressed. She felt as if no one needed her.

When one of her southern Witch friends told her of an opening in a hospital in Tampa, she jumped at the opportunity to follow the advice of the tarot reading. She took the job—and what do you know? The skin cancer began to shrink and finally disappeared. The official language was "remission."

THE STRESS-BALANCING ACT[6]

A Swahili proverb tells us:

> There are three things that if you do not know, you cannot live long in the world:
> 1. What is too much for you;
> 2. What is too little for you;
> 3. What is just right for you.

If a little pressure is a good thing but too much or too little is harmful, then it is obvious that you will be most healthy and will operate best on a plateau between the extremes of no pressure and too much. "Died from stress" doesn't appear on death certificates, but in fact stress is the root cause of death for millions of people. Most of these stress-induced deaths are labeled cardiovascular problems such as heart failure, but the underlying cause is the chronic stress of life in today's world.

You don't often hear about someone who "died from stress" or "died from absence of stress," but think of how many cases you know of people retiring—and within a couple of years, dying. It's almost as if their purpose in living has gone away when they stop going to a regular job. Ginny nearly became a typical example of this scenario. Understress is just as deadly as overstress; though in many ways it is more subtle because very few people realize that it is happening. Researchers have even quantified stress, dividing it into three levels labeled:

---

[6] An instructional videotape, *Pro-Active Stress Reduction,* may broaden your understanding of this subject. It is available through Godolphin House, P.O. Box 297-BK, Hinton, WV 25951-0297, or www.wicca.org.

1. U (under-)   pressured
2. P (plateau) pressured (eustress)
3. O (over-)   pressured

Ironically, symptoms of 1 and 3 may resemble each other. For instance, the person who continuously plays computer games may be wasting time to increase the deadline pressure on a job, or may relieve stress by doing a mindless no-brainer task. Here, instead of "computer games," you can read "too much meditating" or "tidying house" or "useless handwork" or "escapist TV" or "reading" or any other pursuit that buys time to delay the inevitable.

RECOGNIZING STRESS MALADJUSTMENT

Each of us is different. Some people are very sociable; some are loners; some are overweight; some underweight, and so on. So when you evaluate people for stress maladjustment, you should look first for behavioral changes and second for the "overs." This can be overweight, over-dressed, over-indulged, over-petted—in fact, excessive anything. The "overs" are fairly easy to spot, especially gross overweight and over-fearfulness. In behavioral, physical, and mental changes, your job is harder because you do not know what was normal for the patient when his/her health was optimal. Watch for the changes listed in Tables V-2 and V-3.

Changes in appetite	Sweating	Uneven heartbeat
Chest discomfort	Skin rashes	Pins and needles
Stomach upset	Restlessness	Insomnia
Sleepiness	Muscle tension	Dry mouth
Headaches	Nosebleeds	General weakness and tiredness
Need to urinate	Constipation	Pain in target organ
Cramps	Backaches	

TABLE V–2
Physical Changes Resulting from Stress

FEELING OF CONSTANTLY BEING:

Under pressure	Frightened	Tense
In conflict and aggressive	Suspicious	Isolated
Drained	Irritable and complaining	
Unable to make decisions	Frustrated	

TABLE V–3
Mental Changes Resulting from Stress

Usually the first signs of stress show up in the mental area; you can easily recognize the increase in irritability and the inability to make decisions. In your own life the first sign might be the length of time it takes you to write the monthly checks and to balance the checkbook. Do you get angry easily? Are you continually frustrated?

Certain diseases are known to follow stress: for example, skin rashes, yeast infections, migraines, grinding the teeth, and, in crowded living conditions, tuberculosis. Witches believe that the mind causes all illnesses, and it is clear that stress is the most likely cause of many dis-eases.

Each of us has his/her target organ. We all walk around all the time with literally millions of highly dangerous bacteria either inside our systems already or in the air we breathe or on surfaces we touch. Telephone instruments, for example, notoriously spread infection. Most of the time, though, these latent bacteria don't affect us—but sometimes they can be deadly. Much depends on individual life circumstances and on stress levels. Table V-4 lists the illnesses that will most probably develop from maladjusted stress levels.

Hypertension	Rheumatoid arthritis	Eczema
Heart diseases	Pre-menstrual syndrome (PMS)	Tuberculosis
Migraine	Flatulence	Depression
Allergies	Indigestion	Colitis
Asthma	Diabetes	

TABLE V–4
Diseases Recognized as Having a Stress Background

THE OVERSTRESSED DANCE TEACHER

Concepcion M was a very successful dance teacher with her own studio just outside New York City. She started teaching Argentine tango when that craze first began. She was good at it—half-Spanish herself, bilingual, and possessing the physical sinuosity of many young Spanish ladies. She traveled several times to Buenos Aires to perfect an authentic milonga style; so when the craze really took off in New York, she was ready to ride the crest of the wave. She found herself teaching classes seven days a week, and almost every day ran from noon until late at night. She worked in studios all over the New York area. It was as if she had a license to print money.

At first she reveled in this deep-immersion experience. With all the endorphin happy pills she got from her dancing, she seemed to be on a very good track; nor did she lack for companionship when the classes were over. Many men wanted to "improve their style" with the attractive lady. Everything was going along well but she began to lose her voice.

She took all the obvious steps: She got herself a radio-remote microphone and amplifier so she no longer had to shout across the studio floors. Still she grew hoarser and hoarser. Laryngitis looked like a permanent part of her future, though doctors could find nothing wrong with her larynx. One specialist gave her some muscle and voice exercises to do, and for a short time they seemed to help.

She thoroughly enjoyed her work and was distraught at the idea she might have to stop. She called us to confide that she didn't know what to do.

Gavin did a reading over the telephone. Many, many negative cards turned up and even though he toned down the worst of the predictions, still she got the message that she would have to slow down. Eventually, after many hours of long-distance phone conversations, Gavin convinced her to find two or three young women whom she could train to do some of the teaching.

Reluctantly she did that. As soon as she added the teachers' class to her schedule, which we assumed would overstress her even further, her voice began to come back. Her psyche realized that there was a light at the end of the tunnel. No drugs were involved, no special healing herbs, nothing but a minor change in lifestyle. This caper had a very low gasp factor.

HAVE YOU TRIED THE NEW DRUG FOR DEPRESSION YET?

If you watch any television, as we do, you, too, may get the impression that almost every day there's a new drug announced to "cure" depression. Depression seems to be the excuse *du jour* that the body presents to its owner to avoid looking at the life its owner lives. It does seem that finally the medical mechanics' paradigm is moving over slightly to make space for the holistic one.

In depression you have something which is obviously the result of the mind's action, and mind-bending drugs are being used to try to fix it—but often they have little effect, so new drugs must be invented and tried. It's an industry. Yes, we know the inventions don't come every day—but it certainly is on a monthly basis. Hundreds of people write to us asking what our cure is. In most cases, of course, we can't advise them.[7]

Notice that Table V-3, Mental Changes Resulting from Stress, clearly shows the same symptoms that depressed people report. This points up the proximate interconnection between stress and depression. The frustration engendered by the feelings that "I am helpless to change this situation. All I can do is choke back the anger I must not show" results in immediate stress and deep clinical depression.

IT'S NOT YOUR BODY'S FAULT

The body has a built-in mechanism to react to stress. When you are in danger, several automatic systems come into play to tense the muscles, increase the adrenaline, increase the clotting ability of blood, cause the bowels to evacuate, and move the supply of blood around in the body. As soon as the danger ends, all these defensive mechanisms relax. You have experienced that "whew!," that letdown. This group of physical reactions is called the *fight-or-flight syndrome*. The body reflexively tells itself to fight the threat.

---

[7] See Appendix 2 for a thorough discussion of some legal aspects of clerical/counseling work such as the Church of Wicca performs. On medical matters we can advise only members of the Church in good standing. The same is true of counseling and of psychic healing. We cannot advise or heal people who are not active members in good standing of the Church of Wicca. No matter how distressing or deserving the case, our lawyers tell us we must hold firmly to this rule.

Unfortunately when you subject the body to one stress after another, it never gets a chance to relax. It's as if you clenched your fist and kept it clenched continually all day. The muscles get set. Try it for yourself. Just clench your fist and hold it clenched for about five minutes. You will feel a certain resistance to relaxing it.

The muscles in the heart and in your arteries and veins do the same thing when you experience nonstop stress. With today's fad exercises and diets, you pile stress upon stress. You feel emotionally stressed, so you go out jogging with your cellular phone or your beeper clipped to your belt; you come home and you don't allow yourself to eat. This way you pile stress upon stress. You never unclench. The body receives shot after shot of adrenaline. No one in his/her right mind would continually shoot themselves up with adrenaline, but this is what the body's automatic system is doing.

ACCUMULATED STRESS

That final straw piled up beyond the limit of tolerance—the final straw that breaks the camel's back—is painfully relevant in thinking of stress. The first stress sensitizes you, and each subsequent stress makes you more sensitive, until finally stress burnout occurs. The body reacts to many things in the same way. A single bee sting may be an annoyance; the next one slightly more noticeable. At some point (which varies from person to person) another bee sting will send you into anaphylactic shock and kill you. You have become sensitized. The body can develop a tolerance for some irritants; not so for stress.

We tend to assume that dominant male leaders are the only ones who fall over with stress-induced heart attacks; but studies show that people in subordinate positions, especially females, exhibit just as many stress-induced illnesses. Frustration causes this stress. The low-paid waitress is a typical example of the problem. She is caught between the kitchen and the customer, at the mercy of them both with no recourse. She has little influence in the kitchen, and with a demanding customer she has no place to take out her frustrations.

In the world of stress analysis and research, there is a famous experiment:

Take one hundred healthy rats.

Put fifty of them ("Group S") into an ambient temperature of 40°F.

After seven days, take all one hundred into an ambient temperature of 28°F.

In seven days the fifty rats of Group S are dead. The others survive.

This experiment teaches that: You do not build up a tolerance to stress. Research clearly shows that if you are not overly stressed, you can take a little extra stress in stride. When you are stressed to your limit, even a little further stress will push you beyond recovery.

GEORGINE SAVES BETTY'S LIFE AND HER JOB

Georgine and Betty worked together at a high-profile advertising agency in San Francisco. Every February witnessed a major upheaval in the agency because three of its biggest accounts came up that month for review and reassessment. This meant that everyone worked seventy-hour weeks, trying to come up with new and different ideas and approaches to the ads so the agency would keep the accounts.

In January of 1996, Betty's husband left her. For a couple of weeks she bottomed out emotionally, working with lawyers and trying to rebuild her life. She seemed to move forward with her two sons into the new life, stressful though it was, without too much difficulty. She found a lot of comfort in confiding to Georgine. The two had earlier grown close; in fact, during Betty's last vacation, Georgine had watered her house plants and picked up her mail.

Just before one of the major presentations at the agency, Betty got a phone call. She slammed the phone down and rushed out with no explanation, leaving her colleagues to do the critical work on the presentation. Back at her desk the next day, she apologized to everyone, explaining that her teenage son was in trouble; he had been caught buying drugs down in the Castro.

Betty seemed to recover even from this, and gave the impression that she was determined to go on with her work. But Georgine sensed that something was very wrong. She tried talking to Betty but her friend, usually communicative, brushed her off. At home that evening Georgine couldn't get Betty off her mind. Finally she called her. Only the answering machine responded. Later that night as Georgine lay in that twilight state between waking and sleeping, she had a picture of Betty bleeding to death. She phoned again; again the machine.

This time she was not satisfied to let it drift, but got up, dressed, and drove to Betty's apartment. As she pulled into the parking lot behind the building, a police cruiser drew in behind her. "In a bit of a hurry, aren't you, ma'am?" the gray-haired policeman asked politely. Georgine told him she was worried about her friend. "That's no excuse, you know," the officer told her.

Georgine persuaded him to help her learn whether Betty was all right. Together they knocked for admission, but there was no reply. Georgine hastily used Betty's key that she had retained after the house-sitting time, and let them both in.

The whole place was full of gas. The policeman now took charge. He called for backup and crawled across the living room to open the biggest window. Finding it fixed in place, he broke it with a chair. He returned coughing, but after a few moments he crawled back to turn off the taps of the kitchen stove. Again he had to come out for air. By now Georgine was frantic, screaming, "Get her out! Get her out!"

"Calm down, ma'am. We'll get her." The EMT team arrived just then and did get Betty and the two boys as well. A short stay in the hospital cleared their systems of the gas. The following week, Georgine sat down with Betty to talk with her about her attempt to kill the boys and commit suicide.

"I just cracked, I guess," Betty wept. "Just too many things building up."

They talked about how she could adjust her life to lower the stress. Georgine gave her the stress-reduction techniques that a proactive Witch would use.

GEORGINE'S ADVICE ABOUT REDUCING STRESS

The vital key to diminishing the effects of stress in your life is this: interruption of the connection between the instant of a frustrating or stressful experience and the onset of the fight-or-flight reaction. There are four principal coping techniques for doing this. All are proactive. All must occur instantly, before the fight-or-flight reaction kicks in.

1. DESENSITIZING

Typically, when people yell "Witch! Witch! Witch!" at Yvonne and Gavin, they laugh. The harassers are thus discomfited and go away. Laughter always reduces your stress reaction, and bullies tend somehow to wilt when people point and snicker. (Have you ever seen a Nazi giggle?) The media are always searching for ways to startle us and grab our attention with outrageous headlines and vivid pictures of horror.

Here is a technique for learning to desensitize yourself. Watch a thirty-minute newscast, write down each story headline that is negative, and come up with a positive, amusing interpretation of the events. The Senate has screwed up again? They've been doing it since they were first convened in Philadelphia way back when Jesus walked the streets of Chicago. What's new? First, you can be amused at the antics of these purportedly serious, intelligent men and women; second, you can be relieved that in this nation we are able to see them for what they are. So instead of becoming frustrated, be glad and amused.

Do this exercise for seven consecutive nights; you may get to the point where the morning news broadcast won't ruin your breakfast any more. Remember the media saying: Nothing that's normal is news. There is an amusing anecdote from the 1930s about the *Times of London*, when they deliberately wrote dull, nonstressing headlines. Instead of headlines, the front page carried court announcements and advertising. The staff ran a behind-the-scenes competition for the dullest headline. The winner read: "Krakatoa Erupts; Not Many Dead."

On a recent blistering, humid afternoon in St. Louis, Missouri, the weather man used the line, "Let's be grateful for this beautiful summer weather. Let's enjoy it on the river while we can." Isn't that better than lamenting about what a terrible heat wave we were having and the discomfort we were all enduring? We all knew perfectly well we were in a heat wave and were in discomfort! But the weather man significantly lightened the mood.

So Method 1 in avoiding the reactions that stress your body is: *Desensitize.*

2. Renaming Things and People

In an old Muppets episode, Sam the American Eagle got terribly embarrassed when he realized the implications of his announcement, *Everyone is naked under their feathers.*

If you have thought of the president of the company as a king or a god, take a different approach. Think of him as an overworked elderly man who is no smarter than you. Think of him as a premature ejaculator. The waitress' technique, thinking how all the patrons would look nude and bald-headed, might work for many situations, including Congress.

So Method 2 in stress management is: *Rename.*

3. Construct a Magical Safe Place

Here is a technique to abort the fight-or-flight response when you run into a new frustrating situation. It is called "going to your safe place." It is almost tantamount to a meditative approach, but one that you put on fast-forward. It calls on you to use your imagination almost as a child would. We want you to find fifteen minutes of time in your busy life to make your safe place.

Imagine a safe place: one without telephones or beepers or electronics or mail or calendars of any kind. When we say *imagine,* we are thinking in terms of *visualizing in the mind.*[8] When you imagine something, use your dominant sense to start with and then fill in the details, flesh out the picture, with your other senses. To find your dominant imagination technique, think of a baseball game where someone has hit the decisive home run. Do you

> see it—like a movie?
> smell it—like sweat?
> taste it—like hot dogs and mustard?
> hear it—like the cheers and the crack of the bat?
> feel it—in the crowd's emotions?

If your impression combines more than one of these, which came first?

Some 90 percent of people imagine by seeing pictures; some 6 percent imagine by hearing sounds; the remainder are pretty well

---

[8] *Imagination* implies hearing, smelling, tasting, or a combination of all the sensations that human beings can experience.

split up in the remaining 3 percent. (Percentages vary from researcher to researcher.)

However you imagine best, imagine this place, which is very safe. Give the place a very simple name. You can call it "Place" or "One" or "Chamber" or "Meadow" or anything you like. Make the name short and simple. A friend of ours calls her place "Pony" because in childhood she always felt safe when she was riding her pony.

The place in your imagination is unusual in this regard: You can change it at will. Let us say, for example, it is a cave. Inside the cave you can have any arrangement you like. If you want to imagine different music playing in the background, you can have it. If you want a different sort of couch, you can imagine it. If you want a different companion (or no companion), that's what you can have. Examine the place very carefully, without haste, and in great detail. Memorize every single detail that you can. Where are the windows? What color are the draperies? What do the furnishings look like? What scent can you smell? Is the place outdoors? Is it dry or under water? Up a climb or down a descent? Bright or dark? Open or enclosed? Put it behind a heavy door that only you can open. As a final touch, associate with it some pleasurable sensation. Make it anything you like. You may imagine it as the feeling of an orgasm; or of a gentle massage; or as the most delectable food you have ever eaten; or as winning a game. But you need to associate a very pleasurable sensation with the place. Be inventive, but be detailed. Make it real, make it vivid, and make it yours alone.

Now make some written notes about it all. Make sure that there is no piece of the place left unexamined: the sky or ceiling above, the floor or carpet, whatever. Get everything down. In mine, called "Cliff," I like the sea and a beach outside the window. I can hear the waves over some harp music.

Now think of something else, or talk to someone else, or watch a TV program for about ten minutes. In the middle of what you are doing (perhaps when a commercial comes on TV), say to yourself or out loud: "_____" (the name of your place). Can you instantly go back into it? If you cannot, do the exercise again, filling in more detail, like the background music you would like to hear, choosing the scent you would like to smell, feeling the texture of the draperies or the upholstery or the stone or wood that you have put into the place. In fact, if you are a person who does not visualize well, you may want to carry with you a piece of fabric you can feel or a small vial of scent you can smell or even a tiny bell or a seashell. These things are easy to obtain; and if they get you quickly and surely to your safe place, they are what you need.

Using Your Magical Safe Place—When you experience a stressful situation, immediately go to your safe place by slowly saying "_____" (the name you've given it) over and over again while you imagine your safe place. Remember the pleasure sensation you feel there. In this way you will stop the body's reactions in midstream. Instead of the adrenaline rush, you will get a pleasant mind-inspired healing. People going into many situations can think of their safe place ahead of time and dramatically lower their reactions.

All this may sound to you like a mind game for children, but it isn't. It is a useful skill for overworked adults that has been proven time and time again to work for all ages and all genders. Obviously you can't avoid or desensitize all situations; your aim here is to move your stress away from the *chronic* category eventually into the category of *occasional*.

So Method 3 in stress management is: **Construct a Safe Place.**

4. RELAXATION EXERCISES

Going to your safe place is one very good way to get you out of a situation and into another mindset. For some people, though, these meditative techniques are not totally effective. If that's true of you, you need to do some physical exercises to relax. A very simple one is to clench your toes for fifteen seconds and relax them, instead of clenching your fists. Another is to slump. Another is to just totally relax. Drop your head on your chest. Stretch out your legs. Put your heels on the floor and let your feet flop over. Flop your arms down by your sides, as if you were a very soft old rag doll. Take three sighing deep breaths, making each breath last as long as you can sustain it.

So Method 4 in stress management is **Relax.**

PROACTIVE VERSUS REACTIVE

In dealing with stresses, it is important to understand that you must be proactive, not reactive. If you go in to see the boss and you know it's going to be a tough session, go to your safe place *before* you turn that doorknob to the boss's office. Prepare yourself with one of the methods we outline here. Listen to music *before* you start that stressful trip. The better you prepare, the less effect the stress has.

RAGLAND'S SIGN

There is a simple way to find out whether the adrenal glands are performing properly, or they are overstressed and you are in stress burnout. For this you will need a blood-pressure measuring device. Here is how to test yourself:

1. Lie down. Go to your safe place and stay there for at least five minutes. (If you like, use a timer.) While still lying down, take your blood pressure.

2. Gently stand up, but don't leave your safe place. Without removing the cuff, reset your machine and take another reading.

Normally when you stand up the blood pressure should rise slightly. If the blood pressure remains steady or even decreases slightly, you have adrenaline burnout. If it declines more than 5 mm Hg, you need to begin serious work on reducing stress in your life.[9]

STRESSORS IN YOUR LIFE

Table V-5 lists further common stressors to watch out for. Some of these are ostensibly pleasant events or milestones—but don't buy into the assumption that all families live the life depicted in Norman Rockwell's paintings. Generally, the stressors are arranged with the highest stressor at the top and the lesser at the bottom; but of course, since everyone is different, they may not be in the order, or have the weighting, you would select. For a single mother, pregnancy may or may not be more stressful than a car accident. For a battered woman, separation may feel less stressful than carrying on with the relationship. Separation can always be regarded as an opportunity for new experiences and growth—contrary to popular wisdom which insists that adults belong two-by-two as in Noah's ark.

---

[9] There is an online stress test at http://www.medmd.com.

EVENT		ONGOING	
Stressor	**Points**	**Stressor**	**Points**
Death of a lover / spouse / SO	100	Unsatisfactory sex	40
Separation	73	Children/teenagers	10–50
Marriage	65	Driving to work	0–90
Imprisonment: threatened or actual	63	Strict diet	90
Personal painful injury	53	Waitressing	80
Car accident	50	Car mechanic	60
Loss of job	47	Doctor	20–90
Moving	45	Neonatal nurse	50
Retirement	44	Moderate diet	30
Serious illness of a lover / SO	40		
Pregnancy	40		
Sexual dysfunction	40		
New child	40		
New job	40		
News stories (per story)	10		
Money	38		
Death of friend or family member	37		
Change in number of arguments with SO	35		
Christmas	30		
Legal action	30		
School begins or ends	20		
Vacation	20		

Total event stress   _____
Total ongoing stress   _____
Grand total   _____

TABLE V–5
Stressors in Your Life

The set of stressors under "event" was developed by Thomas Holme and Richard Rahe after they studied over five thousand families and gauged their stress reaction to life's events. Stressors listed under "ongoing" were developed empirically by Gavin and Yvonne.

Try changing the tables into the sequence in which you would rank the stressors; then add other stressors that are important to you. Add to the table those things like "trouble with the boss" or "freeway driving problems" that are your special stressors, and give them all realistic weights. Make the table fit you.

When you are subjected to these additional pressures that cause stress, it is vital to take better care of yourself and to use all the stress-avoidance and -repair techniques you can manage. If your regular daily routine is too stressful, you need to reevaluate it and look at changes you might make in your life to reduce the pressures.

To use your table, simply list the things that have happened to you in the past year. If your score is over 300, you are vulnerable to a stress-related illness or mental dysfunction.

AVOIDANCE THERAPY

The first stress-reduction technique is the physical act of avoidance, which might be summarized as avoiding a situation: Why go to the party if you don't like the people who will be there? Why go to church if the minister doesn't make you feel better about yourself? Why go shopping with your SO if you don't need anything? Why go to the lounge bar if you don't like the decor? Why listen to the TV if you don't like the program? Do something better with your life.

Obviously, if there is in your life a situation that causes continual stress, you should make plans to vote with your feet. Why should you be a plankton, helpless at the mercy of every wave and ripple? But in situations where voting with your feet is not a viable alternative, there is still another option: your safe place.

The safe-place technique also reduces your stress reaction. When you go in to see the boss and you think for sure he or she is going to tear you to ribbons, stand for just a moment outside the door and think of your boss as a naked bald-headed clown. Go to your safe place and experience the pleasure sensation that you have stored there. Then go in and face the encounter, avoiding the stress reaction.

SUMMARY

There is no need to go belly up. There are things you can do. A high-school coach—indeed, any authority figure—may have trained a lot of your reaction in. Well, you can train it right back out again, because you realize today that you have options; that now you don't have to react in a negative, competitive, fight-or-flight way to every stressful situation. There are techniques you can use to deactivate your hot-buttons. Remember:

Life happens.
Stress is optional.

The Witch's Healing Grimoire[1]

WITCHCRAFT AND ALTERNATIVE MEDICINE

People are spending more money than ever before on alternative healing methods. On January 17, 2000, *Newsweek Magazine* reported that the outlay in the U.S. now amounts to more than a billion dollars annually. Three reasons are suggested for the trend:

1. The high cost of conventional medicine

2. The lack of anyone to "talk to" in the health-care octopus

3. A lack of confidence in "real" (read: *conventional* or *allopathic*) doctors

The media—especially the tabloid press with their continual scare stories—do the medical establishment and the general public a great disservice. Most of the time "real" doctors do a better-than-ever job. The authors of this book live almost in an alternative universe; yet when they get truly sick, their first stop is a real doctor. Yes, it took a long time to find one to talk to, one who would accept their habit of doing self-medication with herbs, and one who understood that they didn't want the latest miracle cure but were content with older slower medications.

---

[1] A *grimoire* is an ancient book of knowledge.

The recent furor over hospital deaths[2] has pointed up something that the medical establishment has known for a long time: the vital importance of the patient's involvement in his own healing and drug therapy. Many people passively take their physician's advice without question; but that can be a mistake. Make sure you understand the proposed treatment and every letter of the prescription. Verify its correctness when you pick up the medication from the pharmacy. On February 15, 2000, CNN reported that a minimum of 1.5 million prescription errors occur every year in the U.S.

Question your doctor. Get a second opinion. Don't go blindly ahead with a treatment—especially surgery—without knowing the risks and the expected benefits. It is vitally important that you find yourself a physician who will talk to you. This person may not be a high-fashion cutting-edge doctor; but part of the healing process is the confidence you feel in your doctor. So get one who takes time to talk.

As perhaps the original purveyors of alternative healing, Witches everywhere are being inundated with requests for help. For the reasons given in Appendix 2, we have to turn away more seekers than we like. The only positive effect has been that the age-old fear of the Witch is giving way to communication and respect.

HERBS AND THEIR EFFECTS[3]

Natural vitamins, herbal cures, and psychic energies are all coming to be recognized as potent aids in healing. The most dramatic of the "wonder" drugs developed in this century is probably still penicillin—an extract of cheese mold. For hundreds of years the eating of bread, old cheese, and pickles had been known as a cure for fever; yet the two key constituents, the acidity of the pickles and the cheese mold, had not been identified. As your mother may have told you, sometimes the answer is right in front of you!

---

[2] On February 22, 2000, President Clinton announced his task force hoped that the new proposed rules would reduce these unnecessary deaths from 98,000 annually in the U.S. to less than 50,000 annually!

[3] Additional reading on herbs is readily available. One book we like is *Rodale's Illustrated Encyclopedia of Herbs* (Emmaus, PA: Rodale Press, 1987). The School offers a twelve-lecture course in Basic Herbal Healing through Godolphin House, P.O. Box 297-BK, Hinton, WV 25951-0297 or www.wicca.org.

Similarly Eli Lilly has recently developed two compounds from the flowers of the violet that give much hope for patients with cancerous tumors. It is interesting to note that the fifteenth-century *Culpeper's Herbal* recommended these flowers as a remedy that would "shrink and dissolve the swellings." The world's largest pharmaceutical manufacturers now send teams of experts into tropical rain forests to identify and research plants used by native populations in healing.

In all the excitement and enthusiasm, though, remember that an overdose of a "natural" remedy will kill you just as quickly as will that of a prescribed drug. Old recipes often use highly toxic substances such as belladonna, aconite, digitalis, and the like without specifying whether the herb is to be picked (for example) on a dry day or after a rainstorm. Sometimes the toxicity of plant parts is unknown.

Despite all this, work continues, and many herbs are very safe and efficacious.

YOUR SHORT LEXICON OF USEFUL HERBS

It is not our intention for this book to become an herbal guide; instead, we name here a few of the herbs that we regularly use. Many of them are in your kitchen or your garden patch. The best way to obtain most of the others is to grow them yourself because some are rare; some you buy may be unethically harvested. Look for a sunny spot in your home and a decent seed catalog. Plant in clay pots. Enjoy your work—you will soon benefit from it!

===== WARNING =====
**IN NO CASE SHOULD THE HERBS OR POTIONS BE USED
IN LIEU OF PROPER MEDICAL CARE
FOR SERIOUS ILLNESS.**

Make sure that a conventional health-care professional has already seen any prospective patient.

GARLIC (ALLIUM SATIVUM)

This age-old bulb is known to lower high blood pressure; recent research indicates it can retard formation of tumors. Two drops of juice in one ounce of gin is a full daily dose. (For those who do not use alcohol, an alternative is olive oil.) In experiments at Western Research University, garlic-fed mice that would normally have died sixteen days after injection of a cancerous growth survived without fatalities for over six months. In some cases the garlic completely prevented formation of cancerous tumors and thus "cured" the mice permanently. Watermelon seeds and strawberries are also reputed to have anti-cancerous properties.

COMFREY (SYMPHYTUM OFFICINALE)

For hundreds of years it has been reported that comfrey leaves held against wounds, especially burns, could cause amazing cures. Research has revealed that comfrey leaves contain allantoin, now being used in many drugs and salves.

LICORICE, SARSAPARILLA, AND PUMPKIN SEEDS (GLYCYRRHIZA GLABRA/ARALIA/CUCURBIT)

Off your normal sexual activity? If you are a man, drink sarsaparilla; it contains male hormones. We have also had strong anecdotal evidence in favor of pumpkin seeds. If you're a woman, eat licorice for the corresponding reason.

TEA TREE OIL (MELALEUCA ALTERNIFOLIA)

This is Nature's antiseptic. Add a few drops to anything that you like: to water as a mouthwash, to your favorite shampoo to fix dandruff. It will even help with athlete's foot. However, there is anecdotal evidence that it can be hazardous to your health if you are HIV-positive.

ST. JOHN'S WORT (HYPERICUM PERFORATUM)

Crush the dried flowers. Marinate them in pure olive oil, then let the oil sit in direct sunlight for several weeks. This creates red oil, an excellent remedy for muscle pain, minor burns, and wounds. **Caution:** Some people are allergic to St. John's Wort; and its use internally can cause sensitivity to sunlight. The Food and Drug Administration has recently advised that St. John's Wort lowers the effectiveness of prescription drugs including birth-control pills.

GINSENG (PANAX QUINQUEFOLIUM)

This age-old herb is known as the prime Buck-You-Uppo of the herb kingdom. Feeling too pooped to party? Eat raw ginseng and re-spark your enthusiasm.

YOHIMBE (PAUSINYSTALIA JOHIMBE)

Sometimes called Nature's Viagra, this herb's effect is extremely tricky to gauge. One half ounce of the ground bark seems to be enough for most cases. A minute amount too much, and the patient becomes impotent. Hence it is very important to know the potency of your source and to prescribe it in gradually increasing doses until you achieve the desired effect. In some men yohimbe also seems to increase irritability.

MINT (MENTHA PIPERITA)

This perennial breath freshener is also a powerful digestive. Chop fresh leaves and mix with vinegar and honey in equal amounts. Two ounces of the fresh leaves and one cup each of local honey and cider vinegar combine to form an elixir that can be taken one tablespoon at a time either before or after over-indulging.

SAGE (SALVIA AZUREA)

Silver-leaf sage is the desert variety. Made into a tea (one tablespoonful of the leaves to a cup of boiling water) and drunk each morning, it becomes a powerful diuretic. Dandelion root has the same effect; hence, its French name *pissenlit* (wet-the-bed).

ALOE (ALOE VERA)

Every kitchen should have an aloe plant in the window. When you get a minor burn, first apply ice for ten minutes, then break off a piece of aloe leaf and rub the sap onto the burn. For major burns, go to the hospital—immediately.

CLOVE (EUGENIA CARYOPHYLLATA)

(1) Got a toothache? Take four cloves, shake them up in one ounce of gin for about two minutes, then swill the painful area with the liquor. Don't drink it! The mix acts as a surface anesthetic and numbs the pain until you can get to the dentist. (2) Mix the same alcohol extract with one cup olive oil for an analgesic massage oil.

SAW PALMETTO (SERENOA REPENS)

For poor old men like Gavin, this is a specific remedy used to shrink the prostate. Maximum safe dosage: 2 grams per day. Clinical trials show saw palmetto to be as effective as Proscar.

ROSEMARY (ROSMARINUS OFFICINALIS)

Shakespeare says, "Rosemary is for remembrance." To help the synaptic action in the brain, on the night before a test or exam, warm about two ounces of the dried leaves in a cup of red wine for ten minutes. (Do not bring to a boil.) At bedtime, drink ye all of it.

THYME (THYMUS VULGARIS)

To help you sleep and dream, make thyme tea. One teaspoon dried leaf in one cup boiling water with a spoonful of honey, and you'll know nothing until the alarm sounds.

ECHINACEA

There is some evidence that this herb stimulates the immune system. Used at the onset of a cold, it reduces the sumptoms and shortens the duration of the infection. People with suppressed immune system (e.g., AIDS) should not use echinacea.

GINKGO BILOBA

In 1997, clinical trials showed "somewhat" higher performance and "delayed" mental decline in Alzheimer's patients. Results were modest. Ginkgo does not combine well with blood-thinners such as aspirin and warfarin.

EDMUND AND SOO LO'S PRESCRIPTION

Edmund W works for a shipping line based in San Francisco. For several years he had traveled the Pacific Rim drawing new customers to the business. One day early in 1999 he found himself in Seoul, Korea, but his baggage had made it to Osaka, Japan. His faithful pill kit rested in the wandering suitcase, and now in the middle of the night in the Westin Hotel he couldn't sleep. Thinking the time was 11 A.M., his body was reluctant to shut down. He called the desk to ask whether they had anything that would substitute for the Seconal in his kit. They offered the usual aspirin and aspirin-substitute type of product; he knew from past experience that these would not work. The concierge also suggested that around the corner from the hotel in Itewan[4] several drugstores would still be open.

---

[4] One of the huge marketplaces of Seoul.

He said he could summon a taxi for Edmund, or even send a bell-boy to Itewan to make the purchase. Since Edmund was awake anyway, he elected to go himself.

Despite all the rumors of easy access to drugs, he found that the pharmacist would not sell him any powerful prescription-style medication. Instead he recommended an herbal remedy with a totally unpronounceable name. The pharmacist said that after taking this remedy tonight, Edmund should take the little accompanying bottle of tonic the next morning before breakfast. A long three-way conversation ensued involving Edmund, the pharmacist, and the taxi driver. The Koreans finally convinced Edmund that the unpronounceable pills would work. Mollified but still hardly believing, he returned to the hotel.

Those pills did work. Edmund got a sound night's sleep. Duly taking the tonic in the morning, he conducted a very heavy day's schedule with ample energy and alertness.

That evening he returned to the same pharmacy. A different pharmacist was on duty, one who spoke English. After some consultation with Edmund's receipt and the pharmacist's records, he produced more of the same pills and more of the same little bottles of tonic. Edmund asked what the pills contained. He learned that they consisted of the herb thyme. "And what's in the tonic?"

"Ah, that is ginseng."

The one experience taught him both the efficacy and the low cost of herbal preparations.

PSYCHIC HEALING

The body heals itself, just as it makes itself ill. When your life is out of balance, when you have hangups, when you resist dealing with some difficult issue, illness is the body's ready excuse for a no-blame avoidance of the situation. Psychic healers, including ourselves, have some amazing cures to their credit. In some of those cases, though, the patient soon has a relapse or gets another dis-ease. If the patient *needs* his disease, resolution of the conflict is the only cure. Often when the underlying problem is identified and solved, the disease goes away by itself. Before trying to heal, a Witch may do such things as a tarot reading with the patient or perhaps have him/her gaze into a crystal ball with her. These traditional methods get the patient talking. From the psychological point of view (s)he puts her problem "out there" onto the cards or into the crystal and can talk of it more comfortably. Once the Witch understands the underlying problem, once the patient faces up to it and resolves to deal with it, then (s)he can take concrete steps—whether magically or mundanely—to fix it.

THE AURA AND ENERGY FLOW

One can also consider *energy flows* while viewing the psychic component of a disease. Every living creature is surrounded by a force field, the *aura*. Many Witches can see auras; others cannot. Those who can report that a balanced person serenely at rest puts out a little of every type of energy. These combine in such a way that only a pale blue or white "halo" is visible around the person. A disturbed or dis-eased patient, however, manifests a disturbed balance and puts out a preponderance of one type of energy, which appears as a specific color in the aura or in some one region of it. Thus, you can compare an illness to a deficiency disease, because the excess energy that you detect flowing from the patient causes in him a deficiency in energy of that specific color.

Let's say you baked a cake with a nicely balanced set of ingredients; the cake would have a pleasant flavor. If you now had some way of extracting all the sugar from the cake, the cake would not taste so good; it would not be balanced. A deficiency disease works in the same way. The patient loses something that is not being replaced. On the mundane level, a patient can be deficient in, say, iodine; in this case he will get goiter. Energy deficiencies are just as relevant to good health as are dietary deficiencies.

THE WITCH SAVES GLEN

Glen S and his partner Robert live in New Orleans. Glen is a Witch and a well-known healer in the Old Quarter (Vieux Carre). Robert called us one day to say that he was worried about Glen: Glen had begun to have blackouts. Robert had taken him to a regular doctor, suspecting some kind of epileptic seizure—perhaps *petit mal*; but the doctor could find nothing wrong. Robert was so concerned about it that he was willing to have us fly down and talk to Glen. Instead we got a local Witch, Netta, to visit with them.

Netta reported back that Glen's energy felt very low and his aura was almost nonexistent. We batted the problem back and forth and finally agreed that Netta and her group would put Glen into circle and put healing energy into him. Two months later Robert called us again to say that the healing had been successful for about six weeks—but now Glen was having blackouts again. When we talked to Netta she told us that Glen refused to give up his healing work and that he was putting all his energy into the healings. There was little her coven could do, she said, but send him some energy from their monthly meetings. We talked to Robert and finally persuaded him that for the sake of Glen's health, they should move to a drier climate. They did move, and Glen magically recovered. Of course, the move was designed to break Glen's link with all the people to whom he had so freely been giving his energy.

When Glen got better, nothing would do but they had to move back to New Orleans. Of course he started healing people again, and of course he got sick again. This time Robert made him a medicine bag to rebalance his energies. This helped in two ways:

1. It blocked his link to those he healed; and
2. it helped rebalance his energy.

Not only sick people need extra energy; you may need it, too. You can expend too much energy. As you enter the arena of psychic healing, keep that in mind.

MAGICALLY REPLACING LOST ENERGY

Energy from various sources can compensate for excess outflow. Don't hesitate to avail yourself of it. Draw energy from yourself, from a group of friends, or from a range of natural substances. In cases where the patient can be aware of your effort to heal, give serious consideration to using a Native American medicine bag. It will provide appropriately tuned energy from natural sources.

Figure VI-1 shows this. The figure in the diagram is losing energy. (S)he needs to replace it from some source to achieve a better balance, as the diagram shows. Here is where you, the healer, come in. For instance, when a patient emits large amounts of "green" energy, you know that she must get additional green energy to keep her in balance until the illness can be cured. If you supply that energy from yourself, you in turn will experience an energy deficiency. You need to compensate for this by adjusting upward the green emanations of your own medicine bag.

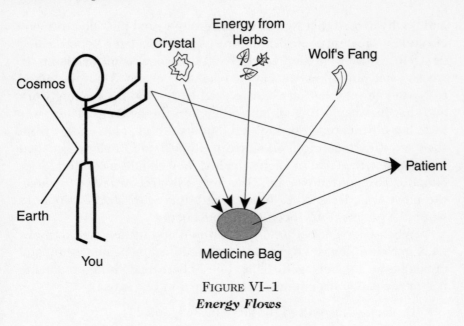

FIGURE VI–1
Energy Flows

If you are particularly interested in healing of this type, you may want to study Reiki. The channeling of energy from the universe into a patient is the path that most Reiki masters recommend.

Every situation you come into has its own little quirks and peculiarities. You must be wide awake to detect interpersonal subtleties so you can supply the right energies to the right people to cure the psychic part of any illness.

MAKING A MEDICINE BAG TODAY

When Great-Grandma set out to heal a case of the flux or the tetters, an essential part of her procedure was the hanging of a little sack of something around the neck of the patient. This practice traces back to prehistoric times. The medicine bag still serves today for many Native Americans and Witches as a potent healing method. The connection between the objects in the healing pouch or medicine bag and the illness often appear arcane. What, for instance, has a rabbit's foot, a wolf's fang, or a chicken neck to do with curing a flux? Having come this far in your study, you know that such articles accumulate and transmit energy, as well as producing energy in their own right. Great-Grandma also put further energy into them which her patient needed for a cure.

Certain metals, crystals, and natural objects (or *talismans*) aid in the treatment of certain diseases; yet, curiously, metal bracelets seem to lose no weight in carrying out their healing task. Thus, we believe that each object sends out special unique energies which affect the human body in a specific way. Each is actually a natural energy store, night and day constantly at work, yet never depleted.

Table VI-1 shows items recommended in the treatment of several illnesses. Specifically for healing, the table expands on the tables of mind triggers given previously. Thus, to get the psychic energy needed for healing, two different techniques are available:

1. The use of the appropriate natural energy sources; and

2. the use of energy from yourself or from your group, either directly or stored in a talisman or medicine bag, which you give your patient.

A talisman can be almost any natural object that gives off psychic energy: a rabbit's foot, a wolf's fang, a crystal, anything. Once you have learned to see auras, you will be able to select these natural objects and match them to the auric color you need.

If your psychic senses do not "see" auras clairvoyantly, be aware that you may "hear" auras or "feel" them, "taste" them, "sense" them, or even "smell" them. Although we use color as a convenient metaphor because over 90 percent of people "see" psychically, we could also have used sounds. Psychic sounds may range from such things as the whispering of silver chains to the bellowing of a berserk elephant. Whatever sense is your avenue of psychic reception, convert it and use it in your reality to feel or *intuit* energies.

Illness	Body Part	Herb	Flower	Stone/ Crystal	Metal	Color	Aroma
Ulcer, Epilepsy, Diarrhea	Ankles	Winter Savory	Buttercup	Aquamarine	Pewter	Violet	Lemon
Insomnia, Tumor (cancer), Irritation	Feet	Thrift	Water Lily	Amethyst	Zinc	Lavender	Lily
Arthritis, Depression, Exhaustion, Blood Pressure	Head	Anemone	Geranium	Ruby	Bronze	Scarlet	Tobacco
Polio, Melancholy, Tuberculosis	Neck	Ground-Ivy	Cowslip	Jade	Nickel	Red	Sandalwood
Constipation, Hepatitis, Diabetes	Hands, Arms, Lungs	Lavender	Orchid	Opal	Aluminum	Yellow	Clove
Bronchitis, Digestion, Circulation	Breast, Stomach	Poppy	Night-Scented Stock	Pearl	Silver	Amber	Narcissus

TABLE VI–1
Mind Triggers for Healing

(Cont'd)

Illness	Body Part	Herb	Flower	Stone/ Crystal	Metal	Color	Aroma
Mononucleosis, Cramps, Thyroid	Heart, Spine, Arms, Wrists	Rosemary	Sunflower	Diamond	Gold	Orange	Rose
Cerebral Palsy, Retardation	Hands, Abdomen, Intestines	Caraway	Snowdrop	Agate	Mercury Amalgam	Chartreuse	Cinnamon
Fever, Hypertension, Blood Disease	Lower Back, Kidneys	Alkanet (Anchusa)	Rose	Emerald	Copper	Emerald	Myrtle
Impotence, Muscle Tension	Pelvis, Genitalia	Sweet Basil	Cactus	Turquoise	Platinum	Turquoise	Orange Blossom
Shingles, Goiter	Hips, Liver, Thighs	Balm	Narcissus	Sapphire	Tin	Blue	Nutmeg
Glaucoma, Palsy	Skin, Bones	Barley	Thistle	Onyx	Lead	Indigo	Civet from onion

TABLE VI–1
Mind Triggers for Healing (Cont'd)

CHARGING YOUR TALISMAN, MEDICINE BAG, OR HERBAL PREPARATION

In earlier chapters you used sensory keys in the construction of rituals. Such keys serve you in the same way when you charge the contents of your healing medicine bag. They serve when you make herbal preparations and when you send energy to a patient.

Table VI-2 suggests keys for chanting and dancing. Remember that you don't have to get every single sensory key, chant, or dance precisely in accordance with the tables. In the early months of your work, of course, the closer you can get to what they list, the better will be your rate of success. As your skills grow, you will learn what works best in your own reality.

To charge any preparation or potion, you first have to raise correct energy; then intensify it and focus it into the preparation you have just made. To do this, use the mind triggers listed in Table VI-2 and pair them with a simple chant. Opposite each complaint in Table VI-1 you see a color and an aroma. To use these triggers, have available a white candle and marking pens in a range of colors, as well as the various aromas. Before you start the charging procedure, color the very tip of the candle in the color appropriate for the best psychic charging of the preparation. Then anoint the candle with the corresponding aroma.

Once you have made any preparation in this way, unbind your body: Remove clothing, rings, any jewelry, and hair fastenings. Place the preparation, and the candle you have anointed and colored, on a work surface and surround them with a ring of salt. If you have a photograph of the patient, put it into the salt ring, too, to serve as a further psychic link.

Stand facing east (the direction of new beginnings), at new moon for growth or at full moon for a decrease. For example, you *increase* good health or *shrink* a tumor. Light the candle. Quietly start a repetitive chant of the syllables shown in the table. As you continue to chant, think of the cure you want and of the person upon whom the cure will work. Continue the chant with gathering intensity. Begin to spin on your own axis at the rate shown in the table. Increase your volume until you are literally shouting out the syllables. When you have built all the intensity you possibly can, clap out the candle and yell at the top of your voice, "Heal!" As you do this, with your dominant hand pick up the preparation you have made and clutch it to your heart.

Illness	Body Part	Pronun-ciation	Chant Pitch	Speed
Ulcer, Epilepsy, Diarrhea	Ankles	Aye-Oh	Very High, Wailing, Spirituoso	Very Fast
Insomnia, Irritation, Tumor (cancer)	Feet	Aum	Low, Largo, Resonant Hum	Slow
Arthritis, Depression, Exhaustion, Blood Pressure	Head	Ka-Ka-Ka	High, Sharp, Staccato	Fast
Polio, Melancholy, Tuberculosis	Neck	Gay-Ah	Low, Largo, Resonant Hum	Slow
Constipation, Hepatitis, Diabetes	Hands, Arms, Lungs	Ah-Bra	Very High, Wailing, Spirituoso	Very Fast
Bronchitis, Digestion, Circulation	Breast, Stomach	Homm	Medium, Legato, Flowing	Medium
Mononucleosis, Cramps, Thyroid	Heart, Spine, Arms, Wrists	Mm-Mm	Low, Largo, Resonant Hum	Slow
Cerebral Palsy, Retardation	Hands, Abdomen, Intestines	Mu-Ah	Medium, Legato, Flowing	Medium
Fever, Hypertension, Blood Disease	Lower Back, Kidneys	Aye-Oh	Low, Largo, Resonant Hum	Slow
Impotence, Muscle Tension	Pelvis, Genitalia	Yah-Weh	Medium, Legato, Flowing	Medium
Shingles, Goiter	Hips, Liver, Thighs	Aye-Oh-Em	High, Sharp, Staccato	Fast
Glaucoma, Palsy	Skin, Bones, Knees	Aye-Oh	Very High, Wailing, Spirituoso	Very Fast

TABLE VI–2

Healing Chants and Dances

This entire procedure takes less than a minute. In timing various workers who heavily charge medications, we find the average duration is 17 seconds. Plan to charge every preparation you use, because the charging is an essential part of its restorative properties. It is what makes herbs, medicine bags, and potions the unsurpassed remedies that they are.

MAKING A MODERN MEDICINE BAG

You can make medicine bags for yourself and for other people. They are bags of linen or other natural fiber, dyed the appropriate color and charged, that contain as many of the items from the tables as possible. Say someone suffers from common diarrhea: Great-Grandma's "flux." Looking at the tables, you can see in the left-hand columns the illness "diarrhea." You see that the medicine bag contains a piece of pewter, some winter savory, either a pressed buttercup or a picture of a buttercup, and an aquamarine, and that it should be dyed violet. These four items in a bag close to the stomach will of themselves help the patient; but if you then scent the bag with lemon and charge it with a high wailing "aye-oh" chant while you very quickly whirl, it will be even more effective.

Popular wisdom has it that a medicine bag should be made of leather and hung around the neck on a leather thong. It has been our experience that this will work adequately with uncharged objects but that when the objects are charged with psychic energy, there must be a minimum of contact with animal-derived substances like leather. Such substances tend to absorb the very energy that you intended for the patient's cure. In hundreds of experiments we have also found that synthetic fibers tend to build up electric charges which sometimes seem subtly to change the healing energy, diminishing its effectiveness. Thus we recommend you make medicine bags from cotton or linen. Hang them on a ribbon instead of a leather thong.

In using these healing aids, remember that they work on the body's psychic energy field. They do not work on the mundane body; but they help the psyche, which then instructs the body to heal itself. If you are under a doctor's care for some specific disease, the doctor helps the body cure itself by giving it substances to use on the mundane level. So your psychic healing is an adjunct to—*not* a replacement for—good diet and the trace elements and materials the body needs to rebuild itself. Nor does it replace the care of a trained physician; instead, it supplements it.

PREPARING YOUR OWN WITCH'S POTIONS

These preparations have been known for hundreds of years; they have been well tested. They are tried-and-true recipes that Witches still use today just as they have for centuries. Such preparations are called *homeopathic*. None contains harmful substances or preservatives.

If you ever have any doubt about the strength of the substances, dilute them instead of strengthening them; for the body generally needs only minute quantities to work with. These are not strong medicines but gentle curatives. We have never known anyone to have an allergic reaction to any homeopathic remedy; however, if you are subject to allergies we recommend you patch-test a small quantity on the inner surface of your upper arm.

These preparations are made of natural ingredients; so in general you should use them immediately after you make them up. If you need to store them, they will last several days covered and refrigerated.

This information is meant to be a practical guide to a few preparations you can easily make in your own kitchen. The preparations are grouped by symptom. In addition to the minute quantities of exotic nutrients and cleansers contained in the preparations, you will want to charge them with energy for the greatest efficacy.

NOTE

These directions suggest gin as an alcoholic extractor of the vital oils and essences of the herbal principles. Vodka or brandy will serve as well.

Acne and other skin problems

Principles—Witch hazel; white vinegar

Usage—Wash face gently with mild soap morning and night. Rub affected area with witch hazel on a cotton ball. Rinse with solution of 1 tablespoon white vinegar in 8 ounces water. Pat dry.

Aging

Principles—Honey; apple-cider vinegar; kelp tablets

Preparation—Dissolve 2 tablespoons honey in 8 ounces warm water. Add 2 tablespoons vinegar. Charge the elixir.

Usage—Drink the elixir and take a kelp tablet fifteen minutes before retiring each night.

Allergy, Pollen

Principles—Cappings from local honeycomb

Usage—Spread cappings liberally on hot buttered toast. Warm under a broiler until they melt. Eat hot upon first rising in the morning: One slice honey-cap toast each day during allergy season. For absolutely best results, search out a beekeeper in your county. His bees will have used the same flowers that prompt your allergic reaction, and this will tune his honey to your specific needs. Charge just before eating.

Arthritits

Principles—See AGING elixir above. Also warm water; red fruit; cod-liver oil pills

Usage—1. Follow directions for AGING elixir.

2. Eat two bowls of red fruit each day. This may be plums, strawberries, cranberries, cherries.

3. Drink six glasses of warm water each day; charge at least one of them. The more glasses you charge, the better; but many people have time and patience to charge only one glass per day.

4. Take six cod-liver oil pills a day.

Asthma and Cough

Principles—Bay leaves; horehound

Preparation—Pre-charge a handful of bay leaves and a handful of dried horehound leaves.

Usage—When an attack of asthma or coughing occurs, wrap three bay leaves and equivalent horehound in a piece of muslin. Crush them thoroughly. Dip for thirty seconds into 1 cup boiling water. As soon as the muslin has cooled enough, place it over the nose and breathe deeply through it. Drink the water in which the bay/horehound mix steeped.

Bad Breath

Principles—Salt; baking soda; oil of peppermint

Preparation—Mix ½ teaspoon salt, ½ teaspoon soda, 2 drops oil of peppermint in 8 ounces warm water. Charge the mixture.

Usage—Thoroughly rinse the mouth night and morning until the condition is alleviated.

Flu and Colds

Principles—Blackberry jelly; honey; apple-cider vinegar; horehound

Preparation—Pour 2 cups boiling water over 1 cup loosely packed horehound leaves. Steep for ten minutes. Strain the liquid into a bowl. Add 8 ounces best-quality blackberry jelly. Add ½ cup honey. Make sure that all ingredients are dissolved. (You may warm the mixture again to ensure complete dissolving, but do not bring it to a boil.) Pour the liquid into a covered jar and let it cool, ideally in contact with the earth. When it is cool, use a wooden spoon to stir in 4 tablespoons of apple-cider vinegar. Ancient lore teaches that as you charge this mixture, you should chant,

> *Berries wild and hore of hound,*
> *I stir my elixir 'round.*
> *Sweetness of berry and acid vile,*
> *Soothe the hurting throat a while.*

Note: We do not recommend *echinacea*. Its popularity is leading to a threatened status. On another level, some evidence suggests it reduces your current symptoms but simultaneously decreases your resistance to colds.

Diarrhea

Principles—Comfrey; cottage cheese

Preparation—Finely chop the comfrey leaves. Mix 1 tablespoon with 1 cup cottage cheese. Charge this internal unguent.

Usage—Every time diarrhea occurs, eat 1 cup of the mix.

Special note: When in a foreign country and troubled with diarrhea, use the whitest, lightest cheese available in this same recipe.

Diuretic

Principles—Silver-leaf sage, or an equal quantity of dandelion root; honey

Preparation—Dissolve ¼ teaspoon powdered sage into 1 cup boiling water; add 1 tablespoon raw honey. Charge the tisane while it is hot.

Usage—Drink as hot as possible in the morning. Maximum usage three times a day.

Earache (for earache after flight or exposure to wind)

Principles—Olive oil; marjoram

Preparation—Add 1 tablespoon ground marjoram to 2 ounces pure olive oil, warmed. Shake vigorously. Let steep one hour. Pour the clear olive oil into a clean bottle. Charge the decoction.

Usage—In a teaspoon, gently heat a small portion of the decoction over a candle flame. Test its temperature on the back of your hand. Pour a few drops into your ear. Cover with a small piece of red flannel and place a hot-water bottle over the flannel.

Elixir of Life (for increased vigor and vitality; also a sovereign remedy for a persistent dry cough)

Principles—Honey; dry "white" mustard (Colman's mustard seems best)

Preparation—Dissolve ½ teaspoon mustard in 1 tablespoon of honey. Add 1 tablespoon water. Charge the elixir.

Usage—1 teaspoon at bedtime as an elixir. For cough, take small portions as needed.

Flatulence

Principles—Fennel; cinnamon; gin; sugar cubes

Preparation—Measure 2 ounces gin into a small bottle. Add 1 teaspoon fennel and 1 teaspoon cinnamon. Shake vigorously. Charge the mixture. Pour off the clear liquid into a clean bottle.

Usage—When troubled with flatulence, place 3 drops of decoction on a cube of sugar and eat it. May be repeated at three-hour intervals.

Headache

Principles—Coffee (freeze-dried, not decaffeinated); honey

Preparation—Dissolve 3 heaped tablespoons coffee into ¼ cup water. Add ¼ cup raw honey. Mix thoroughly; charge the elixir.

Usage—1 tablespoon elixir every hour. Follow with 8 ounces water in case your headache is a symptom of dehydration.

Caution: Some individuals find caffeine a dangerous stimulant.

Hiccoughs

Principles—Cinnamon; dill; gin; sugar cubes

Preparation—In 2 ounces best-quality gin, vigorously shake 1 tablespoon dill seeds and ¼ teaspoon ground cinnamon. Let settle. Pour off gin into a clean bottle. Charge the decoction.

Usage—Take 9 sugar cubes. Place 1 drop decoction on each cube. Eat the sugar cubes in succession, as rapidly as possible.

Indigestion

Principles—Peppermint (leaves or oil); apple-cider vinegar; honey

Preparation—Crush 1 tablespoon peppermint leaves. Shake vigorously in ¼ cup vinegar. If you are using oil of peppermint rather than leaves, add 5 drops to ¼ cup vinegar and shake. Pour the vinegar carefully into an equal quantity of raw honey; warm gently and stir thoroughly until the honey dissolves. Charge the potion.

Usage—1 tablespoon each hour until the discomfort is alleviated.

Sedative

Principles—Thyme; honey

Preparation—In 1 cup boiling water, dissolve ¼ teaspoon powdered thyme. Add 1 tablespoon raw honey. Charge the tisane while it is hot.

Usage—Drink as hot as possible at bedtime.

Toothache

Principles—Cloves; gin

Preparation—Crush 4 cloves. Shake vigorously in 1 ounce best-quality gin. Let settle; pour off the liquor. Charge it.

Usage—Sip a little of this and hold it in the mouth over the painful tooth.

Note: This is an instant remedy. When it touches the tooth it will cause a momentary sharp pain but then will totally deaden the nerve. Of course the patient should visit the dentist promptly.

Warts

Principles—Salt; celandine

Preparation—Mix 1 cup chopped celandine leaves with 2 cups salt. Seal the mixture overnight in a 1-quart Mason jar. Fill the jar with cold water. Shake vigorously until salt is dissolved. Pour off the brine into a clean jar. Charge it.

Usage—Take about 3 tablespoons brine. With a hard toothbrush, scrub the warts until they are sore but do not bleed. Ideally, start this application seven days before new moon. By the night of new moon, the warts should be gone.

DEATH, THE ULTIMATE HEALER

Whether we like it or not, we live in a society that has quite a twisted set of beliefs, especially about death. Yes, Wicca is gaining ground by leaps and bounds; but the old nonsense was ingrained into our ancestors for centuries—and whether we like it or not, into us and into the patients you will work with. Death is defeat, you are told, something to be feared, partially because you are supposed to believe that you may not get to "heaven." The stress that those last few years of life put on your spirit, your family, and all those support people is unimaginable. Hospitals and physicians are now said to make 80 percent of their income from patients in the last five years of their lives, as patients, duped by lifelong propaganda, resist the graduation called death. Western culture keeps people alive on machines—that is, at least until the insurance money and the estate are drained. It's an industry. Yes, our view is cynical, but unfortunately it's true. Of course, there are dedicated people who give up opportunities and sacrifice their lives to care for their aged relatives. And there are those who realize that "death" actually means graduation from this planet.

The fact that has been denied to people is this: *Death is an opportunity to start again: another chance.* The process is a natural one, not something to be feared. Just like divorce or graduation, it wraps up one chapter and begins another. If you haven't made a living will, or your patient hasn't made his or her own, do it! Maintaining patients in a vegetative state when they should pass on is (in our opinion) one of the few "sins" that Wiccans can commit. It harms a spirit trying to graduate. Yvonne sometimes says, "I nominate Jack Kevorkian[5] for Surgeon General."

When you do any of the healing procedures that we outline, always add the line, "or help them release." From Gavin's own experience, he can relate at least three cases in which people released themselves when they felt it was finally time.

1. Dr. Loy Stone was an early Wiccan martyr. When the court case that accused him of murder was over, the jury retired only ten minutes to find him not guilty. After being found not guilty, the parents of the dead girl sued the Stones on the principal their being an attractive nuisance. The Stones lost the suit, their farm, and their livelihood. Loy died. He just didn't want to live any longer in a world that could make him a prisoner for his religious beliefs.

2. When Gavin's father in England knew that he (Sidney) was getting close to the end, he asked that Gavin visit from the States. When the aircraft landed, Gavin called the hospital and Sidney learned that Gavin would be there that morning. By the time Gavin arrived at the hospital, Sidney was gone. He had waited to be sure that Gavin would be there to take care of things.

3. When Gavin's elderly mother in a home was close to the end, she too waited for him to arrive and then, once she had heard his voice, promptly released and graduated.

---

[5] Dr. Kevorkian voluntarily assisted those who wish to commit suicide when the alternative is an existence prolonged on medications and life-support machines.

Many people who are in their last days stay around because of some unfinished business or worry that they have on their mind. If you can talk to them, find out what their concern is. It may be that you will have to get a conventional priest of some sort to come in and let them confess a "sin" that has been worrying them since forever. It may be that they wish to see someone. You will be amazed at how quickly and peacefully they graduate when their worry is assuaged and their unfinished business is wrapped up. And, of course, once they have released, they can return to the next incarnation. In one case that comes to mind, Dame Sybil Leek told Gavin that she was waiting until she was sure that her granddaughter would be born the following day because she was determined to inhabit that child. In fact, Dame Sybil died precisely two days before that grandchild was born.

SUMMARY

We really hope you will not just read this chapter and lay it aside. Healing, both of yourself and of others, is a most rewarding pursuit. Not only can you help yourself to better health; but when you help others, your life will become much fuller and will have new meaning. The steps are simple. Charging a potion usually takes less than 30 seconds. A Jewish grandmother might say, "Could it hurt?"

The Witch's Defragmented Soul

THE SELFISH WITCH

If you were to make your own personal lexicon of words free of positive connotations—words that are used only in a negative sense—surely at the top of the list would be the word *selfish*. In western culture people are not supposed to think of their own needs or wishes; instead they are supposed to put the needs and wishes of everyone else ahead of their own. "Nice" people defer. "Nice" people subordinate their ideas, feelings, or agenda to what other people inflict on them without regard to the comparative merit of "my" agenda versus "theirs." Many Americans have Celtic roots. Being individualists, the Celts do not subscribe to the same agenda as "nice" people do. In today's business world we recommend the Celtic attitude, since the overarching paradigm of business is that *nice guys finish last*.

A FRAGMENTED SPIRIT

Around the globe, native (preliterate) peoples believe that your spirit can be fragmented or broken apart into pieces.[1] Witches also subscribe to this belief. "Civilized" people habitually think of one spirit running one body; but since every little cell of the body has its own

---

[1] Sandra Ingerman, *Soul Retrieval, Mending the Fragmented Self* (New York: Harper, 1991).

145

spirit, it is the sum total of all those spirits (and your own long memory) that compose your spiritual being. Grasping this concept can make all the difference in working magical procedures and in gaining serenity.

The spirits of children usually appear as beautiful, radiant bodies that some Witches feel are pure energy. In older people who fall ill, and in people who reject new ideas, the radiance is often reduced. In serious cases it becomes almost nonexistent. These are the people we refer to in everyday life as people with "nobody home." Even the dullest of nonbelievers can detect this condition.

Several cultures believe strongly that photographs actually take soul pieces, minute though those pieces may be, from the person photographed. Many Buddhist monks in Thailand, for example, avoid having their pictures taken. In a similar way the psychic links we use in our rituals contain fragments of the soul pieces of their former owners.

Many people who have lost a loved one feel as if something is missing from their lives. They no longer feel *whole*. That feeling is valid. When you get very close to someone emotionally, you give away a little of your spirit to that one. And if the loved one leaves—whether through death, divorce, or a traumatic separation—that piece of spirit goes with them. To become complete again, you must take steps to recover the missing piece(s) of your spirit. There are three ways to do this.

1. You can do it yourself.

2. You can get a shaman or a competent Witch to find and bring back the missing piece.

3. You can spend thousands of dollars and years of your life with a therapist who gradually returns each piece.

The concept of soul pieces may seem strange to you; but bear with us a little while. You will see how helpful and valid it can be, and how much sense it can make. In our work people constantly ask us to meet with them and to sort out their lives. We invariably reply, "We will help you by teaching you to do these things yourself." Our reason? If we gave of ourselves to all those who want help, we would soon have nothing left; our soul pieces would all be used up—and the seekers would be no better off skill-wise than they had been before.

Such clamoring and consuming happens to many psychics and healers, and it literally uses them up. They get sick. They get depressed. It takes a lot of effort on the part of their friends to bring them back.

The reverse is true with regard to entertainers. Have you ever wondered how a personality can go on stage and seem to get more and more energy as the performance progresses? It happens because the audience is giving of their spirits to the entertainer. They are energizing and enlarging his (her) spirit. Consequently (s)he can go on for hours; whereas without the audience (s)he would soon be depleted and have to quit.

HOW YOU LOSE SOUL PIECES

In many cases soul pieces are lost because the spirit does not want to experience a traumatic event. Such events can be minor, as in the case of a friend of ours. He didn't like his job of running a jackhammer on a road crew. He learned to detach partially from his body while it kept on working. Eventually part of him left permanently and took up residence in the cab of his truck.

Table VII-1 shows common events that prompt loss of soul pieces. If you feel "out of it" after surgery or any of the other causes listed, you should consult a Witch or a shaman.

Traffic Accident	Divorce or Separation from a Significant Other
Puberty	Surgery (with full anesthesia)
Rape	Abusive Relationships (especially parent/child)

TABLE VII–1
Causes for Loss of Soul Pieces

Very occasionally there will be a psychic vampire around who deliberately steals and keeps soul pieces so (s)he can control others. The good news: They seem to be diminishing in frequency; we ourselves have not encountered one in years.

MILDRED ALMOST DIES

Mildred and Fred P retired to a condominium in Florida when they were well past their golden anniversary. One day they and two or three couples who were their close friends went to Miami to admire the art deco cityscape. Then Fred and a couple of buddies went to a poorer part of town where rumor said they could get good Cuban cigars cheap. The rumor was a come-on, and the men got mugged in broad daylight. Fred died.

Mildred was devastated. She had lost her husband of sixty years—but more than that. They had lived together so closely and so affectionately for all their married life that she felt desperately lost and empty without him. Even though she lived in a retirement community with lots of things to do, now she couldn't be bothered. She hardly troubled to get out of bed each morning, let alone get dressed and venture out to socialize.

The managers of the community often arranged special programs or guest speakers for the residents. One of these speakers was a local Seminole shaman. During his presentation he talked about retrieval of soul pieces, and a friend figured that this sounded a lot like Mildred. "Why don't we set her up with him?" Mildred herself had not been interested enough to attend the meeting, of course. She was certainly not going to put herself into the hands of a native shaman. Only after a great deal of persuasion did she agree to meet with him.

The experience was not at all what she had assumed it would be. The man just seemed like any other business-suited professional, youngish, competent, articulate, low-key. He sat and talked quietly with her in her condominium. As they chatted, he began to walk idly around the living room to pick up Fred's emanations from everything; Mildred felt no pressure or hype from him. Eventually she grew comfortable enough to drift off into a trance. The shaman went with her, guiding her. Although afterward she had no memory of it, she met Fred on the astral planes. On the astral, the shaman convinced Fred that he should give back some of the love that Mildred had given him. When she woke, Mildred felt much better and actually felt hungry for the first time in months. Before he left, the shaman asked Mildred whether she would donate Fred's old clothes to a shelter.

He visited her three more times over the next months. On his second visit he encouraged her to clean out all her Fred-mementos. She kept only a couple of happy pictures. The long-term effect was as if Fred had given her a bag of gold. Mildred was restored and became a whole person again. Recently she remarried; now she and her new husband enjoy the quiet pleasantness of Florida retirement.

WHO OWNS YOU?

Mildred's history illustrates what can happen when someone who is no longer even *alive* controls the life of another. Often children unjustly blame a dead parent for the problems in their present life. Recently a lawyer told us with a straight face, "My Daddy was in the army in Korea when I was growing up. That's why I can't have lasting relationships." Many of us fall into this category. The trend is growing, especially as we realize what a poor job of parenting many people do. After all, parenting is an amateur undertaking; it's all unskilled labor. People in the western world get very little training in how to do it right. We Frosts think this is a gigantic lack in our nation—not that the school systems don't take over the job of parenting, but that individuals get little or no training themselves for the children they eventually have. In earlier times on farms with a much extended family of several generations living together, knowledge of parenting skills passed naturally from elder to younger generations. There was a support system for the new parents. Nowadays a new parent is usually stuck with only two sources of information:

1. What they can glean from Internet chat rooms; and

2. glossy magazines written far away often by nonactive parents or theorists who may never have changed a diaper or treated a skinned knee.

Countless people come to us complaining, "I'm this way because my parents did such a rotten job of raising me." Many of those parents are no longer alive, and often those who survive dwell hundreds of miles distant—yet the people seeking comfort are still totally bound by those old emotional ties.

If you were to visit a Christian church, you would hear a lot about forgiveness: "Forgive them, for they didn't know what they were doing," or something similar. Instead of *forgiveness,* it is useful to strive for *forgetness,* and simply leave behind the pain of the past. As a Witch and a proactive person, the first thing you will need to do is figure out *why* these people still have power over you. If you think about it, it's pretty weird, letting a person long dead or far away still control you. Are they still taller than you? Can't you read now? Can't you blow your own nose? Earn your own living? But this happens all the time.

It's because that person still owns a piece of your soul. They have one of your soul pieces in their possession. To get rid of their influence and to be whole, you have to get that soul piece back. If you can do it, the best way is to get yourself into an altered state of consciousness[2] and travel to the person who (either in spirit or in life) still influences you. On the astral plane when you meet such a person, you can usually see the missing piece of your soul. In most cases the other spirit willingly returns it to you. Occasionally, especially in the case of mothers who have found meaning only through their children, they want to retain it. Then, to get your soul piece back, you need to make several visits and promise to visit again. ("You never come to see me!")

Soul pieces can take many forms. They can look like a child, or an amorphous cloud, or a growth on the other astral being, or like a bag of money that you know is yours, or simply a piece of *you* that you know you own. Once you have done this the first time, you will recognize your soul piece, no matter who possesses it.

When you get that soul piece back, it may not instantly reintegrate with you. You may feel upset and strange for up to 24 hours, but after that time you will get a feeling of completion—that you are now a whole person once again.

YOUR FIVE-STEP SYSTEM FOR RETRIEVAL OF SOUL PIECES

1. List all the people who control you when they are absent. These are often parents or children, although they can be spir-

---

[2] See Appendix 1.

itual leaders or other people who have had big influence in your life. It may be that your boss or a coworker has this type of excessive influence when they are absent. That's a sure sign that they have worked on you and stolen a piece of your soul— whether consciously or unconsciously. Rarely, you may find your soul piece with many others in the keeping of another spirit. To recover your piece in such a case, *get help!* If you, relatively unskilled, match wits with an Evil Sorcerer, you may inadvertently lose more of yourself.

2. Get a *psychic link(s)* to the person who you suspect has a piece of your soul. In many cases you will be able to see something that looks like a fine thread of light leading from you to your soul piece.[3] If you think part of you is missing but you don't know who has it, you may be able to follow such a thread and find the piece without having to have a psychic link to the thief.

3. With the aid of a shamanic drumming tape,[4] enter an altered state of consciousness. Extend your channeling into astral traveling. Strongly hold uppermost in your mind the intent, "Find my missing soul pieces."

4. With the psychic link, find the person or place you seek in the astral plane and retrieve your soul piece. Places may vary among the apartment you rented when first in love, the operating theater where you had surgery, or the site of your traffic accident, or numerous others. If you can't see the aka thread, you need to check out any such place from your past. Occasionally a soul piece may drift in a void, and your specific intent takes you to it.

5. Destroy all psychic links to that person available to you. Mildred had to give away all the clothes, all the mementos, and especially all the pictures of good old Fred. This is very hard for many people to do, but that very reluctance shows you the strength of the psychic link. The link must be broken to reduce its influence. The best way to dispose of much of this detritus

---

[3] Witches and Hawaiian kahu\nas call this the *aka thread.*

[4] An audiotape of *Shamanic Drumming* is available from Godolphin House at P.O. Box 297-BK, Hinton, WV 25951-0297.

of your past is to make a bonfire of it. Light it at midnight on full moon and scatter the ashes before sunrise. As the moon wanes, the influence weakens and dies.

In bringing your lost pieces back, you may well replay a little of the trauma you felt with the original loss. Try to minimize the pain by thinking of the joy of the reunion, not dwelling on the pain of the initiating incident.

AYESHA AND HER FLOWER GARDEN

Ayesha J lives in a small town in southern West Virginia. She and Nick run a landscape gardening business, and she is famous in the area for her beautiful flowers. A stream of visitors praises her annuals, perennials, and shrubs. After even one visit, somehow people can't seem to stay away—they have to come back. When we visited her site, we, too, found it beautiful, but Gavin got some very negative emanations from the perennials. Quite unwittingly, Ayesha was a psychic vampire. When a visitor came and loved her flowers, she stole little bits of soul pieces and stored them in her perennial bushes. Her business grew. Her circle of friends grew exponentially. The peculiar thing was that most of the friends didn't *like* her—but they still kept visiting. This was especially true any time there was a pagan festival in the area.

One winter brought very cold weather with a whole series of killing frosts. Then a rapid spring thaw and a couple of hot days followed in swift succession. All this happened during the time Ayesha had traveled to Japan. The erratic weather, without Ayesha there to put straw down over her perennials and protect them, meant that most of the perennials died. Once they were dead, Ayesha's circle of friends abruptly shrank.

When we went to visit her after her return, Gavin didn't get the same negative emanations from her garden, even though looking at it would almost have made you weep because it was such a sad sight. Yet the garden felt better psychically, even in its pitiable condition, than it had at the height of its summer glory. In a channeling session, Gavin traveled astrally to the forlorn site. He concluded that it was the spirits once trapped there, that had caused his negative feelings, and that they had now departed.

Notice here that it was not the death and destruction of the garden that released the captive soul pieces; it was the abrupt changes from cold weather to warm and even hot. Here Nature used the technique that you can use in your own kitchen to clean psychic impressions off objects. Thermal shock releases soul pieces just as it releases stored energy from a god/ess or from a psychic link.

Despite Gavin's counseling, Ayesha has begun again to trap soul pieces in her shrubbery. Now that he is aware of the situation, he regularly travels on the astral planes to restore any captive soul pieces to their rightful owners. Do we need to say it? Gavin and Ayesha are not on speaking terms.

PSYCHIC VAMPIRES ARE REAL

We are confident that many vampire stories are based in reality, on the very real fact that occasionally, people do actually collect soul pieces. You might expect that a very attractive, charismatic person would have lots of admirers who would willingly give up soul pieces—but a psychic vampire is not necessarily an attractive person. In fact it can be someone who is almost unnoticeable. The dowdy lady who reads tarot cards can be a very capable psychic vampire. (Again, her preying may be conscious or subconscious.) Another example might be the gentleman who leads a local "spirit study" group. They go out of their way to set up psychic links with their victims so they continually draw on their victims' energy.

We knew a case in which two such psychic vampires were preying upon a particularly guileless lady. Once a normal spirited person, now she had become almost a zombie. Physicians had given up hope; though they had treated her for deep depression, the drugs only seemed to make her worse. Only when she met a shaman friend of ours did he realize in looking at her aura that there were two extra attaching auric threads. In a very simple procedure he brought back her soul pieces, one the first week, and the second a week later.

In bringing back soul pieces like this, it can be important not to bring back all the missing pieces at one time. A psychologist does not make you relive the whole of a traumatic experience in one session, brutally ripping open the scars of old wounds. So in retrieving soul pieces, the competent Witch brings in only a little at a time.

Take the case of Mildred and Fred. If all those memories had come in from Fred at once, Mildred would simply have been swamped in emotion.

TINA AND THE ACCIDENT

Tina V was typical of today's first-year college students. She was away from home, she had a new car, and she had left behind the very restrictive guilt-ridden household where she grew up. As often happens, once she had her own mailbox, she enrolled in the School of Wicca. On campus she became a party animal. She knew her grades were suffering, but she felt she could catch up with those once she had sown some wild oats.

One night Tina and three of her girlfriends were driving back to the dorm. For once Tina was designated driver and had not overindulged. She lost control on the icy road. In one of those terrifying crashes that the movies do so well, the car hit a bridge abutment; a girl in the back seat was thrown out and killed. The other girls basically got off with scratches and bruises. The rescue team took the car away in a sack.

Tina left some of herself at the site of the accident. Perhaps because of her upbringing or perhaps not, she felt terribly guilty about Sonya's death. Perhaps if she had driven slower by a couple of miles an hour . . . perhaps, perhaps, perhaps, if only.

The more she thought about it, the more of herself she put into the accident and into the site, which was vividly imprinted into her mind. Finally, after a few days of this, she blanked it off. The mind can take only so much trauma and pain, and finally blanks out the things that cause it the most pain. Tina appeared normal physically—but she was no longer a party girl; and she began to go off into blank moments. She was so unlike her old sunny self that her parents thought the accident must have caused some undetected brain damage. They sent her for a CAT scan and several neurological tests. None showed any physical damage to account for her sudden lapses.

Another semester went by. Though Tina had previously been a good student even with her partying, it looked as if she would earn failing grades. Her parents sent her to a psychologist. After several sessions he identified the problem as this blanking off of part of the brain because of the accident. Gently he encouraged her to observe the tragedy little bit by little bit. He tried hypnosis; in it she would accurately recount what had happened during the accident, but when she returned to consciousness it was all gone again. The moments of catatonic blanking grew worse, not better.

A Witch friend told us about Tina. He asked whether we could do a healing ritual for her. At our very first meeting she went into one of the blanking episodes. When she didn't respond for some time, Gavin went into a trance to see whether he could find where her spirit had gone. He found it at the scene of the accident. This provided the clue that part of her was separated and lingering at the scene. He decided he would try to bring back just the memory of the accident but not the memory of Sonya's death. His effort worked, and Tina immediately became more responsive. After two more sessions, her episodes began to diminish in both frequency and severity. In subsequent meetings Gavin was able to bring back the remaining fragments of her soul that still clung to the accident site. In fact he found one piece in the wrecking yard still attached to the car, which she had loved as many of us do love our own first car.

As Gavin gently brought the pieces back one at a time over three or four weeks, Tina was completely restored. He felt very strongly that if he had brought everything back at once, she would have had an even worse seizure and might never have come out of it. After having experience with many of these cases, we are sometimes horrified at the actions of regular doctors who force full recall on patients who are not emotionally ready for it. The mind and the spirit are in delicate balance, and preservation of that balance is essential to the wholeness of the patient.

THE BALANCE AMONG SELFISHNESS, KINDNESS, AND LOVE

Tina was a kind, caring sort of person. She had grown up to believe wholeheartedly that she should take guilt unto herself. Many people don't have such a loving attitude and could not possibly care less about the rightness or wrongness of their actions. They never feel responsible or guilty when they cause harm. Such people cling tightly to their own soul pieces. Some occultists will tell you they have a tight aura, meaning that their protective field is very strong and drawn in close around them.

As a Witch you must learn to consciously balance your reactions to people and to situations. Typically people give to their first love a large amount of their spirit: large or multiple soul pieces. Then sometimes when the gift is abused, they find they can't leave the abuser because they have so much of themselves tied up in the abuser. This situation may persist even after a divorce or parting. There is still regard in the spirit of one partner for the other partner, even though they have been abused and taken advantage of. We often come into situations where we think, "You should put that SOB in jail!" and it doesn't happen—because of the control exerted through the soul piece so freely and innocently given. A Catch-22 ensues here: Hate has replaced love, but pulling away cannot happen because the abuser still controls you through owning part of your soul.

In Chapter IV, we taught that you can break the link formed along the Web of the Wyrd if you send a neutralizing emanation back along the link and kill the incoming manipulation. If someone is controlling you through unauthorized possession of your soul piece, the link is unbreakable. Remember: Not all control is through hate. Mothers control children (especially sons) through love. This becomes negative only when the loved person loses his/her own volition. Time and again we see people being nice to past abusers for no possible earth-plane reason. It is almost as though the abusees like the pain—or maybe it's all they know, and spiritually they're too mutilated to try anything different.

Getting back your missing soul pieces cuts off that whole communication; don't ever reinforce it again by giving away more of yourself or by turning your thoughts to the detested one.

Give your spirit a physical act that demonstrates your release. Start with a photo of the detested one, or sketch his/her likeness, to give you the strongest possible reminder of that one's appearance. Wrap this image around a candle, and burn the whole assembly to the last ash.

THE "SELFISH" WITCH?

We might have called this entire chapter The Selfish Witch. What we mean here by *selfish* is maintaining your personal intrinsic integrity—keeping your essential being inaccessible to psychic or emotional intruders. When you have built trust with someone you have known for a very long time, then of course you can give of yourself to that person. Otherwise it is only sensible to be very, very selfish. The person may be attractive and even satisfy you sexually, but that doesn't mean you should give away pieces of your own spirit. Giving and loving and being kind are all wonderful things to do; but in the real world you must ration the amounts you give out, or you will

1. Deplete yourself; and
2. become easily controllable.

In this sorry world, there is never a shortage of parasites eager to draw from you as long as you play host. When you are used up, they detach (cheerfully or resentfully) and go on to their next dupe. What's wrong with this picture?

We see it every day. Joe Blow influences Tammy Trusting. It's as if he were a snake transfixing a bird. Moreover, Tammy is controlled and manipulated by three or four other people upon whom she has innocently lavished her love (whether mundane or spiritual).

You can't go through life being controlled by everyone you meet. You owe them nothing. If you let them in, we promise you: The world is not going to run out of sob stories. Yvonne can tell you that she once donated in response to a begging letter from a "good cause" that sought her support. Charities and manufacturers of good causes have long memories and big computers. They talk to each other. Now her incoming mail is over-full of letters from such causes; we can't guess how many times her name has been sold from one to another. Donating to that first good cause is a lot like giving away a piece of your soul. If you want to donate, do it anonymously with a postal money order that you only partially fill in.

CO-DEPENDENCE, POSITIVE AND NEGATIVE

The authors live in a co-dependent relationship. We write books together. We are very rarely apart. Any lengthy separation causes unease. Over the years we have given generously of our soul pieces to each other. Some friends say that this is wrong, that we should be independent, that we should get back our soul pieces from each other and have autonomy.

The problem is—we like it! We think we do excellent work together, and there are very few negatives in our lives. In our own case history our co-dependence works and is a positive force, not only in our personal lives but also in the world at large, where we have improved, illuminated, and brightened the spiritual paths of hundreds of thousands of people. So when does co-dependence go negative?

1. When one partner literally cannot live or function without the other; or

2. when one partner is uncomfortable with co-dependence; or

3. when it is not *voluntary* and *mutual*.

Gavin's late mother, Gladys, was completely dependent on her husband. That was the way relationships *worked* in generations preceding this one. In youth she had worked as a very competent accountant, keeping the books for several large hotels. Yet when Gavin's father died, Gavin realized that Gladys couldn't even balance her own checkbook. Long years in a co-dependent state had robbed her of the self-reliance and autonomy implied in her early skills. They had a good life together; but so far as her spiritual growth went, it was negative. She didn't grow in the relationship; instead, she regressed.

If you give too much of your spirit to another person before you are certain that you will be with that one for a very long time indeed, you risk becoming too locked in to release your co-dependence. In such a situation, you forfeit your autonomy.

The theory of the spirit or soul as something that can be *fragmented* leads to a clearer understanding of our lives and the influence of others on them than does the conventional idea of a unified soul. You may see people doing actions that seem stupid or self-defeating. They make more sense, though, if you realize that the influence of another person—alive or dead—persists because that person owns (or more accurately, *wrongfully possesses*) a piece of the "stupid" one.

GETTING YOUR SOUL BACK TOGETHER

When you go to a trained Witch or shaman to get yourself back together, you will go through a process similar to the one described in the five-step retrieval system above. The shaman usually gets you to sit down or lie beside him/her on a soft warm blanket or rug. He/she holds your hand or maintains body contact from foot to shoulder. Then, with the aid of drumming and talk, the shaman takes him-/herself and you into an altered state.[5] (It may take more than one session to make this successful.)

Once in the altered state, the shaman finds the missing pieces and returns them, often by "blowing" them into the heart or fore-head. This last act may be pure showmanship, executed simply because the patient expects some shaking of the feathers and rat-tling of the gourds. In our experience, the soul piece snaps back into the patient as soon as it comes near.

The process takes time—but so long as you allow the influ-encer to retain a piece of your soul, healing cannot happen. If you start thinking or worrying about the old trauma, you stand a good chance of losing the soul pieces you have just made such an effort to retrieve. Exclude him/her and any other trauma by thinking of other things.

Planning your life must include being "selfish." You cannot help everyone in the world, nor can you give of yourself to every person or charity that claims your attention. Even after the career parasites have entirely consumed you, the world will still have prob-lems. Selfishness should be listed with the other virtues, not left for-gotten on the shelf or called bad names. You owe it to your own spirit to do everything you can to help it develop and grow.

GROWTH AND KARMA

Witches believe that the spirit comes to this plane of existence to learn and to grow. If pieces of it detach, it must obviously degrade. It is the responsibility of the owner of the individual spirit to make sure that this does not happen. At least, it must happen only in such a way that the pieces can be reassembled at death. Again, in ancient cultures many believed that all the pieces of the body must be buried together; otherwise, the uneasy spirit cannot progress, and haunts its old abodes. During the Civil War (1861–1865) many peo-

---

[5] Some shamans insist that you and they use a drug to help the journey. We prefer not to work with people who use this approach.

ple who lost limbs carefully retained them and sent them home (often pickled) lest they be "incomplete" at death.

The spirit itself contains the record of all previous incarnations. Witches generally do not believe in a big record book in the sky kept by some overseeing angel with a quill pen and a green eyeshade. You carry your own record encoded within your spirit. The spirit comes to Earth to grow. Some of that growth comes through suffering; some comes through love. This explains our belief that everyone should aim to get the widest variety of experiences you can possibly pack into the incarnation. The more experiences you can pack into a lifetime, the more your spirit grows. The only time the spirit begins to degrade is when:

1. You refuse new experiences and sink passively into your own spiritual fat, lethargically watching the idiot box.

2. You allow others to steal your soul pieces.

How, then, can you help others grow? First defragment their soul, and then encourage them to have a wider variety of experiences. Propping them up emotionally and pandering to their every self-indulgent need does not help them. In fact, it may prevent their growth.

THE TWO-HAMBURGER PROBLEM

One day on lunch hour you go to a fast-food place downtown. You intend to buy a hamburger; but a two-for-one sale is going on, so you buy two hamburgers to go. On your way back to the office, you see a homeless person begging for money. The question is, should you give him your second hamburger, or should you selfishly keep it? A certain number of people who are homeless *choose* that path as their path of learning. If you make that path easy for them, you curtail their learning. Therefore in many senses it is better for you to be "selfish" and keep your extra hamburger than to give it away.

Of course there is a humanitarian side to this topic. You are human, and one of the higher traits of humankind is the helping of other humans. So you may want to make yourself feel good by giving away your extra hamburger. You have to make that decision, to give or not to give; but it is not an easy decision with a clear-cut answer.

If you see a little girl fall off the sidewalk into the path of an oncoming car, and all you have to do is reach out and pull her back, 99 percent of people are going to stretch out their hand. Only one in a hundred will say, "It's her destiny. I shouldn't interfere."

What if you see an unconscious person lying on the sidewalk, and it looks as if they've just swallowed their tongue and may suffocate? What if you know CPR and know you can save that person's life? Your human side will encourage you to reach down and help. Your Witch side might say, "Now wait a minute. I can't ask this person whether he needs help. Maybe it's time for him to go on."

These are all over-simplified examples of everyday decisions that a Witch must make. If you go through life continually giving away of yourself without regard for the consequences of your actions, you may as well not be here. You will become one of those "nobody home" people.

How a Witch Recharges Herself

UNLIMITED ENERGY CAN BE YOURS

When a Witch completes a lengthy ritual, she feels exhausted: physically, mentally, and psychically. To restore her physical energy, she needs only food and rest. To restore her mental energy, she may choose to do a crossword or to knit or to listen to lively music. The restoration of *psychic* energy is not discussed in books consulted by most workers in the conventional healing industry. In a previous work[1] we talked briefly about standing in the Star Position with hands outstretched and head tilted slightly back, receiving the energy that flows constantly from the cosmos into the earth. In this chapter we will extend the techniques you have used in earlier spell-work and discuss the tuning of energy for your own use.

A Witch uses energy from the earth, from living things, and from the cosmos. Go outdoors and—despite all the smart remarks in today's press—hug a tree. Put your forehead against its bark. Let its serene energy flow around you and through you. That energy is ideal for recharging your psychic batteries and for quieting the jangled nerves that are an inevitable part of today's world.

---

[1] G. and Y. Frost, *The Magic Power of White Witchcraft* (Paramus, NJ: Reward Books, 1999).

SOURCES OF PSYCHIC POWER

Few people know that psychic energy is just as essential to good health as the food energy that serves to run their bodies. You can wind yourself up with endless cups of caffeine-laden coffee and lots of high-nutrient food. You can keep the mind active by having an interest or learning a foreign language. That's all swell, but if you don't pay attention to sources of psychic energy in your life, you will become depressed and fall ill.

There are people who blame their depression on the fact that it's a negative-ion day—and it's true that when you feel sunshine on your face, you feel better. The sunshine recharges your psychic batteries. In the same way, you can recharge yourself by hugging a tree or eating live vegetables or using crystals or even (as you will see) storing energy when you are high, to be called on in down times. Whatever your lifestyle is, you can use these sources of energy to keep your *spiritual* energy in balance with your *physical* and *mental* energies. If you neglect the recharging of your spiritual energy, you are asking for trouble. You will become depressed, snappish, and stressed out; but may be unable to identify a cause for your feelings.

A Witch calls on many sources of natural energy—sources that you too can tap for an extra pulse of energy. This energy can pull you out of a suicidal depression, add a boost to your spells, improve your health, or simply get you back in tune with the real world. Chief among these sources are:

Crystals and stones, which some call the "distilled essence of the earth";

Living things, including plants, familiars, and people;

Earth and cosmic (Gaea) power (the Chinese *chi*); and

Hearth god/dess power.

CRYSTAL POWER

In Chapter III we showed you how to use crystals in your spell-work. This chapter extends that instruction into your sphere of personal need. If you use this power, we recommend you reread the section headed Gemstones and Crystals in Chapter III before you begin your work.

Witches have used crystal energy for thousands of years. One traditional method is to sew a little bag and wear it on a ribbon over your heart, placing in it a crystal appropriate to the energy you need. Some people get better results if they place a crystal in the band of a hat so that it rests at the center of the forehead over the "third eye." Some occultists we know actually glue the crystal to their forehead; but the heart crystal is adequate for most recharging efforts, and is less conspicuous.

GRETA AVOIDS SUICIDE

Greta lives in Austria. As a member of the old moneyed aristocracy, she belonged to the fashionable Viennese demi-monde. In her early twenties she played the madcap heiress socialite; she danced the nights away, frequented the ateliers of Paris couturiers, and led what is best described as an outrageous life.

A couple of seasons of life in the fast lane burned her out. She was jaded. After an unsuccessful suicide attempt, her doctor sent her to Baden Baden, Germany, for a cure, but her depression was more than physical. She simply felt that her life held no purpose or meaning. Physically and mentally she was as healthy as she had ever been, but spiritually she was a wreck. The baths and springs began to work their own recharging magic, and Greta began to come alive again.

At the baths one day she felt a mysterious attraction to a young man who was, quite frankly, ugly. "Homely" was not a strong enough word to describe his plain looks. He had so much energy and so much lust for life, though, that she couldn't keep her eyes off him. At an afternoon tea at the bathhouse they were introduced in the formal German way. When they shook hands, Greta was taken aback both by the energy that she felt in Juergen's handshake and by his "lower-class" accent. She felt the reflexive response of an aristocrat's disdain for a laborer. His ugliness and his background repelled her, but she felt she must gain some of that fascinating energy. Greta had had many sexual adventures in her life, and she set out to get Juergen into her bed. A fling during her stay in Baden Baden could cause no harm, she reasoned, and she would probably never see him again. Once her campaign succeeded, she was trapped; because although he was not a very sophisticated lover, intimate contact with him totally recharged her psychic batteries.

Now Greta was a very pragmatic Germanic type. Trying to determine cause and effect, she assumed that her new brighter outlook came about only because of Juergen's novelty; she had never had a relationship with anyone outside her own social class.

She returned to Vienna refreshed and took up her demi-monde playgirl lifestyle one more time. Fairly soon, despite other sexual adventures, she felt run down again and began to crave her blue-collar lover. Her friends laughed at her, but she went to his village to track him down and to re-establish the relationship. She learned that he mined crystalline sea salt. They took up where they had left off. Then, refreshed once more, Greta went back to Vienna—but now found that she was even more reluctant to end the relationship. She persuaded Juergen to come to Vienna and live with her.

Soon each seemed to be run down, and both went into deep depression. Juergen returned to his village and to his work, and Greta to her wild ways. Drugs followed, and she again tried suicide. At the news, Juergen came to Vienna and almost forcibly abducted her, taking her back to his village. Now they tried living as a couple, one month in the village and one month in Vienna, on a continuous cycle of using energy and recharging themselves. Of course Juergen could not keep his job under such circumstances. Suddenly the recharging that had always occurred in the village stopped happening. Regretfully they thought they had simply fallen out of love. Greta didn't want to believe that, so she asked the local village Witch what she should do.

With an indulgent smile the Witch told her that all they needed to do was wear a pouch of salt crystals over their hearts. They took her advice—and they both became the talk of the Vienna demi-monde for their nonstop energy.

YOUR OWN CRYSTAL POWER BANK

If you have an energy problem, of course see your physician first. Many women suffer from an undiagnosed borderline hypothyroidism. If this is left untreated, health problems can follow and, if pregnant, any children they have may manifest birth defects. If your low energy shows up as a feeling that the world is too much with you and nothing is worth the effort, but professionals can find no physical cause, you need recharging. Probably the easiest way to do this in today's world is to carry the appropriate crystal with you. For just

CRYSTAL	POWER TO HEAL	PSYCHIC/EMOTIONAL ASPECT
Emerald	Hyperactivity, mental disorders	Improves creativity
Fluorite	Arthritis, low energy	Increases intuition and astral travel
Garnet	Heart problems, circulation	Boosts energy
Hematite	Lung and kidney problems	Grounds
Moonstone	PMS and childbirth	Releases fear, increases femininity
Obsidian	Weakness	Psychic protector and shield
Opal	Master healer	Removes guilt
Rose Quartz	Heart disease	Makes more loving
Rutilated Quartz	Broken bones, depression	Improves dreaming
Smoky Quartz	Impotence	Very powerful grounder
Tourmaline—green	Master healer	Decreases stress
Tourmaline—pink	Emotional problems	Stabilizes emotions
Tourmaline—black	Weakness	Psychic shielding
Tourmaline—blue	Confidence	Improves self-confidence

TABLE VIII–1
Guide to Crystal Renewal Power

a few dollars, at any gem and mineral show you can buy more crystals than you will ever need. Resist the big bombastic ones. The chipped ones with an irregular facet or two, and those with a "poor" polish job—that look unfinished—are better for your purposes than the high-priced exquisite ones that conform to traditional ideas of beautiful gems.

Table VIII-1 serves as a guide to crystals that will most help you in meeting specific needs.

RENEWING YOUR LIFE FORCE

You may have met people who drain your energy. The term for such people is *psychic vampires*. They are real, but often they do not realize what they are doing to their friends and acquaintances. You will notice that they are full of energy; it makes you tired just to be around them. In Table VIII-1 you can see that wearing obsidian will prevent such a psychic drain.

The Witch can gain energy deliberately from her friends, from familiars, and from plants in the same way the psychic vampire does it. She simply tunes in to the spirit of the living being and draws energy from it. Since she is skilled, and since her action is a conscious one, from friends and animals she takes only a little. From a plant she may take a little, as from a tree, or all of it, as when she eats a fresh vegetable.

GWEN AND THE PRODUCE MANAGER

Gwen T lives in San Francisco. She used to haunt Golden Gate Park, hugging the trees that grow there, mainly because as a massage therapist she was perpetually using her psychic energy to heal her patients. Gwen was a very powerful healer with her massages. Of course most of her clients attributed their improvement to the physical aspect of the massages, but Gwen knew it was her psychic energy that effected the healing. She was also smart enough to know that she needed to recharge herself after sessions of healing work.

Gwen often bought her fruits and vegetables at the produce market of a mature Korean woman, Mrs. Yung. When she and Gwen started to open up and get acquainted, Mrs. Yung told Gwen that she did not have to hug trees; that instead she could gain psychic energy by eating living vegetables. Gwen could feel her own energy easily enough, and now Mrs. Yung taught her to "read" the vegetables. She invited Gwen to come along early one morning to the wholesale market to buy for the store. Everyone at the wholesalers' knew Mrs. Yung. "They always try to trick me," she confided to Gwen. "But see? I use my pendulum and if the vegetables are still alive it will swing in circles. If not, it will swing in lines." As she went through the cavernous building, Mrs. Yung carefully chose only those vegetables that her pendulum told her were still vitally alive. "You see," she explained, "vegetables don't die when they're taken from the earth; they just go dormant. If they've had their roots or their leaves cut off, they'll live only about another two weeks. So I always select the ones where my pendulum gives the largest swing. I know they're the freshest." Gwen was sure that the wholesalers must regard Mrs. Yung as some kind of harmless freak. Instead, some of them asked her whether particular shipments of vegetables were fresh, or were they being ripped off with old produce?

Mrs. Yung's market did do a tremendous business in fresh produce. She insisted, "My customers know that I sell living vegetables, not dead ones." Gwen began to eat Mrs. Yung's vegetables, but could feel no difference in her psychic energy. She nearly wrote Mrs. Yung off as nothing more than a benevolent fruitcake, but Mrs. Yung kept asking her whether she felt better. Gwen confessed that she could not feel any difference, and that she was still spending a lot of time hugging trees. "You come to my place tonight and eat with me, and we'll see," Mrs. Y. ordered. As they sat down to the meal, Gwen identified the critical fact. She had been cooking the vegetables, and here Mrs. Y. was serving hers raw, with a tiny dish of nonfat salad dressing as a dip. When she began to eat the vegetables raw, Gwen felt an immediate difference in the level of her psychic energy. When she visits Golden Gate Park now, it is for pleasure, not for replenishment.

USING YOUR PENDULUM

The pendulum is about the easiest divining tool you can make or use. One bead and a hair from your own scalp will serve as well as any elaborate artifact. To "read" vegetables, you need only hold it over the vegetable and observe the direction of the pendulum's swing. It will swing either in a circle or back and forth in a straight line. Usually the circle indicates that the vegetable is alive and the size of the circle indicates how much vitality it still contains. Once you begin to do this, and you know which vegetables are alive, you can divine their energy without the pendulum by just passing your receiving hand over them.[2] The center of the palm and under the balls of each finger are the most sensitive areas.

When you get the vegetables home, turn them into what the French call *crudites*. Prepare them no more than three minutes before they'll be eaten, and serve them with only the lightest hint of a salad dressing. Serve plates of cut-up raw vegetables rather than killing them with cooking. Steven Leacock once said that Anglo-Saxons are afraid of vegetables; that's why they kill them by overcooking.

POWER FROM THE EARTH

In the last hundred years we have gone from horse and buggy to the automobile, from crystal-set radios to TV and the Internet. For thousands of years before the Industrial Revolution, human beings were hunter-gatherers and farmers. Imbedded in our race's memory banks are memories of being one with nature. Even though living in the natural world could be difficult, still we tend to forget the uncomfortable moments and yearn for the serenity and the security of our pre-industrial lives.

Not long ago we (Frosts) were in Muir Woods north of San Francisco. In that natural holy place with its giant redwoods, the peace and grandeur were shattered when a cell-phone rang and someone with a very harsh accent began to yell at his broker. Jimmy Buffett calls this *overkill*. If you can't relax and enjoy the serenity that trees and earth create, you will surely quit this planet in a pine box well before your time. Your body was not designed to run at the pace of today's world. The stress of current life causes a plethora of diseases, and the only way you can avoid them is to get back in touch with your roots.

ELLA AND HER HERBS

Ella was an advertising executive in New York City who thoroughly enjoyed her high-stress job. It became clear to her boss that Ella was

---

[2] If you are right-handed, your *receiving* or *secondary* hand will normally be your left hand, while your right hand is the *transmitting* or *dominant* hand. Try both hands, though, because even today well-meaning teachers and parents have bullied many natural lefties into being righties.

getting burned out: She was no longer coming up with those brilliant gimmicks that advertising requires, so the boss insisted that Ella take a month's vacation. After the first week Ella was at her wits' end. She didn't have anything to do! During the second week she had her first heart attack. People seldom admit that to a fast-paced overachiever, forced idleness is very stressful.

Ella recovered from her heart attack, but she took it as a sign that she must slow down. However, when she finally got back to work, wearing her iron suits and her power pumps, carrying her briefcase, she found herself caught up again in a highly stressful campaign for a new line of watches. During the campaign she met and fell in love with the illustrator for the advertisements. Pete was a very laid-back individual who privately swore his illustrations came through channeling. He encouraged Ella to try it for herself. Sitting still for fifteen minutes was a real problem for her, but she managed it for a few nights. What she got in her head were vivid pictures of herbs. Neither she nor Pete could make much sense of it all, but it did turn her attention to the subject. She wondered whether her channeling indicated there was some herb she should take to lower her stress levels.

Between the advertising campaign, and traveling to see her new lover, and forcing herself to sit still, she ended up with a second heart attack. Ella decided the message was clear: "Slow down or die." Her new interest in herbs gave her an idea. She started growing a few of the most common ones, first in boxes in her New York apartment, and then at Pete's place in Connecticut. Then it was, "What am I going to do with all these neat organic herbs I've grown?" She found that herbs in bulk were not very profitable, but packaging them as teas and pills was highly profitable. Applying her advertising skills, she quickly had a very successful little business under way and she gave up her New York job.

She noticed very clearly that she was less content when working in the office of her herb farm than when she was working physically with the herbs, with dirt under her nails and potting soil in her denim cuffs. Wisely, she hired a teenager straight from high school to do the office work. She sensed that someone who had not formed conventional business habits would be easier to train than an older "skilled" worker.

Ella has now retired from actually managing the herb farm in rural Connecticut, but she can still be found puttering among the herbs. Her teas and potions hold a prominent place on the shelves of many herb stores. She has gained serenity and contentment from the earth.

WINDOW BOXES AND GARDENS

You can start bringing the serenity of earth energy into your home by removing the carpets. You can follow up with stone bowls containing sand and a few desert plants. The next step may be to grow your own kitchen herbs in a window box. How long has it been since you enjoyed a delicious *omelette aux fines herbes*? Not officially a herb, but beneficial and attractive anyway, is the classic aloe vera. Handy in your kitchen window, it is a wonderful convenient plant to have nearby in case of minor kitchen burns.

Most herbs are extremely easy to grow, with few natural enemies. Unlike many fancy houseplants that take a great deal of care, they ask only a sunny spot and some water, with an occasional feeding of fertilizer. These babies are survivors, after all. There is an old saying that if you can keep an herb alive for a year, it will own the house the second year. It is true that once an herb has settled into its plot, it takes off enthusiastically. You can mistreat herbs abominably, and nearly all of them will still flourish. When you plant herbs in your garden, you need to be scrupulous about confining them to specific areas. The mints, for example, are notorious for their trait of taking over the whole world; and if you put a sprig of mint into a bed, do not be surprised when its unconfined roots spread throughout the garden.

Similarly, the small sprigs of herbs that you buy from the nursery will soon develop into large leggy bushes if allowed to seed, and may come to resemble a garden pest—but remember that most of them are very marketable pests. Bunches of fresh herbs sell well in all farmers' markets. Rosemary, thyme, oregano, basil, sage, and even some exotics such as artemisia (wormwood or mugwort), and chocolate mint sell well.[3] You won't make a fortune selling herbs this way, but being in contact with growing things and seeing the cycle of the seasons as the plants fulfill their potential will give you great peace of mind. You will come to share the opinion of those who value other things as highly as they value dollars.

---

[3] Often in the market you can trade with others—perhaps your herbs for their vegetables and eggs.

DORIS SAVES HER $50,000-A-YEAR JOB

Doris N grew up in New York City and had all the skills it took to live in that metropolitan environment. Once she earned her bachelor's degree, she took a position in a publishing firm and worked her way right up the ladder to the title of senior sales representative.

That meant travel, and it snatched her out of her normal matrix. Week by week, month by month, her health deteriorated. She saw a physician; she started taking ginseng; she tried St. John's Wort, but she felt worse and worse. Finally her doctor sent her to a psychologist. After many expensive visits, Doris felt briefly as if she were getting better; but soon her heavy work schedule sent her into further problems. Now they centered around allergies—to almost everything.

Among the books she was selling was one by the present authors. She tried doing the Star Position to recharge herself. Then one day she met us and talked with us at length about her health history. We found in her a "yes, but" person. When we suggested things, there was always a reason she couldn't do them.

"Try A."

"Yes, but I can't do that because . . ."

"Try B."

"Yes, but that won't work because . . ."

It was several weeks later that she contacted us again. At her recent job evaluation she had learned that, quite bluntly, she was on her way out. She needed to do something pretty emphatic to turn around her job performance and salvage her career. Apparently she didn't have time to shop, and her diet was a mess, so we suggested she start growing her own fresh plants.

"Yes, but I don't have a garden."

"Use a window box."

"Yes, but what can I grow?"

Now Gavin's European background came into play. "Mustard and cress."

The tiny seeds of these two plants germinate and can be eaten in less than two weeks. They are not common in many parts of the United States, but almost every European supermarket offers little trays of planting medium with the mustard and cress already in and sprouted. The box goes into a sunny window and gets a few drops of water each day. You clip off the green tops and add them to your salad for that psychic recharging that all living plants provide. Nothing could be easier.

We knew that Doris needed even more help than the living plants could provide. We sent her a burst of healing energy and a crystal that she should carry with her at all times. About a month later she called back to thank us and to update us: Her problems were rapidly disappearing and her allergies had gone away.

FAMILIARS

Many of the oldest Witch legends tell of *familiars*—animals that associate with Witches and ostensibly help in "dangerous" activities. Trial reports from later centuries often mention black cats, the cat being a suspect animal from earliest times.[4] The cat is not the only creature accused of sinister abilities: Many other small animals and birds are also mentioned, ranging from the popular raven to toads. It is not surprising that a Witch—perhaps shunned by her neighbors—would turn for companionship to a pet. What *is* surprising is the great volume of folklore associated with this apparently harmless pursuit.

The truth is that any animal can provide rebalancing of our energies. Caring for a sick animal can lead to a (perhaps painful) reevaluation of your life; often people will forget their own problems in their efforts to help the animal.

Traditionally, and still in some cases today, familiars work with us in three ways:

1. To sense spiritual presences or the presence of excess psychic energy;

2. to test potions (very rarely by an individual Witch today, but some pharmaceutical companies still use them); and

3. to recharge their owners.

It is no wonder that cats have always been regarded as the Witch's familiar companion. Almost every town has its Cat Lady. Medieval

---

[4] For example, see Robert Darnton's, *The Great Cat Massacre* (New York: Random House, 1997).

literature contains many references to shape-changing; and the distaste that many men have felt for cats is best summed up in the words of Rudyard Kipling:

> *... and since that time every good man throws his boots at the cat.*

The truth behind these legends is that cats put out a lot of living energy, and that cats give freely of that energy to people whom they trust.

It is true: Cats are instinctive loners, whereas canines live in packs. Feline autonomy does not flatter people who want a creature that will fawn on them. Nonetheless, when you are feeling down or are confined to bed with an illness, your cat will come ankling around, sensing that something is amiss and wanting to help put it right. Stroking the cat, hearing it purr, and feeling its body warmth immediately give you a lift.

GLORIA JEAN'S FAMILIARS SAVED HER LIFE

Gloria Jean lives in southern West Virginia. Like many cat ladies and many Witches, she is not young. She is known in town for taking in all the stray cats that no one else wants to bother with. Unlike many such people, she keeps an immaculate house; and her cats get the best veterinary treatment that money can buy.

When her retirement abruptly removed her from the social atmosphere of the office where she had worked, Gloria Jean went into a depression. It was not long before she was diagnosed with breast cancer. Between the surgery and the chemotherapy, her health sank to a low ebb. Neighbors felt that she did not have long to live. Then one rainy night two kittens arrived at her front porch. It was clear that they had been brutally treated, for they were in very poor condition. Gloria Jean pulled herself out of her depression to care for the kittens, and the three of them, Cat Lady, Mungojerry, and Rumpleteaser, now enjoy excellent health.

It is a well known fact that when visitors to elder-care facilities bring pets, those pets lift the spirits of the residents for days afterward. Some dog-food commercials use this fact to encourage you to buy a specific brand on the grounds that it will help your pet live longer and consequently extend your life.

CHOOSING YOUR FAMILIAR

A cat really is an ideal familiar. They are sufficiently self-tending and -maintaining to demand of their "owners" very little work, and are naturally very healthy animals. In our personal lives, we like the breeds that have some proportion of Siamese, because they have an appealing streak of autonomy—and are more vocal than many other breeds. In choosing your own household familiar, try to get one that has been raised from the beginning around humans; kittens lose the ability to learn social skills earlier than you might imagine. Try as well to choose one that spent at least the first six weeks of its life with the mother. If separated too young, their training may well be incomplete (for example, in litter-box skills and in self-cleaning). Your cat can have a better, longer life if it stays indoors altogether, as our veterinarian recommends. Domestic cats do not belong out there in Flealand or in the land of swift, oblivious vehicles. A last note: Do not declaw cats.

Not all people like cats, and dogs seem to be the natural second choice. Gavin personally enjoys Golden Retrievers for their high intelligence, their amiability, and their courtesy. A cross-breed between Golden and Labrador Retrievers makes a wonderful pet. Choosing a dog from the municipal pound is an altruistic thing to do, but can often lead to trouble. Many pound dogs have been mistreated and can be neurotic. A puppy from the pound may be the best bet of all. Remember that dogs need a lot of exercise and far more attention than cats do.

Any familiar is better than none. Friends of ours greatly enjoy their finches that fly freely in certain rooms of the house.[5] Other friends enjoy their cuddly, intelligent gerbils. At least one man keeps two rats as his composting facility. Before you get a familiar, think long and hard about the amount of time and attention it will need, and whether you can be available *daily* to provide that time and attention.

EARTH SERENITY

The Earth, our mother Gaea, is bombarded incessantly with cosmic power. No wonder, then, that surface soil contains a great deal of

---

[5] In Europe owls and ravens are considered the most useful psychic familiars. Workers often take them caged into the actual circle, where they serve to detect any uninvited psychic presence or vibration.

psychic energy. Some people today even eat small portions of soil mixed into their salads to partake of that energy. If you go into the garden or visit a civic park where a flower bed is freshly dug, kneel down and run your fingers through the loose topsoil. Many people can feel the energy such actions impart. In Korean shamanic practice, it is common to precede a ritual by digging up a patch of earth and then getting the practitioners to tread it down with bare feet or to pat it level with their hands. This may be the ultimate good feeling.

You may scorn the idea of French or Italian workers treading the harvest grapes with their feet, but you will never laugh again if you once try it yourself. It is no coincidence that the grape-treaders follow such a day's work with a night-long session of vigorous dancing. The treading simply makes them feel good. They get a surge of psychic energy from their work. Like any freshly picked fruit, those grapes are full to bursting with earth energy.

You can avail yourself of that same energy. Treading newly turned earth with bare feet is one of the easiest ways, but placing a bunch of grapes in a plastic tub and treading them with your feet in the privacy of your own apartment will give you an even bigger lift, especially if those grapes are freshly picked. Yes, we know: What would your associates think? Who says they have to know? Wouldn't it be fun to have a little secret life on the side?

Of course if you do this regularly, you run the risk of taking that next step and bottling your own wine.

A WITCH'S MORNING EXERCISE

Are you one of those people who have a great deal of trouble getting your motor started in the morning? Even if you come wide awake and ready to roll, it is still good to take a few minutes to welcome the new day with gratitude, and to consider the day past and the day to come. We do this ourselves by thinking in terms of six directions.

1. The first direction is the Center. That is you yourself. Our Native American friends say, "You are the center of your own universe." Look at your reflection in the mirror and be grateful for being alive. Think about the earth and about your roots in this specific place. Be grateful to the earth for all it gives you.

2. East—This is beautiful, green, living foliage. It is the direction of new beginnings and of children (youth). Review your life actions of the last twenty-four hours. Decide whether you have made any worthwhile beginnings in projects, friendships, relationships. Or did you let something slide, when a word or a small gesture might have started something whose results would have been very positive in your life or in theirs? Our Native American friends say, "Judge the effect of your actions unto the seventh generation." They mean that a friendly word to a child will be passed on to that child's children, because a child learns its behavior from you.

3. South—This is heat and warmth and home, the fire of desire in the loins, the fire of inspiration. Is your house warm and comfortable, or are there problems? Has there been something disturbing in it? Are you spending enough time in your "cave" with those who are dear to you? Think about all your actions and your words. Have you shown any leadership, or has it been all negative? If love is the willingness to help another develop, have you done anything in the past twenty-four hours to help those around you develop? Are your relationships at home warm and friendly, or would an observer detect a coldness or indifference?

4. West—In the west you have rocks, and especially things made from rocks or minerals, such as metal and all that electronics stuff you probably own. Gemstones, too, belong here. It is the area of craftwork. What is going on in your work place? What is going on in your job? Are you just putting in time, or are you being creative in your trade and craft? Sometimes we think of west as black and red; at other times, a deep beautiful sunset color. Apply yourself to thinking about both relationships at work and the work you do. Could you do it better? What mistakes have you made? How can you improve relations with your boss? Is something awry that may never be fixable?

5. North—This direction is generally thought of as white—the color that contains all colors of the spectrum. It is all the wisdom you have accumulated. It is your store of knowledge. In the last twenty-four hours have you added to that store, or have you just drawn on it without expanding it? See what your guides think

here. Look for other sources of information on subjects that you enjoy. Think about the future and your retirement, how you are going to live, whom you will live with in that future. Have you done everything you can toward making it secure? Again in relationships, think in terms of whether your current relationships are those that will continue into the future.

6. Spirit—The sixth direction is up. If you like, you can think of this as heaven, or as your next incarnation, or as your spiritual growth. Its color is usually the light blue of a North Carolina coastal sky. Are you developing your spirituality? Have you done anything to help others toward a more spiritual path? Have you meditated on other incarnations of your own? Here again the guides can be of great help in prodding you along to take the high road through life, not the easy path of least resistance. This world is not kind to idealists, but you have to try.

LIVING ON THE HILL

Psychic energy flows from hilltop to valley. If you live on a hillside, that energy will flow through your dwelling. If your patio faces uphill to the south, energy from the east (new beginnings), from the south (fire and fiery inspiration energy), and from the west (craftsman energy) will all bombard it. Then the energy will flow out through the house and into the north (which we hope is downhill). In the north all wisdom accumulates, equating to old age.

You will be surprised to observe how many Witches' homes are situated in this arrangement. Intuitively the Witch chooses such a siting. Without necessarily knowing anything about the Chinese art of *feng shui*, still she "feels" more comfortable in a place where she can sit on her patio and effortlessly recharge with the energy of direction.

If your dwelling is not oriented this way, or if you live on a flat plain, you can take steps to ameliorate the situation. Keep a candle burning in the southernmost room of the house. Have new seeds sprouting in the easternmost room. Site your workshop in the westernmost room. Place your study in the north.[6]

---

[6] For a house on the east coast, see Figure IX-3.

HEARTH GOD/ESSES

Many things besides crystals and living things emanate psychic energy. Some people swear by the old-fashioned rabbit's foot. Others would not be without a token of their deity. Hanging a Snoopy or a Garfield on your keychain will give you a lift. These images work on the mind by amusing you with their harmless absurdity. They can be called mascots. In times before the invention of comic strips, people formed little statuettes and stood them on the household hearth. These grew in importance and became known as hearth gods. Archaeologists at buried Pompeii have found bodies of fleeing people who stopped to retrieve nothing in the eruption of Vesuvius except for the hearth gods—the *lares* and *penates* that guarded the well-being of the household.

When early peoples felt optimistic and benevolent, when things went well, they praised the little statuettes and put happy or loving or healing energy into them. In Mediterranean hunting societies, hunters might pray to an image of Diana for success in the hunt. "Praying to" actually amounts to *putting energy into* the god/ess image. The more people you can get to pray to your god/ess-mascot, the more energy it contains. Gradually the idea went further. People offered first food, then valuable objects, then human sacrifice, to the mascot-god/ess of their choice. At each step on this path the shaman/priest gained more psychic power and control of the people.

Now let's say the tribe's hunters have returned from expedition after expedition empty-handed. Their tribe faces starvation. Their priest—with whatever degree of showmanship—throws the mascot-god/ess into the fire, releasing the psychic energy it contains. Suddenly the hunts become successful. (We should point out here that a successful hunt is a successful hunt. It doesn't really matter whether the energy from the mascot affected the hunters' minds, or magically made their arrows hit the prey more accurately, or caused some other literal effect. Starving people aren't going to quibble. The magic worked. At the very least it inspired the hunters to try one more time.)

The concepts we discuss here seem outside the realm of everyday experience in the "paycheck" world. They do not lend themselves comfortably to conventional labels. What we call *god/ess* and *hearth god* and *mascot* are entirely distinct from any concept dealing with spiritual aspects of human experience. You probably have a concept of Deity in the spiritual realms that you feel comfortable with, whether it be a male deity(s), a female deity(s), or something genderless. Whether your personal belief is any or none of the above, the religion police may probably not come after you.[7] The intent of this book is not to interfere with your spiritual beliefs or to trespass upon them; it is to suggest ways in which you can improve the future you face in the paycheck world. If we knew conventional terms that served as useful labels instead of *god/ess*, *hearth god*, and *mascot*, we would use them. In the meantime, we're stuck with what we can offer. What we can tell you, the aspiring Witch, is that the concepts and labels we articulate do work and are ethical. Seize the baton we're handing you, and run.

EDNA AND HO TEI

Edna and Joe V were moved to Tokyo by Joe's employing firm. Joe's demanding position left Edna alone for long hours with nothing to do but keep house. They lived not near some American military base, but, as the expression goes, on the economy. They rented a Japanese house, shopped in Japanese stores, and used Japanese transportation. The firm provided their housing, of course, and a generous cost-of-living allowance; they lived comfortably.

Once the first novelty of their new situation had worn off, Edna became depressed and lonely. She worked at learning a few words in Japanese but not enough to communicate adequately with anyone beyond the few shop clerks who spoke English. She felt altogether cut off: isolated completely from any social life, without even the camaraderie of the military community.

She took several long trips back home—at company expense—and Joe began to worry that their marriage was breaking up. He was working well and had brought about many successful joint contracts between his firm and various Japanese *zaibatsu* (conglomerates).

One day Edna's gardener found her sitting in the backyard weeping. In his broken English he tried to learn why, and to cheer her up. As he left Edna, he said the puzzling words, "Ho Tei fix." He

---

[7] As they observe politicians, many thinking people fear it's only a matter of time. Hey—it's working for the Taliban. "Live on my terms or go to hell."

returned quickly with his wife. She led Edna into the kitchen and signed that she was to boil a large pot of water. Once the water boiled, the pair led Edna to a little statue in a back corner of the garden. It was a statue of Ho Tei, the Happy Buddha. They showed Edna how to pour the boiling water over Ho Tei.

Suddenly Edna's outlook improved. With the improvement she became friendly with the gardener's wife—who could speak no English. Communication between the two women grew more fluent, half in English and half in Japanese, and Edna became part of the local village society; for even in cosmopolitan Tokyo little village enclaves exist. From a depressed outsider Edna became an active insider in the little world of her neighborhood. Joe was delighted and relieved beyond words.

She often reflected in wonder, "Just a pot of boiling water . . ."

MAKING YOUR OWN HEARTH GOD/ESS

Ho Tei is so popular in Japan that hardly a garden lacks a statue of him. You can get your own little Buddha image in a garden and gift shop or through the catalog of an occult supply house. It will serve to store the optimistic energy you need to draw on from time to time. When you come into the house happy, hold him for a few moments in your hands. Store a little of that happy energy in him. Pat his bald head. Rub his round tummy and just feel good about him. When things go awry, put him into boiling water or pour boiling water over him where he sits. Things get magically better.

A Witch stores other sorts of energy in appropriate mascots or hearth god/esses. For instance, you can store anger in a red candle. Then when you want to do a ritual and send the angry red energy out toward the target of the ritual, you can burn the candle and send the energy out.

"Why would I want to send angry energy out?" you're asking. Angry energy is also the energy associated with curing blood diseases. Both are related to aspects of the warrior god Mars/Ares. Thus, if someone important to you needs energy to heal their leukemia, you can draw on the energy stored in that red candle to send healing energy of exactly the appropriate vibration.

In a similar way you can store and use other types of energy. Lustful energy can be stored in a model phallus, wealth energy in a coin, and so on.

Table VIII-2 lists traditional examples of hearth gods you can make and use in this manner. Among serious workers these are known not as hearth gods or mascots, but as *psychostores*. They function like batteries which you charge with your emotions. When you need to draw on that stored energy, you can do so. Crystals, too, can serve as *psychostores*. In this mode, when you are very up and energetic you can put some of your good energy into a crystal and then wear it for a sustained flow of energy; or for a sudden burst you can drop it into boiling water to release its energy quickly.

Many Witches keep their god/ess figures on an altar. They meditate for a few minutes each day at the altar to gain a substantial amount of new energy.

Capability	God/ess	Statuette	Psychostore
Gives vitality	Mars	Warrior	Red candle
Removes guilt	Leo	Lion	Ho Tei
Makes more loving	Venus	Lovely lady	Green candle
Improves creativity	Odin	Lusty young man	Candle like a phallus
Increases wealth	Gaea	Old woman	Gold coin
Protects	Jehovah	Fierce old man	Black obsidian
Improves business	Michael	Scholar	Textbook

TABLE VIII–2
Hearth God/esses and Psychostores

SUMMARY

We have described ways to bring your psychic energy into balance with your physical and mental energy, and ways to charge and use your psychostores. Living, growing plants are an immediate source of energy, as are crystals.

In today's climate of medical uncertainty, many people who anticipate elective surgery bank their own blood in preparation. They know that their blood contains no surprises—that it can safely be returned to their own bodies without fear that unsuspected diseases come with it, as they might with blood donated by some stranger. Exactly the same thinking governs the use of hearth gods. You store your own energy in them and draw on it later for yourself or for use in your rituals.

The Domain
of the Witch

YOUR HOME'S FORCES

In this chapter we will talk about your own environment and suggest methods to make your dwelling serene and welcoming. As you will see, the methods we suggest will also help you sell your home—when you're ready—for far more than its apparent market value. Finally, there are guidelines on setting up your ritual space.

WALLS HAVE FEELINGS, TOO

Psychometry is the science of reading traces of the Force—the "vibes"—that have been impressed either deliberately or accidentally on objects and places. Police forces around the world use psychics or Witches in reading crime scenes to give them leads on suspects. Perhaps the most famous such case is the one that the media called "The Boston Strangler." In it, famed psychic Peter Hurkos played a major role.

You already know that you can store your innate energy by holding an object between your hands and willing your power into it, as when you make a stone god/ess. Few people realize that the Force can also be impressed into walls, furniture, objects, and carpets within a room. Things have their own force fields that they have developed over their history; and if a room is to feel serene, those emanations must be balanced within the room.

Apart from such impressed forces, natural flows of energy occur along rivers, geological fault lines, and artificial roads. People the world over have "known" about these energies since time immemorial. In selecting places to live—and more important, in placing and building their temples—they have made use of them. In the west, builders used *geomancy* in their construction. In the far east, *feng shui* procedures keep buildings in harmony with their environment. The Chinese art of feng shui[1] and the western art of geomancy deal with these interactions that both create and interfere with energy flows. Recently workers have synthesized much Chinese knowledge with the Witch's skills in a new approach called *neogeomancy.*[2]

We all have to live and work somewhere, and we all know that certain places feel right and good whereas others turn us off with their bad, negative feelings. You may not have a lot of choice about the area in which you live; if that is true, neogeomancy can make great improvements in your domain.

In summary, therefore, you will want to consider five factors in making any domain serene. They are shown in the pentagram of Figure IX-1:

1. The impressed leftover thoughts and emotions of past inhabitants of the space

2. The balance of forces emanating from objects in the space

3. The possibility of trapped spirits (ghosts) in an area

4. The relationship between your domain and surrounding terrain—fault lines, rivers, power lines, and roads; most important, the orientation of rooms relative to north

5. Your relationship to the domain

These forces can be the source of positive or negative feelings; and, of course, they overlap one another. Some people spend thousands of dollars balancing objects in a room, but fail to consider leftover emotions or the possibility of trapped spirits. As a budding Witch now conscious of the major forces involved, you want to consider all of them.

---

[1] T. Raphael Simons, *Feng Shui Step by Step* (New York: Three Rivers Press, 1996).

[2] *Neo:* new, *geo:* the earth, *mancy:* magic.

FIGURE IX–1
Your Pentagram of Room Balance

DONNA'S $100,000 HOME-IMPROVEMENT PLAN

Donna E lived in Baltimore. When her marriage ended, she was left with a dilapidated house, a baby, and no job. To keep food on the table, she got a second mortgage on the house; then she set about improving the property. Despite the advice of fashionable shelter magazines, she didn't spend a fortune on the kitchen or on enhancing curb appeal; instead, she went through the house with some textbooks on feng shui and adjusted it so that it "felt" attractive, felt like a place where anyone would like to live. An important part of this process was the de-cluttering of every room and the removal of all objects that reminded her of fights with her ex-husband.

Now Donna is a Witch, fully conscious of the Force. She washed down the walls with hot salted water and had all her curtains and slipcovers cleaned twice; she also threw out the old carpets and replaced them with throw rugs. Donna also learned from a friend that in selling a house she should be selling a lifestyle, not bricks and mortar. So just before she listed the house for sale, she threw a party as upscale as she could manage. Then she invited her new boyfriend to an orgiastic weekend in the master bedroom. After the brokers' viewing day, it sold so quickly that she had to scramble to find another place to live. It felt great in the living room and sexy in the bedroom, so why wouldn't it sell?

Her real estate agent showed her another property in the same area that, as she said, needed a fixer-upper's touch. This property was available through the city for back taxes. Donna bought it with almost no down payment and in less than three months sold it at over $100,000 profit. The work she did on the property was minimal—mostly cleaning, painting, flowers, some rearrangement of the rooms and their functions, and impressing the right forces on the rooms. Her approach emphasized whatever improvements she could effect through her own labor, instead of relying on cosmetic big-ticket improvements such as new bathrooms and kitchens. She groomed up the yard; she made sure that every square inch of the interior was sparkling clean—and that it felt and smelled right.

Today Donna is still buying and selling properties. To master all the intimidating jargon involved, she earned her real estate license. She plunged into the field in earnest, though without the sense of urgency that she used to have. She has a comfortable income, both from her own property sales and from her work with other brokers in improving properties on the market so they will sell more readily.

This latter talent is a two-edged sword. Brokers have learned that the sellers of property often take them off the market as soon as Donna fixes them up! Of the first five properties she worked on for other brokers, the owners of three decided they didn't want to move—their houses now felt serene and content, more "homey" than ever before. Donna has begun to charge by the hour for her consulting work on making a house into a home, instead of relying on split commissions.

DONNA'S FIX-IT-UP METHODS

When a Witch such as Donna decides she is going to fix things in a house, the first thing she does is "feel" the emotions in each room; that is, she psychometrizes it. Then she channels in each individual room. By using all her senses in that psychometrizing and channeling,[3] she detects the areas that may feel negative or positive. Then she tries to remove everything that feels negative. If there are ghosts, she tries to get them to move on by filling their requests—helping them wrap up their unfinished business. Most rooms in

---

[3] See Appendix 1.

American homes contain memorabilia of one kind or another, and every single one of those souvenirs is loaded with Force, either positive or negative. So you remove all the negatives. If you cannot bear to give some of them up, lock them in a metal drum in the basement.

A big problem in many rooms is the carpet. Carpeting absorbs vibrations as if it were just one big flat sponge. From its very nature of having a lot of end fibers and a rough surface, it is a natural psychic accumulator. If you can afford it, the best approach in any room is to strip out the carpet. Replace it with smooth polished wood and an occasional throw-rug that you can take outdoors to shake or send to the cleaners.

Many carpets have been laid down over subfloors of perfectly presentable wood. Those floors may need only a simple refinishing. If not, ask your dealer about new flooring to apply over an inferior subfloor. Putting down wood parquet tiles is often less expensive than installing new carpet and underlayment. When you have a nice polished wood floor, the occasional stripping and repolish will remove any negative vibrations that have come in; and keeping the center of such a floor bare gives a great feeling of spaciousness. In neogeomantic terms you are expanding the center, the earthy influence.

If you can do just one thing in fixing a house to be sold, get rid of the carpets. That's one of the things Donna did, though her impressing of forces on the rooms was more dramatic; and it's the practice that made her wealthy. If she had pursued it more actively, it could well have made her a literal fortune.

LET THE WALLS SPEAK

Once the house is balanced, it's time to add that psychic blast that will turn it into a real home. Each major room in a house has its specific tuning requirements. Typical tuning keys are shown in Table IX-1.

If you list your home for sale, use the table to reinforce the feelings in each room on the day before the brokers' walk-through. Bake bread in the kitchen; arrange a fresh bouquet of golden chrysanthemums in the living room; have sex in the master bedroom; burn a lavender candle in the child's room; burn sandalwood incense in the bathroom.

Room	Basic Force	Color	Scent	Thought
Kitchen	Fire	Brown	Baking Bread	Good Food
Living Room	Earth	Gold	Chrysanthemum	Fun
Master Bedroom	Water with a Little Fire	Emerald and Red	Poinsettia or Geranium	Lust
Child's Bedroom	Metal	Blue/Pink	Lavender	Comfort
Bathroom	Water	Blue/Green	Sandalwood	Clean

TABLE IX–1
Characteristics of Rooms

BALANCING THE FORCES IN A ROOM

Many rooms have a single dominant element. A large fireplace, an armoire, a big dark couch can appear very heavy and visually tip the room to one side. In the rooms of readers, the bookcases can be almost overwhelming. In the rooms of those with other interests, a big entertainment center or wall of electronics focuses everyone's attention. In China, since living space is in extremely short supply, rooms tend to be small and very cluttered with family memorabilia. All these things put out their own psychic emanations.

When people redecorate, their individual preferences often take one of the two most popular paths, as do our own at home. Yvonne's path is to strip the room empty and paint every surface in a pale sunlight yellow or in white. Gavin's path is simply to let the clutter accumulate and balance itself out. Such preferences can lead to interesting decor.

YOUR CIRCLE OF BALANCE

When you drive along a road, you want the wheels to be smooth and regular; otherwise, the car will bump and vibrate. In the same way, when you are balancing energies in a living space, you think of a symmetrical circle, not one that is lopsided or that has jagged parts. In Figure IX-2 various energies are assigned their respective places around the perimeter of the circle. The five principal elements are

Air, Fire, Metal,[4] Water, and Earth. Air dwells in the east, Fire in the south, Metal in the west, and Water at the top in the north. At the center is Earth. These directions are not arbitrary or whimsical; they correlate with where you live. For instance, if you live in eastern United States, Water energy is to your east, Fire energy to the south, Air energy to the west, and Craftsman energy to the north. Figure IX-3 shows these changes. When you think about it, this makes sense. If you live in the east, the Waters of the Atlantic Ocean are to your east; the Fire of the noonday sun is to your south; prevailing weather patterns bring Air mainly from the west; and the big industrial Craftsman cities of the rust belt are to your north. Earth is below you.

On the west coast of the United States, Water would move to the western side of the circle; Air to the north; Craft to the east. Fire would remain in the south.

On the East Coast the rooms in an ideal house will follow the pattern of the appropriate circle, as shown in Figure IX-4.

However, most houses are not built like that, so think about reassigning the function of respective rooms; or introducing other energies into rooms. It's easy enough to introduce new energies into the appropriate rooms through such things as

1. Fountains for Water, and blue-green paint

2. Candles for Fire, and red paint

3. Potted plants for Earth, and cream paint

4. Metal sculptures for Metal, and silver paint

5. Fans for Air, and white/green paint

Is there a bedroom to the north? Bring some Water energy in, maybe by adding a little fountain, and perhaps a touch of fire energy by burning red candles. In effect this will subdue the craftsman energy and increase the loving and sexual energy of the room. Once you have gone through the house and fixed the big picture, you can go into each room and, knowing the directions, fine-tune the balance of each individual room. If you have a huge area of books, hide some of them behind sliding doors. Is there a massive electronics center? Install a heavy curtain in front of it; or, as some suggest, put it under wraps with a carpet, or in an entertainment center with doors. Such moves will take the bumps out of the wheel.

---

[4] Metal correlates with craftsmen and electric/electronic appliances.

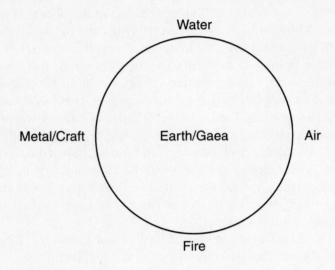

FIGURE IX–2
Your Circle of Balance

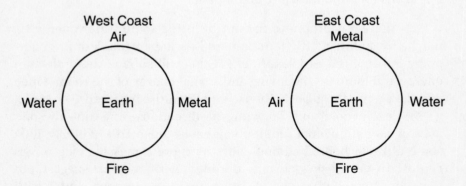

FIGURE IX–3
Circles of Balance for East and West Coasts

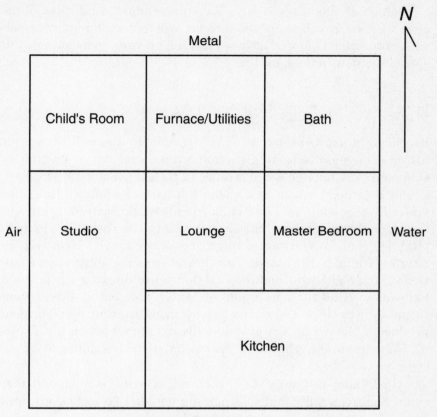

FIGURE IX–4
Ideal Layout for a House on the East Coast

Perhaps you have a room with absolutely no Water energy. Again, a small fountain or an aquarium will lead to a better balance. If you absolutely cannot have a bare floor to bring in Gaea Earth energy, bring in some clay pots containing sand and maybe a few little desert plants or succulents. In any case, you can work toward balance by repainting the walls or even just the trim.

If something in the room particularly reminds you of a very negative episode, get rid of it. Yes, I know it's Aunt Ethel's favorite and she'll be very upset when she misses it—but in an unbalanced environment, your life will continuously lack harmony.

Much of this work is simple common sense. And most of us, after we have psychometrized a room, will *feel* its bumps of imbalance. You will be amazed at how cleaning up your environment will give you a new outlook on life.

BEN AND THE FRIENDLY SPIRIT

Ben lived in a small town in West Virginia. He was well known for his unwillingness to leave his home, even to eat out or go grocery shopping. Any time he could arrange it, he had friends shop for him. Locals regarded his trait as a quaint but harmless foible. "He's born under Cancer, after all," his Witch friends would say indulgently.

One day Ben broke his pelvis and had to be rushed to the hospital. He sent for Gavin and in great secrecy asked Gavin to look after his friend in the house. The "friend" was the spirit of an affectionate little girl who had died in the house decades earlier, and Ben was worried that she would be lonely and scared. Gavin went to the house. He was expecting some manifestation that Ben had produced. Instead he was able actually to contact a little girl's spirit. She was much relieved to learn that Ben was going to be all right.

In talking to Ginny, as she called herself, Gavin found that some cretinous bully had told her she couldn't go to heaven until she had learned her multiplication tables all the way up to twelve times twelve.

Gavin knew that she could and should go on, but hesitated to help her because of Ben's love. Anyway, he discussed it with Ben and got his approval for a friendly exorcism. This meant telling Ginny to try going on, and suggesting ways to do it. She did, and promptly left to a higher plane. Ben was happy for her, and is no longer so housebound. He was fortunate, because often spirits become malevolent when they feel trapped.

CONTACTING SPIRIT PRESENCES

Channeling, channeling, and yet more channeling *with the appropriate protection* will get you into contact with spirit presences in a house. In most cases they haven't progressed because they:

1. Have unfinished business on this plane.

2. Have been told that they can't go on, for whatever reason.

3. Don't realize they are "dead."

Most of these spirits will depart when the psychic worker reasons with them. Occasionally, though, workers will need to do a house-cleansing ritual (see Chapter XI).

A spirit that is friendly and contented will impart a good feeling to its house. Many property owners do not necessarily want such a spirit removed. It lends a certain cachet to the property. Many Witches spend a great deal of time releasing trapped spirits, especially around graveyards and churches or battlefields.

When you channel in homes, if you find trapped spirits, you and the homeowner will want to decide on the course of action that is most beneficial to the spirit. It is ethical to encourage the homeowner to work for the spirit's release and progression. Whatever you do, do not totally banish a trapped spirit without assigning it some appropriate new home.

PREPARING FOR YOUR MAGICAL LIFE

Latest estimates from the Baptist Church say that there are over a half-million Witches in the nation. We live unsuspected in every neighborhood of the land. If you drive down a residential street or walk by a block of apartments, you can be sure that a Witch lives in at least one of them. Yet from the exterior you may not be able to tell at first glance that this is a Witch's abode. In fact those who practice this way of spirituality might tell you that you often *can* identify a Witch's house because it may look a little less compulsively tended than its neighbors and there will be an extensive garden in the rear—or at least window boxes containing herbs.

Some differences may be apparent indoors as well. Often there will be a lot of books lying around, and it may even (perish the thought!) be untidy and dusty. One room will be quietly off limits altogether to the casual visitor, and when you look behind that closed door you might find an altar with candles burning and signs, in an otherwise plain room, that circles have been cast on the floor. This will be the Witch's ritual room—her studio or her worksite.

At first, it may seem incongruous, but many non-Witch homes also contain altars or ritual shrines to one deity or another. Setting aside an entire room in today's space-starved cities may seem like an awful lot to give up for a way of life; but having that sanctuary where the modern world does not intrude is as essential to the dedicated Witch as food itself. The artist has her studio; the chef has his specially fitted kitchen; the Witch has her retreat.

Many Witches have to make do with nothing more than a closet for their magical space. Some of us use patios; others use a shed in the backyard. So we might say that the first requirement for embarking on a serious study of the Craft and making things happen is to find a space that you can confidently regard as your very own.

MACK AND WENDY RECLAIM AN OLD HOUSE

Mack and Wendy met in the workplace and found that they shared an interest in "occult" matters. When they first met, each occupied a single apartment. It rapidly became apparent that they wanted to combine their households; and even though Wendy's dog didn't do too well with Mack's cat, they all moved into a larger apartment together.

The first ritual they tried in their new place was an attempt to heal Wendy's mother. Both had done spell-work before; but this spell seemed to have no effect, so they knew they had to channel to learn what might be the cause of their "failure." When they began to channel they went through the usual stages of worrying about day-to-day problems in their relationship, but after a couple of weeks this settled down. Yet still they got nothing. Meanwhile Wendy's mother grew weaker. They invited the Frosts to their apartment. When we sat in their living room, it was immediately apparent that the *psychic noise* was horrendous. The previous occupants had been a very quarrelsome couple, and remnants of their ill temper were imbedded in the room. To make matters worse, the building was heavily framed in steel—and a major high-voltage power line ran nearby.

We told them the news; to wit, that in order to clean up the apartment psychically all the walls would have to be stripped and painted, and the carpet taken up and cleaned at least twice, or replaced. Even then, because of the building's steel frame and the adjacent power line, we could not guarantee that their results in ritual work would be much improved; although we could tell them that their meditative efforts would bring better results. Since they lived only a couple of miles from us, we suggested that they come for a few nights and channel with us in the enclosed patio we had just built.

Their results in meditation were immediate and dramatic. They were guided to an old property in a town nearby and told to repeat the healing procedure for Wendy's mother on our patio. The healing ritual they did on our patio worked in a powerful way. When they finally found the owner of that house, the house could be had rent-free in exchange for hard work and some painting. They fell in love with the old house and finally arranged to buy it on a private mortgage. When all this came true, they found themselves with a whole large ritual room on the top floor that was psychically quiet. Meditating in that room was comfortable and productive. They had no need to make any changes in the room to make it "work" for them. Over time, though, they have repainted it and made it more comfortable.

Giving up apartment-style living for home ownership was a major step for Wendy and Mack, especially since the house obviously needed quite a little renovation; but the rewards were outstanding. Not only do they now have over four thousand square feet of living space; their mortgage is the envy of all their friends who, ironically, live in no better housing.

Many Witches are recyclers and fixer-uppers. Members of the Craft are probably the most ecologically-minded group of people on the planet. They can't stand the waste and the truckloads of perfectly good materials going into landfills as perfectly good older homes get destroyed to make new upscale developments. Old homes in an older, settled part of town often become available for a comparatively low price. Most of these are more strongly built than modern "boxes of ticky-tacky." Yes, they need insulation. Yes, they need a new furnace or wiring or windows or whatever. So, you spend $25,000 or so that you saved in purchase price on materials, and fix it up yourself. Your reward will be low monthly bills and lots of square footage of living space, as well as a neighborhood of mature trees and settled population.

YOUR OWN MAGICAL ROOM

Whether you want to become a full-fledged Witch, magician, or occultist, or none of the above, still it really is essential to have a space that you can call your very own, that is never invaded by aggression or other negative thoughts; a space where unauthorized persons will not enter. In most houses you can find such a space— perhaps a basement or an unused attic space that can be converted. You don't even necessarily need full-height standing room because much of the time you will be sitting. When you think you have identified such a space, the first thing to do is to psychometrize the space and then do at least a week's worth of channeling in that space. You may receive, as we did at Wendy and Mack's, many disjointed or negative impressions. This is a sure sign that the space needs to be psychically cleansed. If the room has an old carpet, we recommend again that you strip that out and if possible stay with a bare wooden floor, maybe with a throw rug to break it up.

If the walls are papered, strip the paper off. Do not install new paper over old, and do not paint over old paper that inevitably carries imbedded impressions. New paper or paint over old will not prevent the impressions coming through. To clean paint of psychic impressions, use a scrub-down of hot salted water. Add one pound of salt to a gallon of water and use it as hot as your hands can stand. Or you can rent a steamer designed to remove old wallpaper, and go over the paint inch by inch with that. The hot steam will also remove most psychic impressions from old paint. When you have psychically cleansed the painted walls, you can repaint the room.

Do not use the room for your computer or for other electronics. Make sure there is no heavy electrical cabling running along the floorboards. Try not to bring into the room anything that would disturb its serenity. Books, newspapers, people, animal products such as bone or horn, can all impress their negative energies into the room. If unavoidably something negative happens in the room, you will have to start cleansing again, from square one. If you absolutely must do a spell in that room today, you should drape the walls with fabric in the appropriate color; then when the spell is complete, have that fabric cleaned twice.

If your channeling reveals a trapped spirit, check to ascertain whether the whole house needs cleansing.

DECIDING ON YOUR PRIORITIES

The quality of your life depends on many things. In today's world saturated with advertising, you may feel that your happiness depends on the number of possessions you can surround yourself with, and that your family's happiness depends on the number of toys they own (however each member perceives his or her playthings). The kids want toys and videos to go with the latest rage, whether it be Pokemon or Morphin, Power Rangers or Ninja Turtles or Dungeons and Dracula Dinosaurs or whatever else the hucksters can think up. You are told from every side that you should drive a sport/utility vehicle because, the ads tell you, the kids get a better view of the world and are safer when they ride in such transportation. The advertisers would have you believe that love and happiness are intimately connected with money and with inventory. Until very recently, college counselors fought a constant battle with students over which courses they should take. Students demanded courses that would put them into high-paying, fast-track computer or engineering careers. The counselors could tell from their psychological test scores that this would be disastrous for many of them. Recently a counselor friend told us that finally students are getting smarter and are looking at quality of life, not just at the paycheck.

When you start your magical life, you will find many of your priorities shifting. You will become far less dependent on material things—that inventory—for happiness and more concerned with quality of life, with quality time for learning and for channeling, and with living respectfully on the Earth.

JANICE HAPPILY QUITS HER JOB

Janice W was a computer programmer living the good life on Mercer Island, a suburb of Seattle, Washington. She was a member of what is often called the Mercer Island software subculture. She worked long hours and thought she enjoyed her work even though it meant driving the causeway to the island in the middle of the night or before dawn. Occasionally she stopped on her way home to decompress and have a drink in one of the bars just off the island. Gradually this became something to look forward to, and she spent longer and longer in the bars and less and less time at home with her husband, Stu. Inevitably their life together waned and finally flickered out. Stu sued for divorce. Janice sank into clinical depression.

Eventually the plant nurse persuaded her to visit a doctor. This began as a psychological interview, but the doctor was sharp enough to notice that there was more to Janice's lethargy than simple depression. When a cutting-edge Buck-You-Uppo drug didn't work, he sent her for a full physical checkup. It revealed leukemia. The experts predicted that she had a very limited time to live and that she should enjoy herself while she could. When she told Stu this, it hit him hard. He withdrew his divorce petition. Janice quit work and started living the lifestyle of a homemaker. Stu now took on full responsibility for the almost overwhelming payments on the house, the two cars, and the boat, indeed the whole Mercer Island lifestyle. Soon he in turn began to stop at the bars on his way home. In a moment of epiphany, Janice realized that the whole scenario was about to start again, though this time it was Stu's turn to be overworked.

About this time Janice found our web page through the Internet and asked for a tarot reading. The news was extremely negative. All the cards showed that Janice's, and now Stu's, continual crossing of water would eventually lead to disaster. In a follow-up reading, when Janice asked what would happen if Stu gave up his job, too, the cards showed great monetary loss and bankruptcy—but predicted a long and happy life for both of them.

Janice started channeling. She channeled a healing ritual for herself—and an Internet startup idea on computer programming that would let her stay home. Within six months she needed help with her website, so Stu quit his job, too. They quickly realized that the Mercer Island lifestyle was sucking them dry financially. They moved back to the mainland, into the Seattle suburb of Kirkwood. Happy to say, they are both still alive and well. Their lifestyle has shifted from power suits and briefcases to tee shirts and sandals.

THE GAEA CONNECTION

It is rightly said that all competent Witches work in their own locale, for within that locale they are familiar with the feelings and currents of power that can work for (and against!) them.

Within every environment there are certain natural earth currents. The most powerful is the Earth's own magnetic field. Interacting with the magnetic field are the forces, called *chi* in the east and power in the west, that flow along the surface of the planet. These forces are influenced by such things as the planet(s); local disturbances within the field such as roads, railroad tracks, dams, fault lines, power lines; magnetic disturbances coming from cabling in your house; and a thousand other manmade and natural barriers to, and conductors of, the flow.

People who deal in buying and selling land have one overriding mantra: The three top selling factors for a property are Location, Location, Location. This thinking is equally valid for locating a house relative to surrounding force lines. Here are some characteristic traits of the Force:

1. The Force likes to travel in straight lines.

2. It tends to flow downhill to water.

3. It can be reflected by mirrors and by living plants.

4. It flows along artificial ley lines.

5. Rivers generate both positive and negative Force.

Let us look at these characteristics one at a time.

1. *Straight lines*—If the front door of your dwelling aligns with its back door (a "shotgun" house because a bullet fired at the front door goes right out the back), the Force will flow straight through, not stopping, and will suck all the psychic energy out.

2. *Flowing downhill*—Inside the house, force will be generated by, and will stay near, fountains and aquariums. If you leave the toilet lid up, it will flow down the toilet every time you flush (really!).

3. *Reflection by mirrors and living plants*—In a shotgun house, you can prevent a complete draining of chi if you mount a large mirror in its path or arrange a screen of living plants to interrupt the flow.

4. *Artificial ley lines*—If the house faces directly onto a road, the "river" of traffic on the road will draw energy out of the house.

Put a hedge of living plants before the front door, and replace any straight path between street and front door with a curving path. Power lines, especially major cross-country ones, are death, both to the Force and to channeling. Do your best to live well away from them.

5. *Rivers*—As you learned in Chapter III, the west bank of a south-flowing river is a place of positive force; likewise, the north bank of an east-flowing river. Living between two rivers leads to very high diversified energy, like that in New York City. Living in the junction between two rivers causes the most negativity and depression.

SUMMARY

In any dwelling, you can get rid of the negativity and enhance positive forces by using the techniques we describe. The enhanced serenity these steps afford is well worth the relatively minor one-time effort and the cost involved.

Occasionally you will find spirits living with you. As a general rule, you should encourage them to progress. If they won't go, you will have to clean them out.

There are things you can do to balance the psychic energies within a dwelling and within individual rooms. Not all dwellings are ideally situated (on a hillside above flowing water) as ours is; however, there are things you can do with mirrors and hedges to improve a dwelling's retention of energy. Remember: High levels of energy are vitally important to the effective working of spells. To use your magical room for spell-work, drape it.

Foretelling Your Future

THE WITCH'S MAGICAL GUIDANCE

Improving your future may not need all the spells in the world. That future may be bright even though it looks bleak from today's perspective. You need to know what it looks like before you set out to change it; in other words, don't fix something that isn't broken. This means, invest some of your efforts in expanding your sense of prophecy. At the dawn of recorded history, prophets and soothsayers were already working to obtain some view—even just an inkling—of future events. Current methods can work for you as well as they did for earlier travelers on the Path. Some people scoff at the idea that the future is predictable; but certainly in such simple matters as the weather, prediction is possible—indeed, necessary. Animals in the wild know when the weather is going to change, one or two days ahead of the actual fact. Animals and forecasters base their short-range predictions on atmospheric changes detectable to those who feel sensitive. The longer-range predictions such as those surrounding the Kennedy assassinations are truly remarkable; and when a Witch works one on one with a querent/seeker, the results are often more than 75 percent accurate.

In the Frost household Gavin is the predictor. Letter after letter says, "His tarot reading was accurate. I wish I had taken more precautions. Then I could have handled the situation more easily." We have to warn you, though, that predicting for yourself often does not work. Somehow the conscious mind gets in the way of those subtle unconscious signals. In channeling you can often get clues to future events, and you will find that getting answers for other people is a lot easier than getting them for yourself.

MOTHER SHIPTON AND THE CARDINAL

Mother Shipton and her humble carpenter husband dwelt at Knaresborough in Yorkshire, England, late in the 1400s. She got into difficulty with the Church, especially with Cardinal Wolsey, whose death she predicted. The great Cardinal sent the Duke of Suffolk, Lord Percy, and Lord Darey to question her. They got her story out of her and told her that when the Cardinal came he would have her burned as a witch. Hearing this, she threw her linen scarf into the fire. "If this burn, so shall I!"[1] When the scarf was retrieved, it was not even singed. Mother Shipton was not burned; she lived to a ripe old age—while the great Cardinal died as she had foretold.

Mother Shipton's rhyming prophecies were considered almost folk tales, entertaining but insignificant. Yet when read today, they present a stunningly accurate glimpse of what the late 20th century would be like.

> *Carriages without horses shall go*
> *And accidents fill the world with woe.*
> *Around the earth thoughts shall fly,*
> *In the twinkling of an eye.*
> *Through deepest hills men shall ride*
> *And no horse or ass be by their side.*
> *Under water men shall walk*
> *Shall ride and sleep and talk.*
> *In the air men shall be seen*
> *In white and black, and also green.*
> *And in those wondrous far-off days*
> *The women shall adopt a craze*
> *To dress like men and trousers wear,*
> *And cut off all their locks of hair.*[2]

---

[1] Justine Glass, *They Foresaw the Future* (New York: Putnam, 1969).

[2] In those times "proper" women wore long hair and long skirts. Anything else was unthinkable.

YOUR AUTOSCOPE: GATEWAY TO PROPHECY

Mother Shipton gazed into the fire to do her prophecy. Nostradamus looked at the smoke rising from his tripod brazier. Many predictors use such things as tarot cards or crystal balls. Any such device occupies the conscious mind with the view while the unconscious mind goes free to find the information you need. The more complex the autoscope, the more busy-work the conscious mind is kept doing, the better is the result. That is why the complex symbology of the tarot cards works so well; you can see things in the patterns.[3] Here, then, is the basis for making your personal choice of autoscope. It must keep the conscious mind preoccupied to let signals from the unconscious mind come through.

In considering how prediction works, consider the way the lower levels of the mind communicate with the conscious level. Interpretation of a picture or a shape vaguely seen while scrying, or even a series of numerological calculations (in which you might unconsciously make errors) allow an almost direct communication. In the more mechanistic techniques, such as the pendulum or the casting of the I Ching with coins, the power of the unconscious may affect the swing of the pendulum and the fall of the coins. Russian work shows that mind power can physically move weights up to $2\frac{1}{2}$ pounds; and Dr. Rhine demonstrated that the mind can influence the fall of dice. If mind power can affect physical objects and their movements, you must arrange your readings to let the unconscious minds of querent and reader have full play.

Bringing the information you have gathered from the unconscious, and making it a part of your prophecy, happens through the *consciousness connection.* You get data both psychically and mundanely; you filter the data; then you use them psychically (influencing the dice) or mundanely to give your prophecy. Figure X-1 gives you some idea of the process. You, the reader, face a subject, the querent. You use your developed psychic ability to help the querent. The present-world data that you receive come in two forms:

---

[3] As usual, *see* includes "hunches," hearing, scent, and the rest of the avenues through which you can receive impressions.

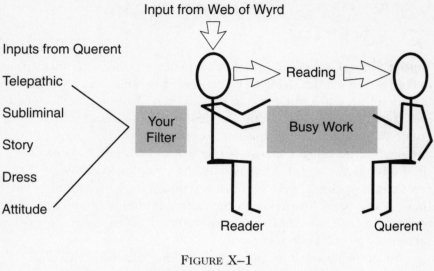

FIGURE X–1
The Reading Process

1. The data that the querent gives you mundanely and directly, both verbally and in subliminal body language that accompanies the verbal input. These data are always suspect; for only a rare querent will tell the whole story up front.

2. The telepathic data picked up by your psychic sense. Often these data will not be confined to input directly from the querent; they may include input from psychic keys the querent has brought to the reading pertaining to other people involved.

ZENOBIA QUITS

Zenobia C worked as an executive secretary in a division of a major electronics firm in Orange County, California. She practiced Spiritualism and regularly attended meetings of a Spiritualist group in Santa Ana. One night during their dark sitting (seance), a voice told her to quit her job. Now although she believed in Spiritualism and in the results of dark sittings, she could hardly just up and quit her well-paid job on the authority of a disembodied voice. Another attendee was surprised, too, by what the voice had told Zenobia. She referred Zenobia to a psychic who had been successful for her. That's exactly what Zenobia did—she sought a second opinion.

The psychic also told her that she must quit her job—if possible, that very day. Well, that was not possible. Zenobia knew in the real world that if she didn't give proper notice, she would never get another good job. What she really wanted was to get a transfer within the firm to preserve her seniority.

Fortunately she heard about an opening in another department that would be a promotion. She applied for the job and moved to the new department. Imagine her surprise when the same voice came through the next month and said, "Zenobia, quit your job." Again she went to the psychic and again the psychic said, "Yes, you must quit—and it looks as if you must leave the company altogether."

This time Zenobia did quit. She moved to a small downtown firm that supplied parts to her former employer. Yet again the voice said, "Zenobia, quit your job" and a third time the psychic confirmed it; but this time with Zenobia's persistent questioning it became apparent that she should move to an entirely different industry. One more time she quit, this time taking quite a pay cut. In the following months her first electronics firm laid off more than one hundred thousand employees, and the second actually went bankrupt when its contracts were canceled.

Zenobia still has the position that she found after her three moves. She looks back on that time with amusement and gratitude. Unlike most of her fellow workers, she did not have to endure the trauma of moving her household. Nor did she suffer the emotional turmoil of a pink-slip layoff.

IN YOUR OWN HEAD

It is often said that your brain is the most under-used organ in your body. You very rarely use its full capacity. Some psychologists and researchers say that in everyday use we employ less than a quarter of our full potential. On the mundane level, sensory inputs bombard you from all directions; and your mind unconsciously files them away, calling on them only in such things as flashes of inspiration and in dreams.

One illustration sums up much of this: In a Washington hotel an elderly gentleman rode the elevator to the fifth floor. After he completed his business, he summoned the elevator to go down again. When it arrived, the three passengers already in it looked to him like skeletons. He was so stunned that he waved the elevator on. It crashed and the passengers were killed.

This was probably not a future psychic insight. Instead, when he rode up he unconsciously detected something amiss. The awareness came through to his conscious mind as the vision of three skeletons.

Thus, most of the information you need to prophesy mundane events such as a traffic accident or a company going bankrupt is already in your head. All you need is a way to pull it out. Gavin likes the tarot because of its complex pictograms. Yvonne likes Norse runes because of their simplicity and clear statements. Investigate the various traditional autoscopes and anything else that you think might work for you. Find the system(s) that suit your personality and your major psychic receiving sense. In an earlier book we briefly described the following systems of prediction:[4]

The pendulum	I Ching
Numerology	Tarot
Domino divination	Palmistry
Dice divination	Scrying
Astrology	Dream analysis

Please investigate several before you decide which you favor. Your principal answers come through channeling, of course, but occasionally to reinforce those answers you need to use an autoscope.

OMENS AND PORTENTS IN YOUR LIFE

Men still enjoy making jokes about women's intuition. Well, here's a bulletin: Men have intuition, too. In a simple example, capable drivers often seem able to predict the craziness of other drivers. They pick up the little signals that say the driver ahead of them is under the influence, asleep at the wheel, or just a plain bad driver. Signals may be very subtle, sometimes so subliminal that the alerted driver can't really pin down where they come from.

If you get a "feeling" that something is wrong—*honor* the feeling. All too often people disregard a feeling or deny it because it "isn't realistic," or it's "too subjective." In case after case of violence—domestic, in schools, and in the work place—when investigators closely question associates and witnesses, they find that there *were* signals, that people *were* worried. Yet they suppressed

---

4 G. & Y. Frost, *The Prophet's Bible* (York Beach, ME: Samuel Weiser, Inc., 1991).

their instincts. They thought that person who finally came off the spool was "too nice" to do harm.

The Unabomber case illustrates this perfectly.[5] When one of his bombs arrived at the California Forestry Association, it turned out to be wrongly addressed, to a *former* president of the Association. The new president decided to open the package, but his assistant manager, a Mr. Taylor, said (in words he will always remember), "If you're going to open that bomb, I'm going back to my office." Taylor had hardly reached his office when the bomb exploded.

In a second incident, Mr. and Mrs. Mosser arrived at home to find an unexpected package with no return address. He asked her what she bought him. She replied the package was not her doing, that she had bought nothing. His last words were, "Well, I'll open this bomb you bought me anyway."

What might be called black humor is often a sure sign of intuition at work. In a world such as today's, you *must* pay attention to those intuitive feelings. In literally thousands of cases, if people had followed their intuition, lives would have been saved.

YOUR GUIDE TO INTUITIVE FEELINGS

Fifteen minutes a day. That's what you need to set aside if you are to do adequate channeling. It pays you to heed your intuitive insights. In one case, the doctor worked at the city's top hospital, but the mother still didn't want him to operate on her child. She kept quiet, and the child died.[6] The mother had let her conscious mind and social training override her intuitive feelings. It wouldn't have been "nice" to question the competence of the doctor and the hospital.

Analysts now call these intuitive feelings PINs or *Pre-Incident Indicators*. They know that such feelings come in several forms. In the two Unabomber cases we have quoted, they were manifested as black humor. These happen every day—and they've happened in your life. "Don't crash the car tonight." "Don't get picked up for speeding." Guess what!

Some other forms in which intuitive messages come through are listed in Table X-1.

---

[5] G. de Becker, *The Gift of Fear* (Boston: Little Brown, 1997). This is a book *everyone* should read!

[6] An actual case.

Feeling	How It Manifests
Black humor	Verbal
Fear/apprehension	Any sense[7]
Anxiety/gut feelings	Stomach upset
Hunches	Any sense
Persistent nagging thoughts	Interrupted thought patterns
Hesitation	Physical stopping before taking a step

TABLE X–1
Pre-Incident Intuitive Feelings

MEN, WOMEN, AND DANGER

Men and women have entirely different attitudes about going across that dark parking lot to their car or down that dark alley to the subway station. A man with a group of his buddies fears that his friends will laugh at him if he tells them he feels uneasy, so he looks at the darkened area and tells himself, "It isn't far, and I'm the very essence of John Wayne." He puts himself at risk—and he gets mugged.

A woman looking at a dark area worries not about the opinion of her friends but very simply whether she's going to get killed—or, even worse, raped and killed. She is right to be wary. Still, time and time again she takes the risk—because her significant other would be impatient if she's late, or the kids are waiting, or for some other reason that surely is of less importance than her very life.

---

[7] *All senses* means that it comes through in your dominant mode as a picture, a sound, an odor, a taste, or an emotional feeling.

PHYLLIS AND THE HIT MAN

Phyllis is a Witch, trained and initiated. Homeward bound on a flight from New York to Cleveland, she experienced an incident. This is what she wrote us:

> I was so thankful that I listened to my intuition the other day. I was on a plane in the window seat in coach, and a really attractive guy sat down next to me. As soon as he sat down I had horrible shivers about him. Still he seemed very pleasant. When the drinks came around he inadvertently spilled mine on himself as he passed it to me. Even though I said I didn't want another drink, he insisted that the stewardess get me one. Of course this started the conversation.
>
> I have to tell you my antennae were itchy and the shivers hadn't gone away—but still he seemed so pleasant. He admired my makeup, which I thought was a little weird but still quite flattering. He asked me what I did. I told him I was a paralegal. "When will you be a full lawyer?" he asked me. Somehow this came across as a real putdown. I told him that with a husband and kids I didn't have time to study for the bar exams. Then he asked me about getting to the Cleveland suburb where I lived (Cleveland Heights) from the airport. I told him I thought there were plenty of taxis and buses but I didn't know because I had my car parked at the airport (stupid of me).
>
> As we left the airport terminal, I found my car in the parking lot and I was completely dumfounded when my traveling companion arrived at the car just as I was about to get in. "Look," he said. "There aren't any buses. Taxis are too expensive. We could travel to Cleveland Heights together. Would you do it or are you too paranoid?"
>
> At that point *all* my alarms went off. I stepped back from my car door (which he was actually reaching for), slammed it, and in one motion hit the remote lock and the alarm. Now my car isn't fitted with one of those wimpy alarms that just uses the horn. It has a police siren and a blue flashing light in the back window. In the enclosed parking garage, the racket was just enormous. Between the noise and the blue light, my hit man ran, leaving his suitcase where it stood. When Security arrived I turned off the alarm system and told them what had happened. They later told me I had been lucky. The stuff in his suitcase identified him, and the guy was wanted in three states! Because of my action they caught him, right in Cleveland.

THE IGNORED "NO" AND FORCED TEAMING

Phyllis was more than a Witch. She had also taken a course at an IMPACT studio in Cleveland.[8] The IMPACT program not only emphasizes how to defend yourself physically. It also teaches some signs you can watch for to reinforce your intuition that the guy you are dealing with is a bad one.[9]

Phyllis's case is very nearly a textbook illustration of those guidelines. Because she regularly meditated and channeled, she immediately picked up the low-level emanations from the hit man. It happens with both men and women, so let's look at some of the things you can watch for and be aware of.

★ Con artists and hit men always choose aisle seats in the airplane. The aisle seat in an aircraft traps the (target) person sitting on the inside. So what if you have to make do with an aisle seat? That takes you out of the space he controls. Granted, you won't get to look out the window—but which is more important, looking at the tops of clouds, or the risk of your very life?

★ The ignored "no" is probably the most important single red flag. Phyllis told her hit man that she didn't want a drink refill even though he had spilled some on her. He ignored the "no."

Time and time again in mugging cases we hear from women, "He was so helpful! Even though I said no, I didn't want him to help, he still helped." Typically in this ploy he offers to help with the groceries. "Let me carry one of those sacks up the steps into your apartment house." The woman says "No," but he still takes the sack of groceries. What does she do? Call the cops—or let this friendly, helpful person right into her apartment? When expressed in these terms, it does sound naive and stupid, but in actual contact it is much more difficult to turn around, get back into your car, let him have the groceries, and drive away. Ten to one he'll put the bag

---

[8] IMPACT offers training for women in full-contact self-defense. Learn the location of the studio nearest you through (800) 345-5425.

[9] Most muggings and rapes—in fact more than 80 percent—are committed by men. So we are not being politically incorrect or sexist when we write of "he" as rapist and "she" as victim.

down on the top step and leave anyway. When you return with a backup person, if he is still there he'll see that his con didn't work.

★ Another thing to watch for is "we." This theme has many variations. In Phyllis's case it was "Help me get where I'm going. You told me there'd be buses, but there aren't any. You have a responsibility to help me and *we're* going to get me out of this situation."

No, *we're* not! He's a stranger! You don't know this guy from Adam's ox. You've never met him before. *Stop being nice.* Professionals who analyze violence call this *forced teaming*. The hit man tries to get the victim to be part of his team. We've all heard that many victims of kidnapping eventually start to identify with their kidnappers. They get force-teamed into joining the kidnappers' team. This happens in many, many situations; not the least of them is the work place. There, the teaming is done against management. "We could run this place better than they're doing." "We hate the boss." Creation of a shared enemy is a typical forced-teaming strategy. We are reluctant to mention labor unions here, but the ploy is clearly illustrated during negotiation of a contract.

DON'T LAUGH IT OFF

It's an unwelcome fact, but every human being contains seeds of violence. "I'd never shoot anyone!" a woman told Gavin virtuously in one of his workshops at a pagan gathering.

"There's a bonfire over there. This horrible-looking fellow comes up, steals your baby, and says he's going to throw it into the fire. He's dashing toward the fire so fast you can't catch him. And leaning against Bob's tent over there is a rifle. Now tell me again?"

She sat down.

We live in a violent society, and the frustrations of today's life make it worse. This, coupled with the fact that we are a mobile society, has taken away what little protection used to exist when everyone in the village knew everyone else and was accountable for their actions.

We all felt terribly shocked by the Oklahoma City bombing in which fifteen children died. We feel shocked when a gunman enters a school in Scotland and twenty children die. But in the United States *seventy-plus* children are murdered *every week*. And in an average year over *four million* cases of reported batterings and attempted rapes are reported. No one can estimate how many go unreported.

The numbers are slowly getting better. But the numbers mean that if you sit in a park with two hundred people, ten of them have violent tendencies—and may have been involved in a battering or a murder. When you walk down the street or through the mall, keep your head in gear and your intuition running.

The mother pushing the baby in a stroller poses no danger . . . probably.

The couple engrossed in the wonder of each other pose no danger . . . probably.

That single well-dressed guy smiling at you on the seat by the fountain? He's where the danger lies . . . probably.

THE SMELL OF FEAR

It is rightly said that dogs smell fear. Hit men are intuitive, too—and they're looking for the fearful person, the one who will be an easy victim. You're walking down a dark street and you suspect someone is following you. You take a hesitant look over your shoulder, quickly turn back and continue, perhaps a little more hurriedly. This is a fear reaction. If your car or other safety is near, it's fine. However, your body language encourages the hit man; it clearly tells him that you feel afraid. What if, instead, you turned abruptly, looked straight down the street in a challenging manner with your hands in front of you, and then turned back? When you turn to look in this way, you put your emotions into anger with all the attack symbology you have learned in foregoing chapters. Your body language speaks volumes. Suddenly you are no longer the fearful victim, no longer the deer in the headlights, but someone who is definitely going to fight back. And more: You get a good look at the street to see whether your fears are justified, and you now know exactly what your stalker and other nearby people look like.

EXPANDING YOUR BRAIN'S INTUITIVE CAPABILITY

Your brain is an amazing organ. Only recently have scientists begun to understand the amount of control it has over the body and its hormone balance (for example), and over its own capabilities. Research is beginning to show that the brains of stroke victims can be retrained so that function can be restored to limbs which otherwise were useless.

The procedure is fairly simple. The good limb is restrained; then the damaged or nonfunctional limb begins to work again. The need to work, the urgent *necessity* to work, makes the brain use other parts of itself—makes it reroute its commands—to control the limb. This approach is called *strain-induced movement therapy.* Notes Professor Taub at The University of Alabama–Birmingham, "The sling we use to constrain the good limb is not a magic talisman. It induces use of the affected limb, which in turn induces brain reorganization."[10]

In a similar way, studies of people who learn a new skill, like reading Braille or doing ballroom dancing, show that trainees use more of their brain when they learn the pattern. The earlier assumption was that if one learned a skill, it became somehow "natural" and that the brain would use less space to repeat the skill. It turns out that the reverse is true. More of the brain wakes up when you learn a new skill. "It means that you create the brain from the inputs you get," explains Paula Tallal, codirector of the Center for Molecular and Behavioral Neuroscience at Rutgers University in Newark, New Jersey.[11]

Those sections of the brain that control language and visual arts apparently also apply to recognition of telepathic and intuitive feelings. Thus, one way recommended to improve your intuition is to practice intuitive thinking! Another way? Learn to paint or to speak a foreign language. Amazing results have been obtained in the field known as *neuroplasticity.* It is expected that the impact of Alzheimer's disease can eventually be minimized or postponed. Further, workers studied children with deficient reading skills. In such children, six weeks of "brain training" gave over two years' worth of improvement in their level of reading. Thus, it seems you should practice such things as reading the tarot cards to improve your capability for reading the tarot cards, and you should listen to your intuition more closely so that intuitive feelings become stronger and more accurate.

---

[10] Edward Taub, "Rewiring Your Gray Matter," *Newsweek,* January 1, 2000.

[11] Ibid.

VIOLENCE IN THE WORK PLACE

Of course violence does not always occur at the work site. Typical is the case of USAir employee David Burke, who caused an airliner to crash, killing himself and 43 other people, just to get back at his boss. Yet Burke had a history of violence and crime—not a person you'd think an airline should employ. Does a work colleague of yours constantly try to force-team you into disruptive acts against management? Does he read a lot of macho magazines? Does he proudly tell you about his collection of weapons? Does he seek to control people? *Talk to the company security officer.* You may avert a disaster.

The signs always exist. In every single case, later investigation turned up people who "knew something was wrong." Besides intuition and psychic examination, there are mundane signs to watch for: specifically the SAD individuals, those who are *Sullen,* continually *Angry,* and hopelessly *Depressed.*[12] Oftentimes, though, your intuition alone tells you when a SAD individual is ready to break.

To members of middle management, to workers in personnel, and to executives, we offer some suggestions:

★ Give your intuition free rein. Do not promise a job until you have meditated for at least fifteen minutes on the applicant and his attitude.

★ Do everything you can to see the *aura* of an applicant. Try to set off negative reactions by asking about previous positions, why he left, and what he would have accepted to stay in that previous employment. All this gives you some idea whether the candidate is a team player or disruptive.

★ The most overlooked thing in employment seems to be verifying the references. We speak mainly of those that the candidate has volunteered, but also of *developed* or *second-tier* references. As you talk with the people voluntarily mentioned as references, ask them for the name of somebody else who knows the applicant.

★ Written references from earlier employers often contain hidden messages. The most blatant of these is "Call for further

---

[12] C. de Becker, *The Gift of Fear* (Boston: Little Brown, 1997).

information." In the executive old-boy network, this means "Danger. There's something wrong about this prospect that I don't dare put into a letter." There is a growing list of things that personnel people cannot say about a potential employee without risking litigation.

Over and over, people disregard these signals of danger and their own intuitive feelings. Over and over, in situations such as hiring babysitters, one never checks references. This nation has learned to its loss in recent years that high school kids, too, act violently. Cases of teenagers abducting children and severely injuring them are unfortunately on the rise. A baby is a precious thing. Surely it's worth a couple of phone calls.

One last word to business executives: If you have to fire or lay off an employee, plan to do it very carefully.

★ Do it late Friday afternoon.

★ Make sure that a security man escorts the laid-off person all the way to the gate and collects all company property—including all IDs—before the ex-employee leaves.

The weekend can help as a cooling-off period. It can help avoid violence and can provide time for psychic healing to the person who is laid off. Dismissal late on Friday can be less traumatic than a mid-week dismissal because he hasn't expected to go in to work the next morning. Living through his normal weekend pattern can provide time to stabilize.

In one recent shooting incident the firing was mis-handled from the outset. The secretary sent to collect the guy to be fired said casually, "Joe wants you in his office. He's going to lay you off." By the time he arrived at that office, he felt furious, and the interview went downhill from there.

THE MARRIAGE SWITCH

Chapter IV discussed Hans and the way his personality seemed to change after marriage. But with careful analysis and use of your intuition, you can cull out the potential control freaks before you get yourself into a legally binding contract—a life sentence. A controlling nature shows up in many ways even during courtship. Who drives the car? Who pays at the restaurant? Who decides what "we" will eat? How much influence does he exert on your attire and hairdo? Does he monopolize your entire weekend? Does he second-guess your decisions? Can you still see old friends without grudging resentment from him? Look at his emanations when you meditate. How much "red" is in that link, showing suppressed anger? Listen to yourself describe this new acquaintance to a friend or relative.

★ "Well, yes, he belongs to the gun club and he always carries a weapon, but I like that because he's very protective."

★ "No, he doesn't have a very good job now but once we're settled, I'm sure he'll get a good one."

★ "Well, he's a musician. But courting me has put his life in a turmoil so he can't compose right now."

★ "He picked this dress out for me. I didn't want it, but he made me buy it anyway. He said he'd pay me back as soon as he finds work."

★ "I was happy to lend him X hundred dollars. He'll soon be working."

These are typical remarks about what we call a "fixer-upper" control freak. With the love of a good woman, this obvious loser will soon become Prince Charming. And once he makes that transition, of course, he'll lose his controlling attitude. Sure he will.

If the relationship is serious, do what a Witch does. Don't even consider marriage until you two have lived together for a year and a day. We as ministers can conduct a marriage (a *handfasting*) ritual—but our year-and-a-day rule cannot be broken. And when we do conduct such a ceremony, it is for a limited time, with a maximum of five years. That contract shows a firm, definitive expiration date. If you are now married and if it is obvious that you made a dreadful mistake, you may well need help in getting out of it. Consider it a learning experience and move on. Unfortunately the police are not the place to go unless it is very, very serious.

When you break, you must plan well ahead. *You must disappear.* If you go to the police, they will tell you, "If he's threatening you, go get a restraining order." Sometimes that restraining order pushes the guy right off into even more violence. In fact, in over 50 percent of cases the target person simply ignores the restraining order and it causes more harm than good. The fact that his battering or manipulative behavior has now become public knowledge breaks down his final remnants of reserve and drives him right over that cliff. Use your intuition to decide whether a restraining order will or will not work. What does ordinary stress do to him? A restraining order will make him berserk. You won't want to be within reach.

In some cases a restraining order discourages the guy from further stalking or harming. In other cases it is disastrous. Almost every week we can read of a woman being shot with the restraining order in her pocket. In most of these cases the ex-husband or stalker shoots himself, too, though that doesn't seem to bring her back to life. His ego is shattered. He figures his associates will laugh behind his back. She cannot be allowed to win, even at the cost of his own life. Nicole Simpson had a restraining order; O.J. broke into the house, battering the back door off its hinges. The police took no action.

As with the employee, so it is with a significant other. Do not let him (or her!) into your life in the first place if you have doubts.

Witches are not big on virginity and believe in sexual freedom, so long as it *harms none.* However, you must be aware that the sex act sets up strong psychic links between the partners. Mother Nature probably built that trait into women so there would be some help in looking after the offspring. And even when the woman does not get pregnant, somehow Mother Nature's trickery is still in place. Women continually go back to men whom they should dump. The percentage of these situations that result in a change of the man's attitude is minuscule. Because she ran away, he usually becomes even more of a control freak, not less—and now it becomes even more difficult for her to get out of it. This results in such occurrences as the desperate woman who poured gasoline over the marital bed while he slept in it and set him on fire. The courts hearing this woman's story held that she was justified and would not punish her.

SUMMARY

For a serene life you need to use every psychic skill in your repertory. Nowhere is this more important than in protecting yourself and your loved ones from the freaks out there, and in forming new relationships. Gentle Reader, if in this chapter you see a little bit of your own behavior toward your significant other—stop it now! Get real!

A Witch's Spells

THE ETHICS OF WORKING SPELLS

Spells can serve almost any purpose and may vary widely in their ethics. The companionship spell below, for example, cages. Once you have done it, you may never know whether the target person comes into your life because (s)he wants to, or because of the spell. You may harm the person by imprisoning him/her; yet your need may be so desperate that you do it anyway. If that is true, remember: In doing it you leave yourself open to being trapped in turn by the target person. We do consider this dangerous.

Always be clear on what you are doing and why. Do your absolute best to follow the Wiccan Rede.

If it harm none, do what you will.

WHY USE SPELLS?

There are two basic reasons to use a spell:

1. To attune the mind, the body, and the spirit, psychologically and physiologically, to what is going to happen. "When I hear the kettle whistle, I know it's tea time," says a British Witch. Red roses and candlelight mean it's time for romance. When you smell sulfur in the air, it's time for circle.

2. To make sure that all the necessary steps for the procedure are included, and they are done in the correct order.

We all practice little rituals in our lives. Most of them go unnoticed. Brushing your teeth—brush—water—toothpaste—water—mouthwash. It doesn't vary. You have already taken part in many individual routines such as bathing, and group rituals such as graduation.

In any given spell, all participants need to understand clearly what is going on and to feel undistracted by the beautiful robes and the hoodoos, not turned off by esoteric words they don't understand. They should share a strong unanimous intent for the spell to come true. Keep it simple. Plan ahead. It works.

A SPELL FOR COMPANIONSHIP

ITEMS REQUIRED

Tight-fitting yellow bodysuit or leotard

Parchment-type paper

Swan quill pen

Dark green or orange candle

Saffron scent

Salt

Red ink

Picture of the type of person you want to attract

PROCEDURE

With the quill pen and the red ink, write on the parchment the name or description of the companion you desire. The picture should remind you positively of that companion. Sew the picture into the body suit over the heart. Place on the table the garment, the candle, and the saffron scent. Surround the collection of objects with a ring of salt. Light the candle. Raise your emotional level and visualize power flowing from your fingertips into the garment. Visualize yourself in the embrace of your chosen companion. Charge the bodysuit by putting all this love-affection-desire energy into it. When your thought energy reaches its climax, clap out the candle flame.

Put the charged garment into a steel box until you are ready to wear it. The next time there is a chance you may meet the companion you hope for, put the garment on. The tighter it fits, the better. It should fit you like a snakeskin, so that every movement of your body makes you conscious all over again of your intent.

A SPELL FOR WEALTH

ITEMS REQUIRED

Dark orange pouch, made of linen or cotton

Black or dark brown India ink

Sandalwood

Orange candle

Linen thread

Ground-ivy (nepeta faassenii) or carpet-bugle (ajuga reptans), a few leaves

Piece of yellow jade

Piece of gold

Soil

Gold-colored cloth

PROCEDURE

With the India ink, on one side of the pouch draw the symbol of the bull (Taurus); on the other side draw the symbol of the earth. Into the pouch put the gold, the soil, the jade, the sandalwood, and the leaves.

Spread the gold-colored cloth on your altar. Beginning at new moon, every morning light the orange candle and place the pouch on the altar before the candle. Stand facing south with candle and pouch between you and the South Pole. Go to your safe place[1] and visualize yourself covered in money. Chant four times:

Money, money! Come to me!
As I will, so let it be.

---

[1] See Chapter V.

Make each repetition of the chant louder than the one before. At the end of the fourth chant, clap out the candle and leave the arrangement until the next morning. After five succeeding mornings of this charging spell, wear the pouch on a linen thread around your neck for the next seven days and nights.

This next step is a most important one. From the time the moon is full until it is new again, lock the pouch away in a steel box and bury it. Try not to think of it; this is the time when the influence is diminishing, and obviously you don't want to draw thoughts of shrinkage to your wealth.

If you need to repeat the spell, you may do so at next new moon.

A SPELL FOR HEALING

This spell is for self-healing, whether of your body, your psyche, or your life. It is useful when you are ill or have parted from a loved one. Most illnesses are caused by stress problems, so the repair of your psyche will result in healing.

ITEMS REQUIRED

Black altar cloth

Nude photos of yourself:
 front and back

A new name[3]

1 cup fresh mint leaves

Black candle[2]

Brazier

Salt

1 cup white vinegar

PROCEDURE

Chop the mint leaves fine and steep them in white vinegar for 24 hours. At noon on the day of new moon, bathe in heavily salted water. Go to your spell area.

Anoint yourself all over with the mint vinegar. Light the black candle. Take a tiny sip of the vinegar. Slowly chant "Aye-oh, aye-oh,

---

[2] Black pigments contain all possible colors. Since self-diagnosis is often difficult, it is better to use something containing all colors than to risk missing a significant one.

[3] Select a name that represents who you want to be in the future. Discarding your old name gets rid of all its old associations.

aye-oh, aye-oh," gradually getting louder and louder. When your chant is as loud as you can stand, yell, "I AM WHOLE!" Instantly clap out the candle flame. Look honestly at the photographs of yourself. Use salt to write your new name on the altar cloth. As you carefully form the name, concentrate on what you are going to become: healthy, vibrant, a whole new person.

Burn the photographs in your brazier. Affirm:

> *From the ashes of my old self and life*
> *let a new healed person arise.*

As the fire dies down, pour the salt from the altar cloth onto it. Continue to concentrate on your new name and your future life, mentally placing yourself very clearly in the near future in greatly improved circumstances.

For the next seven days, bathe at noon in salted water. As you leave the bath, wipe yourself down with mint vinegar. Say your new name aloud and concentrate again on visualizing yourself in your new improved state and environment.

A SPELL FOR PERSONAL PROTECTION

ITEMS REQUIRED

Polished disk of stainless steel, about 1″ in diameter, with hole for suspending

A recent photograph of yourself

Super-glue

Salt

4 red candles

PROCEDURE

Have the Pentacle shown in Figure XI-1 engraved on the face of the stainless-steel disk. Fasten your photograph to the back of the disk with super-glue.

At noon on the day of the next new moon, draw a ring of salt about one foot in diameter on a plain wooden table or on the ground. Put the four candles at the four cardinal points: east, south, west, north. Place the Pentacle in the center of the salt circle. At exactly noon light the four candles and affirm:

> *All-Father above, All-Mother below,*
> *I place Me in your care.*

FIGURE XI–1
Protective Pentacle

Chant this nine times: the first three facing south, the next three facing west, and the final three facing north. Face east and affirm:

At each dawning, Spirits of the East,
Recharge my amulet.

Let the candles burn. After one hour, move them closer to the amulet. After a second hour, move them closer to it until they actually touch it. Let them burn out.

For the following fifteen days, at dawn greet the sun nude and wearing your amulet. Stand in Star Position and affirm:

Lady Queen, Lady Queen, Lady Queen —
Shining Maiden, Strong Woman, Wise Crone:
To You I offer reverence and gratitude;
From You I learn wisdom and compassion.
Yours are dominion, power, glory;
Yours are grace, nurturing, justice.
Thus it is. Thus let it ever be.

A HOUSE-CLEANSING SPELL

Your home may feel as if it is full of bad memories. It may have a spirit or two dwelling in it. Here is a very nice spell that you can use to make the home feel much better and brighter. The simple equipment is easy to obtain. The spell is especially fun to do at the end of a party, when you can clean all the people out as well as the unwelcome influences.

ITEMS REQUIRED

200 feet of silk thread	Alcohol
2-quart bowl, fireproof	Chicken wishbone
Aluminum tray 30″ × 18″	Cooking oil
2 quarts dry sand	Bread
2 beeswax candles	Glass of wine
A box, 2 feet or more on a side	Sea salt[4]

PROCEDURE

On the evening of full moon, tie one end of the thread to the front doorknob. Leave the door open. Take the thread in a counterclockwise direction into and out of every room in the house, including the basement, attic, upstairs rooms, every bathroom, and all storage closets that have a door.

Carry the end of the thread out into the yard. Tie it to the wishbone and put it into the box with a beeswax candle, the glass of wine, and a piece of bread. The box is the spirit house. Position the

---

[4] Or kosher salt.

box on a post or some other elevated pedestal, which may be as simple as a wooden chair.

Put some sand into the fireproof bowl. Pat it down to make a mound in the center. Saturate the mound with a mixture of alcohol and cooking oil, mixed in the proportion of 1 cup alcohol to ¼ cup oil. Put the bowl and the second candle on the tray.

At exactly midnight, light the two candles and the alcohol mix in the bowl. Let it burn outdoors for a couple of minutes before you carry it indoors. Be very careful with the alcohol fire, because the bowl will get astonishingly hot. Standing at the front door, affirm loudly:

> I have prepared a home for any spirit who may need one.
> Come, follow the thread. Go to your new home.
> Go in peace.
> If you do not go in peace, I will curse you and banish you to the outer shades.
> Follow the thread. Go in peace.

Walk forward along the thread repeating:

> Follow the thread. Go in peace.

Carry before you the tray on which both the candle and the bowl of alcohol/oil are burning. If you like, as you go, a second person can sprinkle salt behind you. As you move through the home, have someone follow behind you, winding up the thread.

Eventually you will come to the spirit house. Wrap the thread around the spirit house. Say:

> You have everything you need in this house.
> Everything you need is in this house.
> This thread will bind you in. This thread will bind you in.

When all the thread is wrapped around the spirit house, carry the spirit house away from your property, collapse it, and burn it. Or, you could bury it at a crossroad; or put it snugly in the woods.

Your home is now cleansed. If you want it to remain cleansed, you may scatter salt or sulfur clockwise in a protective circle around it. If you want to keep the spirits as guardians, build a small wooden house 2′ × 3′ × 1′ high with a peaked roof. Put the house on a pole or into a tree in your front yard.

P.S. Do this spell only when all else has failed to rid your house of unwanted spirits.

A SPELL FOR SERENITY

Select a small room or an area in your home. This may be just one piece of a wall. Remove from the area all distractions such as books and electronics. Paint the area in a pale ivory color. Put into the area a small wooden table or altar and a comfortable chair. On the altar put a picture or a statue of some god/ess image that you like, with a single small potted plant and a white candle in a nonmetal[5] holder.

Every evening when you come in from work, remove all your clothes and jewelry. If possible, bathe. Go to the area. Light the candle and sit for ten minutes doing nothing. Contemplate the plant. Allow no interruptions.

A SPELL FOR REMOVAL OF ENEMIES

Occasionally there may be someone who causes such anger in your life that you decide the best thing for your own mental health is never to see that person again. This full-moon spell is designed not to harm, but to remove that obnoxious person from contact with you. It falls into the general category "attack," though "education" might be a more accurate label.

ITEMS REQUIRED

Sea salt	Red ink
Pen	Parchment
Small crucible	Wooden matches
Burlap	Chili powder
Red candle	Snuff or cigar
Photo of target person, or a psychic link	

PROCEDURE

1. Set up your altar. Cover it with burlap.

2. Arrange on the altar as many of the sensory keys as you can assemble from "Items Required" above.

---

[5] Instead of metal, use a candleholder of ceramic, glass, wood, or pottery.

3. Place the candle and crucible on the altar.

4. Close to midnight on full-moon night:

   a. Turn off the lights.

   b. Light the candle.

   c. Cast a salt circle around yourself and the altar.

   d. With the pen and red ink, write across the picture "Begone." On parchment, write the signs of the full and new moons above and below the name of the person. Vigorously cross them all out.

   e. Burn some tobacco. Eat some chili powder. Stroke the burlap. Get as angry as you can at the person.

   f. Hold the parchment facing the picture. Gaze into the candle flame. When you can no longer hold the intent, when the candle begins to flicker, start your chant and whirl.[6]

   g. At the height of the chant, scream out:

   > *Get thyself gone from me! I turn my back on thee!*
   > *We'll grow better separately. As I will, so let it be!*
   > *GO!*

5. In the crucible, burn the picture and the parchment. Hold the crucible between your hands, letting the rest of the power flow into it.

6. Divide the ashes into three piles: large, medium, small. Put each pile into an envelope. At nine-day intervals, mail them to the target person, the largest pile first, the smallest pile last.

7. Clean all the tools and burn any leftover consumables.

A SPELL FOR HEIGHTENED AWARENESS

It is time for you to get your familiar. Tradition tells us that Witches prefer cats, small dogs, and ravens as familiars. The familiar provides you with a focus for this exercise. Let us say you choose a cat.

Sit in meditation with your familiar on your lap. (A raven or an owl might well sit on your shoulder instead.) Experience its weight

---

[6] See Figure III-2 for Generating HEDE.

and its warmth. As you sit quietly, understand that (if your choice is a cat) this is a cat's weight and warmth—but not just any old cat; this one is special. Experience the cat's essence. Open your mind; delve down into the cat's mind. Feel its essential cat-ness. Think of its hereditary panther-like stalk and pounce, its jungle heritage, all its feline stealth, its hidden hooded claws that from time to time may be red with blood. Think of its sensuality, its nature that has both gregarious and loner aspects. Feel the cat-smoothness.

Experience the sound of a cat. Stroke it gently; talk to it softly. The cat begins to purr, but stops when you stroke against the fur. The feeling changes abruptly, but the sound and the feeling are still Cat. Become aware of the cat's smell. This is not the scent of the litter box but the lighter, psychic smell of Cat. Think of the flavor of Cat. Many people associate it with fur: a dry taste that you want to spit out; others taste it more as fish or uncooked meat.

Now you can open your eyes and look at your cat and physically see it as it is.

These are the first steps in developing awareness of your familiar. You will want to become attuned to its moods. When is it angry, and why? When is it peaceful? How do you affect its mood? Can you call your familiar telepathically? As you progress from one stage to another of your development, your awareness will grow. Most people find within a week that if they spend an hour a day at this, their awareness grows beyond any expectation they had at the start.

A SPELL FOR ACCEPTANCE OF THE FUTURE

Use this *guided meditation* in the final moments of any ritual working at full moon. Place yourself so that the moon shines on your face. Follow the path described in these words:

> Come with me. We will follow the path of the moon's light. As we rise without haste along the moonbeam, look back and remember what has happened in the ritual. Remember the excitement, the dancing, the music, the scents of the ritual. See yourself sitting content, meditating. See the others in the ritual meditating with you: a strong protected group. As you gently move further away, you can still see their auras and their power as a pinpoint of light in a dark world.

The moon looms large and bright behind us. Still looking back at the bright spot that is the ritual site, we bump gently into the moon. We reach behind and hold the disk of the moon. We return down the moonbeam to the ritual site. We realize we carry on our back a disk of full-moon light. Carrying the disk, we stand before our bodies in the ritual site. The disk of light that we carry illuminates a tunnel through time. We move leisurely forward along the tunnel.

We hear faint music calling us. We travel to our home. We let the light that we carry transform the home into what it becomes so we can see what it will be like in the coming months. It may not be what we wish to see; but we remind ourselves that the future is variable and can change. So if we do not like what we see in the light of the moon that we have drawn with us, we can change the future for ourselves. Perhaps we simply make the home more comfortable or more serene. Wherever we put the light we have drawn with us, there the future for us is illuminated.

We travel back to our ritual site, still carrying the light with us. Now we know the future has been changed. We know what it holds. We turn and face the moon and send her light back. To her we say,

> Thank you, beautiful Goddess of the Night,
> For all You have shown us here.
> I will keep some of Your light, beautiful Goddess,
> That it may illuminate my path
> And make my future serene and secure.

As you say these words, imagine the moon's light traveling back from you to the moon. Remember to keep enough to surround yourself with. The closing prayer of the ritual meditation then becomes even more meaningful:

> I am surrounded by the pure white light of the Moon.
> Nothing but good shall come to me;
> Nothing but good shall go from me.
> I give thanks. So let it be.

A SPELL FOR REALITY

In your present reality construct, both your body and the seat on which it rests are solid. Yet you know that the amount of solid material in these bodies is actually minute; in fact, less than the point of a finely sharpened pin.

When you travel astrally into the future, you learn that your thoughts can influence the reality in which you find yourself. When another entity is in the same area, the resultant *consensus reality* combines the effects of your thoughts with those of the other entity.

The fact that we all perceive a wall as "solid" means that it looks and feels solid to you in this time frame. If your emotional feeling is strong enough about any given reality, you can impress your ideas on it to such an extent that it changes. In the working of magic, intense visualization of the object or person in the changed state results in accomplishing the change. The more energy and intensity you invest in the effort through the work of several people, god/esses, or other aids, and through your personal intent, the more likely you are to succeed in your work. Do not, however, single-handedly take on the consensus reality of the rest of the world to try to accomplish your end abruptly. Instead, do it a little at a time.

A SPELL FOR SELF-SEALING

This spell is designed for your own personal sealing and protection. If you wish, you can also use it to seal a friend or your children. As given, it addresses a Celtic deity. Feel free to substitute another god/ess if you wish.

ITEMS REQUIRED

Altar or wooden table

Glass bowl

Asparagus

Statuette or drawing or picture of a Centaur (a human-headed horse)

Sapphire-blue candle

Sapphire-blue cloth, about 3 feet square

Ground nutmeg

Narcissus aroma

PROCEDURE

Spread the altar cloth and arrange the items. Light the candle. Put the asparagus into the glass bowl and sprinkle it with nutmeg. Add some scent. Face the east with your hands at your sides and your eyes open. Turn around once in a sunwise direction (clockwise in the Northern Hemisphere). Say this affirmation:

> On this night of new moon, I ask you, Ceridwen, Goddess of Fire,
> To bless me and seal my body against all negation.

With each affirmation, dip the tip of your right middle finger into the asparagus liquid.

Touch each eyelid and say,	Let my eyes see only beauty. Let me witness honestly.
Touch each ear and say,	Let my ears hear truth.
Touch each nostril and say,	Let the very breath of life be for good.
Touch your lips and say,	Let my mouth utter truth and kindness.
Touch your heart and say,	Let my life be lived for good.
Touch your genitalia and say,	Let my life energy be used for good.
Touch your anus and say,	Let my body remain healthy, that I may grow spiritually.
Touch both hands and say,	Let my hands work for good.
Touch both feet and say,	Let my feet walk in the way of growth.

Turn round once more to the right. Affirm:

Ceridwen, Goddess beloved of the Celts,
Witness now my intent to commit my life to growth and to good.
Recognize my mistakes as a part of learning.
Guide me in the way I should go, and shield me against negation.
So let it be.

Let the altar cloth and all objects remain where they lie for 24 hours. Then bury them at a deserted crossroad; or burn them, mentally offering the vapors to the work of the Elder Ones.

A SPELL FOR THE PSYCHIC CLEANING OF TOOLS

The various materials of your tools—fabric, wood, and metal—may hold imbedded psychic noise: vibrations of one kind or another. Before charging the tool, remove all such noise. The process is physical, not psychic.

At full moon, exactly at the time it crosses the meridian, put the dirty tool into the freezer compartment of your refrigerator. Leave it there until the moon next crosses the meridian; that is, until it is directly over your head 24 hours later. Remove the tool from the refrigerator and put it under a heat lamp, at such a distance that the tool grows hot to the touch. Leave it under the heat lamp until the moon again crosses the meridian. Take it out from under the heat lamp, let it cool slightly and hold it against your chest. Affirm:

> As the moon grows smaller,
> So will the energies imbedded in this tool disperse into the ethers.
> As I will, so let it be.

To cleanse a robe, have it dry-cleaned twice: once at each of two different dry-cleaning establishments. Schedule the cleanings to occur at full moon.

A SPELL FOR THE PSYCHIC CHARGING OF TOOLS

The tool most often charged is the athame. Occasionally one charges the ankh as well. As a male-type tool, the athame is best charged by a female acting as the Goddess. There are two methods of charging cleaned tools:

1. Sexual Charging—The Witch acting in the role of the Goddess holds the athame between the palms of her hands at breast level. At the moment of orgasm she charges it with these words:

   > Let the energies of the Life Force flow from me
   > Into this most sacred tool.
   > Let the tool be used only for good, never for evil.
   > As I will, so let it be.

2. Pyramidic Charging—This calls for a pyramid with each side 2.72 feet long, made from bronze rods $3/16$-inch thick. Put the tool into the pyramid at new moon when the moon is crossing the meridian; that is, at about noon. Leave the tool in the pyramid until the moon next crosses the meridian. As you remove it, affirm:

   > By the life-giving power of the sun and the energy of the growing moon,
   > May this tool be forever charged.
   > Let it never be used for negative purposes.
   > As I will, so let it be.

SUMMARY

As you can see, spells are easy procedures. We encourage you to do these and to invent your own. When you are involved in working with someone else's spell, make sure that you:

1. Understand what the intent is.

2. Feel right about the equipment being used.

3. Agree with the procedure.

4. Agree with the intent.

5. Harm none (including yourself).

Your Fulfilled Life

DO YOU TRULY WANT TO BE PRESIDENT?

We Frosts have gotten to the stage where we avoid driving near any major metropolitan area. It's simply too dangerous. We see people tearing along, usually driving at least ten miles over the speed limit, talking on cell phones, shaving, doing makeup in the rear-view mirror, and a dozen other things. The hands-free cell phone is really a great advance. Now drivers can drink their coffee or shave with one hand while they drive with the other—and still talk on the phone. Perhaps we two are getting too old to appreciate such a multi-tasking lifestyle, but we have to wonder what ever happened to good sense. Don't people understand how much road information they get through their hearing? Have they never seen a serious traffic accident? Have they never lingered to smell the flowers? Apparently not.

Yet as writers we are exposed to this high-adrenaline attitude all the time. With the media and with otherwise sensible people in publishing, everything has to be *now*. If you can't e-mail your autobiography (and even whole books), you just ain't with it, Baby.

Where are all those people going in such a hurry? Maybe the answer is: one more step up the ladder in their own profession. They don't take vacations for fear someone may take their jobs. They work long, long hours and totally neglect their families—all for more power in the company and a few more dollars in the paycheck so they can buy more and more toys. The one who dies with the most toys or lives in the most fashionable area of town, wins! Yes, we know that many readers of this book are not like that, but the seeds are there—the seeds of stress, the seeds of addiction to adrenaline, and the seeds of totally out-of-control behavior.

Gavin worked as an executive in an international aerospace firm and Yvonne worked as an executive secretary; that's how we met. We gave up that life in the fast lane, with its access to the best restaurants and its gold credit cards and its first-class air travel, to raise pigs in rural Missouri. For a time we qualified for food stamps. To keep the pigs fed we had to sell many things that we didn't want to part with; among them a restored 1936 Buick sedan. But the quality of our life changed dramatically. Suddenly we had time for each other; and in the School of Wicca we knew we were doing necessary work.

THE PRESIDENT GETS DEMOTED

Josh L was the president of a division of a major multinational corporation. One day in 1998, as the presidents of all the firm's divisions gathered for their annual conference, a telephone call came for Josh. The gist of it was that his daughter had doused herself with gasoline and set herself afire in a protest demonstration, and was now in the hospital burn unit, not expected to live. Josh went to the hospital and stayed at her bedside until she died later that night.

That was the end of his career. Within a week he was given an "advisory" job and his whole multimillion-dollar division got a new president. From the corporate point of view, anyone who even takes a phone call during the annual meeting is suspect; and someone whose daughter is "obviously unbalanced" and who takes time to go to her bedside doesn't rank the corporation first and consequently can never be fully trusted or promoted.

We assure you this is a true story. Are you ready for the level of commitment essential in the executive suites of major corporations? We state quite honestly that neither of us is willing to make such a commitment, no matter what the perquisites and salaries might be. The female executive, too, in a major corporation has to play by these rules. At those levels of management, there is no allowance for her ties to children and family.

When faced with the possibility of a promotion into these levels, many men in middle management fall ill or have a heart attack because they know that "success" will be literal hell. This well known pattern is called the *fear-of-success syndrome*. In middle management, being right a reasonable percent of the time is regarded as adequate and good performance; but in *upper* management, one mistake can lead to involuntary early retirement. Many jobs in smaller firms, especially those that have a significant proportion of female management, are not so merciless.

THE ENDLESS SEARCH

We believe that many of the people so driven face imbalance—not necessarily in the mundane sense that a psychologist would use the word, but unbalanced because they feed their egos while totally starving their spirit. In the Witches' holistic healing way of life, we try to give equal weight to the physical body, the ego, and the spirit. We believe that people get unbalanced when they concentrate on one aspect to the detriment of the others. The athlete concentrates on the body; the business executive concentrates on the ego; the other-worldly swami concentrates on the spirit. In his own way, each lacks balance.

The real question boils down to:

When were you last truly content?

You can adjust your life in many ways with the magic power of Witchcraft, and adjusting your endorphins and other peptides gives you a short time of contentment—homeostasis, if nothing else. Many people feel an undefined lack in their lives. Perhaps they have lost soul pieces.[1] If that is true, they need to recover them. When they have recovered them, that feeling of an empty place in their hearts will probably diminish—but still there's that yearning in all of us to gain total contentment. Today, most people in the western world have the best lives we've ever had—far better than our forebears had, and certainly better than people have in "emerging" nations. We can accomplish many of our dreams. We can turn our visualizations into reality—but still, despite all this, we are not content.

---

[1] See Chapter VII.

This problem stems directly from that imbalance in the three parts of your being. Those three parts, *Body, Mind,* and *Spirit,* are depicted in the intersecting spirals of a shaman's fan, as in Figure XII-1. When you get the three of them into balance, you find that the thing you are looking for to ease your restlessness is actually inside you, not outside. The only person who can make you content is *you*—and if one of your parts is not content, the whole feels distressed.

Satisfying one of the three parts is easy. For instance:

★ For the *Body,* you can go out and have a wonderful time and become a party animal; or have a shopping orgy and max out your credit cards; you can sybaritically, gluttonously eat and drink and have lots of sex; you can get into improving your body and do lots of exercise and body-building; or a thousand other things to pander to your body.

★ For the *Spirit,* you can become an ascetic, spending your time on your knees before your prie-dieu feeding your spirit through meditation and communion with The All; you can become a missionary to darkest New York; or you can simply give your life to the god/ess' work.

★ For the *Mind,* you might follow the road of the intellectual, and become totally wound up into exercising your own brain through puzzles or word games; you might do original research; or learn a foreign language.

It's intriguing to watch current trends. Athletes bring in psychic healers and meditation gurus. High-powered executives begin to take great care with their diets. Gradually, the swamis begin to pay attention to the real world. Yet even with these changes, in each case you can see that they are balancing only *two* points of the triangle of holistic living. Some Witches balance their lives with magic to bring in the energies they lack; and you can do that same trick. You must understand what is missing, though, before you can effectively replace it. The little quiz below deals with three sections: one each for mundane body, for mind, and for spirit.

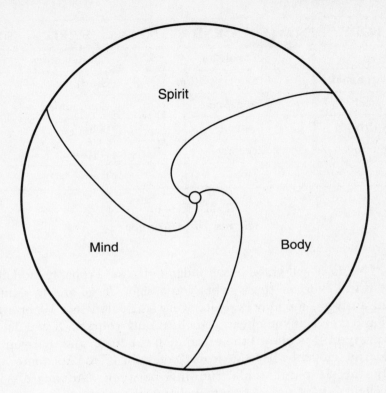

FIGURE XII–1
The Three Parts of Your Being

SCORING YOUR BALANCE

Use Table XII-1 to help you judge which parts of your being are over-indulged and which are getting short-changed. Evaluate yourself. Assign each item an individual weight between 0 and 10. Let 0 represent something that you are not doing well and 10 something you do very well. Just give yourself points in the 0-to-10 range for each answer; then add up each column. From that, decide where you need to do some magical work while you improve your lifestyle to correct the balance. Yes, the magic works. Yes, it brings you closer to the balance—but we urge you for the long term (the rest of your life, in fact) to rebalance yourself by changing your lifestyle.

BODY	SCORE	MIND	SCORE	SPIRIT	SCORE
Diet		Expansion		Altered States	
Environment		Concentration		Gratitude	
Physical		Acceptance		Communing	
Sex Drive		Esteem		Being	
Endurance		Feelings		Spirituality	
Time		Time		Time	

TABLE XII–1
Scoring Your Balance

This is a self-graded, self-judgment test. Probably no other human will ever see the weights you assign. There are no right or wrong answers. You may evaluate every single item as a 10, or every item as a 0 or 1. If you cheat, you cheat only yourself. If you decide that everything is toward the top and off the scale, and that you are wonderful, move the baseline from "Not doing it" to "Adequate" and apply the 10-point scale running between "Adequate" and "Excellent." It is up to you to balance the parts of your being. Whether you do it magically or mundanely, until you achieve that balance you will not feel truly content. Remember that old Greek thinker? "All things in moderation."

Examine each item in turn. Here are some notes to clarify what we mean.

TIME

The *time* section appears in all three columns. It is the amount of your life you give to this area of balance. Enter zero if you give no time to the area—and enter near-zero if that area gets an excessive amount of your waking hours, or if you are totally consumed by the area. You net a 10 when you consider that you give a reasonably balanced amount of time in any area.

BODY

★ *Diet* means your daily intake of food and liquid. Take into account all medications, snacks, and everything else that passes your lips. This is not to make you into a fanatic about diet or nutrition. We believe that the ideal is a diet such as early evolving humans consumed for millennia. This means, essentially, eating fresh, not processed foods (processed foods count lower than whole). It means minimizing the chemical additives that are unavoidable, and running like the wind from anything labeled "genetically modified." How many toxins do you eat, drink, or inhale on any given day?

★ *Environment*—What are your surroundings like at home, in the work place, or where you do recreation? How much full-spectrum sun-like light falls on you in midwinter? Is your residence power-balanced? If your home is balanced, are the two rooms where you spend the most time (the bedroom and the kitchen) also balanced? If your work frequently exposes you to hazardous materials or if you use exotic fertilizers or weed killers, and you don't work in a smoke-free environment, clearly you need to grade yourself way down in this area.

★ *Physical*—What is your body like? Do you like it, or are you concerned that you are overweight (whether that's true or inflicted by advertisers)? Do you have pain? What steps do you take to keep fit? Do you get exercise naturally, or are you into some grim jogging and machine-assisted regimen of torture? If you sit all day, you don't need us to point out that you would benefit from exercising—but get it in pleasant ways! Walk beside a river. Go dancing. When exercise becomes a chore, it doesn't happen. Millions of dollars' worth of fancy machines are rotting in garages and attics while their purchasers sit before the TV, telescoping into their own fat. What's wrong with this picture?

★ *Sex Drive*—Do you have an active and healthy sex life? Do you reward your body with sensual pleasures such as massage and touchings? Do you think you are sexually attractive to potential partners? Can you surrender yourself in sexual fulfillment?

★ *Endurance*—When you start to work on a project (maybe painting a room), do you have the physical strength and agility necessary to complete it? Can you walk a couple of miles without getting tired? Can you run up several flights of stairs?

MIND

★ *Expansion*—Are you doing anything to exercise your mind, learning another language, for instance? Or learning to play another game? The mind is like any other organ or muscle: If you don't use it, it atrophies.

★ *Concentration*—How good are you at focusing your attention on a project? What level of persistence can you show? How long can you sustain interest in a given activity? Does focusing your attention make you feel very tired?

★ *Acceptance*—Children and teenagers readily accept new ways and different ideas. Somewhere in the twenties, people get hardened, but the onrush of technology forces people to become adaptors. How easily do you adapt to new technology, new ideas, new ways of doing things? Do you respond to new ways as Dorothy Parker did? "What fresh hell is this?"

★ *Esteem*—Do you realistically accept the fact that some people are smarter and quicker than you are at a given task? Where do you rank yourself compared with other people? What do you think of your intrinsic merit as a human being, living in the 21st century? Are you an elitist, or are you self-deprecating?

★ *Feelings*—Can you govern your emotions, or do you have uncontrollable urges? Can you accept all your feelings, including those coming from intuition and dreams, even if those feelings are not always pretty? Can you relax, or must your mind always be running at top speed? Have you dumped the feeling of guilt that people may have used to disfigure your childhood?

SPIRIT

★ *Altered States of Consciousness*—Can you enter an altered state of consciousness? Have you been halfway there in meditation and channeling but pulled back? Are you working at this?

★ *Gratitude*—Do you regularly express thanks for being alive? Do you acknowledge that the spirit within you is a gift of immeasurable worth?

★ *Communing*—How well do you communicate on a spiritual level with your significant other, your children, your pets, or with Nature? Can you communicate through actions or music or body language in a nonverbal way? For example, are you telepathically connected with anyone?

★ *Being*—Do you meditate on the reason for your being? Do you discuss with others the reason for your existence? Do you have a firm, comfortable spiritual philosophy that guides your life? Some people would say, "Do you walk your talk?"

★ *Spirituality*—In making decisions in everyday life, do you consider the effects they might have on the growth and well-being of succeeding generations, as our Native American friends say, "unto the seventh generation"? If you discipline a child, do you stop to remember that physical discipline means that the child will visit physical discipline on his/her own children in turn? Do you regularly attend spiritual rituals that uplift you? Or are those you attend meaningless save for the little doses of piety and guilt they dispense?

YOUR ACTION LIST TODAY

When you complete the table, total each column. See whether the aspects of your life are in balance. Yes, it's easy to go back and change numbers, but you cheat only yourself if you do that.

Find the three lowest items in each column and fill in Table XII-2. Jot down things you will do, within your comfort level, to improve that category. You might even want to make notes on file cards or stick-it labels and put them on the refrigerator door or other conspicuous place to remind yourself of what you hope to do toward bringing your life into balance.

No one can do it for you.[2]

AREA	PRESENT SCORE	ACTION TO BE TAKEN

TABLE XII–2
Your Today Action List

JERRY SAVES HIS SUV AND HIS FAMILY

Jerry B lives in Boston. He worked as sales manager for a biotech firm which also supplied sickroom supplies for invalids: rental tilting beds, wheelchairs, oxygen tanks, and the like. The company's dual product line seemed to mesh quite well, and the company was moderately successful. Then Jerry received an offer from a major

---

[2] No one can do it for you—but no one else can claim credit for the improvements you make.

agri-business firm in Missouri. He jumped at the chance, even though it meant uprooting his wife, Danielle, the kids, and the dog and moving them all to the midwest.

When Jerry could catch his breath, he realized he was going to earn a lot of money now. The new firm's relocation specialist persuaded him that he needed a half-million-dollar house in an upmarket suburb. "All the company executives live here," she told him. "You really don't want to be anywhere else." Danielle didn't like either of the two houses on offer; but after a rather heated discussion, they did buy the one closer to the kids' new school. Winter came with a vengeance that year, and Jerry persuaded himself that with all the snow and ice he needed a sport-utility vehicle (SUV). Nothing would do but a Mercedes, spanking new, in fire-engine red. Jerry was proud of it, proud of his new house, and proud of his position in the agri-business conglomerate. Of course he was working long hours and traveling quite a bit. "Don't worry, honey," he assured Danielle. "In a couple of months I'll be able to relax. I'm just on a steep learning curve right now."

Winter went, and summer came. One very hot afternoon a frantic call came to Jerry's desk. "The air conditioner's quit. I called a repair man, and he says we need a whole new unit!"

"Well, what do you expect me to do?"

"Should I buy it or not?"

"You make the decision," he told her firmly.

The $2,000 for the unit wasn't in the budget, and in his new position Jerry was expected to work a lot of late hours but didn't get paid overtime. To make matters worse, he didn't feel he was getting the kind of support he expected from Danielle. And more: The kids in their new upscale school had definite cases of "trenditis"— whether they wore this week's designer sweatshirts and shoes was now a matter of life and death.

In the evenings Danielle often wanted to go out, while he wanted to stay in and rest. The constant low-level bickering led to a downturn in their sex life. Inevitably, perhaps, Jerry began to look with greater interest at the attractive secretaries at the plant.

If he hadn't gotten ill, this would just be another story of a broken marriage and a bunch of unhappy people—nothing very creative. But Jerry had a mild heart attack. For all the doctors could do, he couldn't seem to get the zip back into his fast-track career.

Danielle consulted us. Gavin sat and talked man-to-man with Jerry. He simply advised him to take some long baths with Danielle in their new whirlpool tub and add to the bathwater some lavender essence. Then after the bath she was to rub him down with a mixture of arnica and essence of peppermint. He also advised them to start going as a family to local events and to the Unitarian Church. Gavin rode roughshod over Jerry's "Yes, buts," warning that he would never get his energy back unless he took time for these simple remedies.

The first result of the baths and the rubdowns was an abrupt improvement in the sexual relationship. Jerry actually began to look forward to the time in the bath, the rubdown, and the adjustment of his endorphins. The effect of the family outings and church attendance was dramatic. Now they could rationally discuss as a family the budget and their lifestyle. He agreed that he would give back (or at least look into returning) his hot SUV. Danielle determined to look for a job outside the home, to give her something to think about besides her isolation, and at church the kids found a new set of friends with an entirely different set of values.

Returning the SUV, buying out the lease, proved to be way beyond their budget; and Danielle failed to find a job whose pay level would make a significant difference to the budget. Since Gavin's earlier advice had worked out so well, Jerry and Danielle consulted him again. His tarot reading clearly indicated a return to Boston and to Jerry's old firm—at a distinctly higher level. Gavin told them that in one or two weeks at the most, the job would become available and that Jerry should call his old boss right now to put in his bid. Again overriding their protests, Gavin even insisted they use his telephone to make that call.

Jerry was pleasantly surprised at the invitation back to Boston the next weekend to discuss the possibilities. The company was so eager to get him back that they agreed to pay all relocation expenses, including any loss he might have in selling his executive home. Since their old home in Boston had not yet sold, they moved right back in and as far as we know have been happy to this day. Jerry still proudly drives the fire-engine-red SUV.

MAMMON AND THE ADVERTISERS

There might be some excuse for Jerry to have an SUV in Boston with its difficult weather and abominable traffic. The chief of the city's police department told us face to face, "As you enter any traffic circle here, whatever you do, don't make eye contact with any other driver. If you do, you lose." But that aside, it's not difficult to figure out that Jerry bought his SUV as an ego booster. He boosted his ego so far that he almost totally ruined his life.

The higher you get up the executive chain, people assume, the more executive toys you must own. If you don't own your own Gulfstream airplane or a yacht, well, you're a nobody. Somewhere along the line you pick up a personal masseur, a hairdresser, a nutritionist, a barber who visits you in your office, a tailor, and all the other expensive entourage of a top-level executive. (So far as we've heard, few to date have a personal chaplain.) The company totally owns you and your life. And to keep the ownership fresh, they provide you with every comfort they can think of, including a "social secretary" as well as hot and cold running flunkies. Million-dollar bonuses are becoming almost commonplace in this dizzying world.

Sometimes we ask audiences, "If you won the lottery, what would you do?" Invariably the first response is, "I'd go on a world tour." This is rapidly followed by "I'd buy . . . a new house" or "a new car" or "a new . . ." well, you name it.

Then we ask, "So, after you've toured and cruised the world, and bought everything, what then?"

The usual answer is a long silence, or maybe an "Ah, uh . . ."

Where does the line between glitz and reality lie? Certainly it doesn't exist in the minds of the TV advertisers. We are intermittently stupefied by the home-fix-it shows: "Buy a shack for a hundred thousand dollars, pour in a million or two further, and you have thousands of square feet of unusable living space to heat, cool, and furnish." And all of it is decorated in a way that plain hurts our eyes. These people use a beautiful catch-phrase current in the industry. You hear it all during the time they're creating something between a theme park and a museum display, with your money, that you would never in a million years choose for yourself. They say,

Trust me. I'm a decorator.

That phrase doesn't play in *our* lives, nor, I suspect, does it play in Sheboygan.

Let's look under the surface for a moment and decide what's going on here. It's probably true as claimed, that if all advertising were canceled today, the American economy would grind to a halt. Of course most of the citizens (if they still had a job) would very rapidly move out of debt and start living within their budgets.

Mammon is the god of material possessions and greed. The credit card is his emblem and the advertiser is his high priest. Are you or are you not a slave of Mammon? In society as we know it, most of us, to one degree or another, are slaves to this most relentless master.

THE CONSPIRACY

You may not have realized that you are living under a hidden regime designed to make you an industrial slave. From your earliest childhood you are trained to obey and to conform. "Don't color outside the lines." And, "Life is like a football game. Winning is everything. There are no prizes for second place."

To make people more malleable, to enslave them more deeply, companies tend to move any promising employees around the nation. This cuts them off from the support group of their family and friends, so they become more dependent on the job for all their social life. And there's more. The companies also require those same employees to work unreasonably long hours and add stress on stress so that very often relationships break down. Then the employees get even more isolated, now having not even their nuclear family for emotional support. All the while, advertisers bombard them with messages encouraging consumerism. "You are what you own. Live the American dream! Live in debt to your eyeballs!"

It works to the advantage of manufacturers in two ways, of course, to have families break up:

1. The employee is more dependent on the corporation for social well-being.

2. Now there are two households to buy goods where there used to be only one. The company sells more of its products: two washing machines, two hair dryers, two sets of linens, two stereos, and on and on.

In a similar way, churches have found that singles in church support groups are more reliable parishioners than the married couples who tend to stay comfortably at home on Sunday mornings. The deck is stacked against you. Guinea pigs in lab cages are better off.

Politicians, the people who make the laws (and carefully exclude themselves from having to obey them), also gain by having more singles. Singles don't vote! Why else do you think there is a tax penalty to being married?

Does all this sound cynical? It's not a paranoid fantasy of ours; it's the real world behind the scenes.

You owe it to yourself to break out of this malevolent cycle of control. Wrench yourself free. It takes a violent effort. You will feel afraid at times, uneasy. Psychologists tell us that the early training in conformity you get in school is so strong that it takes real trauma to break through. Sometimes the trauma manifests as the executive heart attack. Sometimes it results when the marriage breaks up under intolerable pressures. Many things may trigger it. We believe that with care you can perceive the trap you are in and take steps to elude it. Associates may label you nonconformist (high praise, if they but knew it!) and fear your difference—for Different is Dangerous.

Be an individual. Be proactive. Be free. Certainly it can be done. We did it. And yes, it's difficult and scary. But once we saw the situation clearly, and recognized all the people who gained by our brainless acceptance of life as it's "supposed" to be, in less than a year we had broken out. Gavin will be glad to tell you that he hasn't donned an executive suit since.

V, AS IN VICTIM AND VACATION

Owen J lived a high-pressure life in London. He was born in a small valley in Wales and was always a writer. He found his niche as Welsh correspondent to the *London Times,* and settled quite happily into the relatively high-pressure job, which still kept him in touch with his roots and let him regularly visit his beloved mountains. The *Times* assigned him to cover an event in Washington D.C., and he took the opportunity to have a two-week American vacation. During those two weeks, as the French say, lightning struck. He fell passionately in love with Zoe, a fashion designer from New York City. She was smitten in turn by the romantic Welshman. After a whirl-wind courtship and many long hours of to-ing and fro-ing, Owen gave up his position with the *Times* and moved into Zoe's New York loft. He found a job with a Manhattan advertising agency. He didn't feel much difference in pressure between his London job and the Manhattan position. Although he mourned for his mountains, he made do with visits to the Catskills.

After about a year he began to realize that nobody in the agency took vacation time. He talked to his colleagues to learn that none of them even considered taking time off. They usually took extra pay in compensation.

Owen gradually got grayer, and more and more depressed. Zoe was no longer happy with her dour, depressed Welshman. As with nearly all Welshmen, when depression hit, it hit hard and black and deep. It may be a uniquely Celtic trait.[3] Owen talked to Zoe about vacationing in Europe, returning to Wales for a couple of weeks. Her design world demanded just as much of her as his world of advertising demanded of him. She could see no way to justify taking time off for personal pleasure. Owen quite frankly couldn't understand the American attitude toward vacations. He had been accustomed to his regular two weeks and had been looking forward to his tenth anniversary at the *Times* that would give him three weeks—and then eventually four weeks after fifteen years. All his European friends talked of the vacation time coming to them, and sometimes took unpaid leave to stretch it for a couple of days.

Zoe convinced Owen to visit a psychologist. The psychologist passed him on to a wellness doctor, who prescribed high-intensity light. He convinced Owen that he was spending too much time out of sunlight whereas he had spent most of his youth outdoors. So in the fixtures in the loft, and over his desk at the agency, Owen arranged to have the fluorescent bulbs exchanged for full-spectrum lights. This indeed helped. His depression soon disappeared and he settled down again to his job and his life in New York.

At that time, the *Times* decided to do a piece on Zoe's designs. Of course Owen met some of his old colleagues who were assigned

---

[3] "Believe me," Yvonne says, "when I say I know. Gavin is Welsh. They're masters at what I've learned to call the 'Scorpio Blacks.'"

the job. They talked of sunny vacations in dry Tunisia, and of walking holidays in Nepal. They asked him whether Banff was a good place to go at this time of year, and similar questions. All this put him into one of his blackest moods so far. Even Zoe and the light therapy couldn't pull him out of it. Then one of his journalist friends speculated that Zoe's designs would be a hit in Europe. To make a long story short, Owen convinced her that being in Europe would much improve the visibility of her designs since most American big-store buyers looked at the European fashion shows before the American shows.

Owen and Zoe moved to London. After the usual hassle and settling-in time, Zoe leased a studio outside London in St. Alban's. Soon she became well known in the world of London fashion design. Owen found a cottage near Caernarvon in Wales where they tended to spend long parts of the working week. Zoe regarded their time in Wales as her weekend, and did her design work in St. Alban's on the real weekends. With their new relaxing lifestyle and their new practice of taking extended vacations, Owen's black depressions have become only a memory.

EXISTING, LIVING, FLOURISHING

What sort of life do you lead? Are you balanced? Are you growing? Or is everything just the same old grind? In other words, are you just existing, or are you living a good life but one that's really going nowhere? Or are you flourishing, getting up every morning with joy and anticipation of what the day will bring?

YOUR SPIRIT

Although the body seems to have the appetites, and the mind seems to control the body, Witches do not think in those terms. Your *spirit* is in control. In your heart of hearts, and in your everyday thoughts, you recognize that your spirit "owns" your body and mind. You say "my arm," "my leg," "my mind"—but "I sleep," "I have"—and when you want something, you say "I want." It is your spirit "I" that owns your body.

Thus, even in your everyday speech, you recognize that the spirit, the mind, and the body are separate entities. In the oldest sacred scripture known, the *Rig Veda*,[4] are written these words:

> *A human being is like a driver in a chariot.*
> *The immortal soul is the driver;*
> *The chariot is the body;*
> *And the reins of the chariot are Wisdom.*

You may already have noticed that the spiritual part of you does not seem to age. The spirit of an "older" person still wants to do all the things it did when the body was younger. It gets somewhat frustrated that the older body cannot perform the tasks which the spirit assigns it; and it is still subject to feelings assumed to be the sole property of youth—-anger, joy, bewilderment, hope, surprise— the whole gamut. In facilities where old people are warehoused, visitors may be surprised to observe the youthful thinking (and sometimes the youthful behavior) of the inhabitants. Of course, attendants discourage the residents' behaving in inconvenient or embarrassing ways; they are told, "Act your age!" In fact that is exactly what they are doing; the problem is, they act the age of their spirit, not the age of their body.

The most important part of YOU is your spirit, the "I" or consciousness. Thus, if you fail to pay attention to spiritual things, you doom yourself to a mere existence.

MOON PUPPY AND PATRICIA

Leaders of the Wiccan community have a range of sobriquets to describe various types of persons inhabiting their world. Each type comes in all genders and orientations.

★ *Drama Queen*—These are the people who blow a situation completely out of proportion—they ratchet up the gasp factor, if you will—because (for example) they see a fundamentalist behind every tree and a Klansman under every bed. Many of these individuals grew up in strictest conformity to their parents' conventional norms; thus, when they see anyone coloring outside the lines—deviating from what they have learned to

---

[4] A holy scripture of the Hindu religion.

define as proper behavior, and (worst of all) enjoying it—they get a real knot in their knickers. Their first knee-jerk response is to gasp in horror. The second is to run and tell someone about it, awfulizing the tale by some large factor. In general these are mind-overbalanced, since they have never experienced physical pleasure or developed any spiritual awareness. They also get a great deal of attention for their adrenaline clamor. This is surely the lowest form of psychic vampire—those who crowd into the spotlight at the expense of others.

★ *Turkey Dog R. D. or R. C.*—Use your imagination about what "R. D." and "R. C." stand for. Let's just say that, in an excess of enthusiasm for the new world of adulthood they've discovered, they've rubbed themselves raw. Most of the Turkey Dogs are male, though some are not. They parade around displaying themselves (especially their raw parts), hoping to conquer[5] everything in sight. Here we have the archetypal body lover, not awfully long on thought processes; and spirituality might as well be on another planet.

★ *Moon Puppy*—Moon puppies tend to run young in years. Whatever their age, they believe the spirit and magic can do everything—including balance their checkbook, prevent the spread of social diseases, serve as contraception, and feed the large friendly canine accompanying them.

Jenny is a moon puppy. She is typical of a certain kind of Witch—and curiously enough, nothing really disastrous ever seems to happen in her life.[6] When she dropped out of college, Jenny started to hang around with rap groups. At one point, she went to Europe to become a constant attendee at rave events. The stories she tells about this phase of her life are enough to lift any parent's hair clean off their head. To hear her tell it, she was smuggled across borders when she had no passport; the group continually moved drugs back and forth; there were all-night gigs involving a range of strenuous activities. A brief stay in a Tunisian jail helped her grow up in a hurry, and she gratefully returned to the States.

---

[5] *Conquer* is a euphemism.

[6] We speak of Moon Puppy as a female, although there are quite a few males in this category. We do not mean to be politically incorrect, but we have hundreds of examples in our files of Jennies and only a few male types.

Although she realized that Daddy, her local senator, and the State Department had secured her release, she still felt that her spiritual life was everything. Now Jenny wanted to settle down, but she was still a moon puppy; she still believed that her spirit would lead her and that magic would solve every problem. Of course her problems included such mundane matters as no job, no significant other, and no money. For a long-term address she used her old room in her parents' home.

Jenny decided that as a first step she would spell herself a new companion. Let's watch over her tattooed shoulder.

For all her colorful lifestyle, Jenny was at heart a pleasant, intelligent girl with only a couple of notches on her headboard. She and her best friend, Patricia, had met in high school. Pat was the flip side of Jenny: She held a responsible middle-management position in an electronics factory. Pat and Jenny usually managed to go out together once or twice a week. On one of these regular evenings out, Pat brought along her latest conquest, Erin. At the moment of introduction, lightning struck Jenny. Erin seemed interested, but not enamored. On a date the next week Pat confided to Jenny that Erin was much too much a fixer-upper for her; despite his attractive bod and his skills in bed, she was looking for a way to dump him.

Jenny confessed she was very interested. "I don't mind," Pat said. "You're welcome to him."

"Can you get me a picture and maybe something personal?"

"Oh, sure."

Pat lived up to her promise and Jenny set out to ensorcerelle Erin. After some thought she decided on a candle magic. She used a red stubby candle to represent Erin, believing that it adequately represented male fire. She carved his name on it. She positioned it on the pair of jockey shorts Pat had given her, and while she looked at Erin's photograph she rubbed oil of orange into the wax of the candle with a caressing motion while she thought intently about fire in his loins.

To represent herself she used a spherical green candle. She laid out the shorts on her altar and set the two candles on them to rest until new moon. At midday on new moon she sited the candles on a table covered with velvet, with the photo Pat had given her and the jockey shorts well in evidence. She put the candles about a foot apart. Thinking bold thoughts, she lit them. After 15 minutes she blew them out and went on her way.

She repeated the procedure for the following 15 days, moving the candles closer together on each day. She replaced the candles as needed and saved the stubs. On the day of full moon she melted all the candle stubs together while she chanted "Ja-Weh." Then she slowly danced a pleasant waltz while she looked into the melted candles.

After her next date with Pat and Erin, Erin went home with Jenny. They were together longer than most—altogether Jenny needed two years to figure out that Erin was never going to work and that she had to get a job to support them both.

At last she admitted to herself that it had been a mistake. Her counter spell required almost six months. She had made her original spell nonreversible, after all, by melting the candles together. Eventually she broke the old spell and was free. Now she realized that she could not put everything into the spiritual side of her life. She finally learned how to balance.

PROGRESSIVE REINCARNATION

Who has not asked himself, "Why am I here? Why is this particular load of dung falling on me at this exact time in my life? Why are some people gay? Why are some children born deformed or diseased or addicted?" Why? Why? Why? So many questions, and seemingly so few satisfactory answers!

One very simple theory, *progressive reincarnation,* offers an answer to all such questions. It suggests a way to understand your path through life.

You already know that you have a spiritual part, the "I." Reincarnation theory postulates that this "I" started out in a simple body at a lower stage of development; that after the death of the body it inhabited, it reincarnated in a new body. There are literally hundreds of cases in which such reincarnation of the spirit is the only explanation for the observed facts.[7, 8] Hypnotic regression is now widely used to explore and heal emotional and physical problems. In every case, the subject recalls previous lifetimes. In many cases, earlier identities can be verified from records that still exist in the physical world.

---

[7] Gina Cerminara, *Many Mansions* (New York: Signet, 1999).

[8] J. Fisher, *Case for Reincarnation* (New York: Somerville House, 1998).

In order to protect their position and to make people come to the church or temple, throughout history religious leaders have preached against reincarnation or have used it to threaten their people. All major religions, including Judeo-Christianity, originally had a strong belief in reincarnation. In fact, if reincarnation were not a valid belief, claims of a second or third "coming" would have to be censored from the Judeo-Christian belief system. It is not difficult to trace the way the belief was erased from Christianity, first by Constantine and later by Pope Gregory. As Bishop Smith[9] pointed out,

> *You can't sell real estate in heaven*
> *If people don't believe they're going to stay there.*

Thus the Judeo-Christian hell became a fiery threatening place where you dwelt forever in torment,[10] rather than a temporary place to synthesize your experiences before you reincarnated.

Similarly in Buddhism, to bully people into coming to the temple, Manu the Lawgiver invented *transmigration,* the threat of reincarnating at a lower level as a repulsive animal if you were naughty. Then *karma* became the threat system. Manu claimed that your every act was recorded in the great akashic record, where it remained to judge you through all future incarnations.

In progressive reincarnation, as it inhabits a progression of ever more complex bodies, "I" grows through the lessons it learns in its identities. That fact gives a reason for being here and an explanation for all the difficulties we experience. Those painful experiences are not some random punishment inflicted by an irritable god with a prostate problem. They resemble term papers: assignments that are not necessarily fun but are essential to growth.

We are here so that our spirit "I" can learn. It learns, for instance, by inhabiting microbes, plants, and animals including the human identity. The spirit guides the actions of the body. The spirit reincarnates on the earth plane specifically in this identity so it may learn what it is like to run a body around, what it is like to feel such emotions as pain, hunger, anger, love, and disappointment. When it has learned all it can in a given incarnation, it leaves the body behind, laying it aside as it would an outgrown garment. It spends a time at home—on the other side of the Invisible Barrier—before returning to inhabit a more complex body with more challenging assignments.

---

9 James Smith, *Pearly Gates Syndicate* (New York: Doubleday, 1971).

10 A hot place sounded good to the Eskimo, so in northern Canada, a Christian's Hell is cold.

We do not know how many incarnations we spend at each level. Personal choice comes into play here. Obviously, if you lead a very sheltered or locked-in life (think of a couch potato watching TV for a lifetime), or a vicarious existence in which you live only through others, you learn very little and have to undergo many incarnations. Refusing an assignment by quitting or by committing suicide means only that you do it all again. Conversely, if you overcome your problems, face your challenges, and live with compassion toward other spirits, you get more done in fewer reincarnations.

Upward, progressive, rational reincarnation is a cornerstone of Wiccan belief. The belief is well expressed in a 12th-century Sufi poem, the *Mathnawi*. It reads, in part:

> *I died as a mineral and became a plant;*
> *I died as a plant and rose to animal;*
> *I died as animal, and I was a Man.*
> *Why should I fear? When was I less by dying?*

Sequences of "I have been . . ." are also found in many bardic poems and Celtic remnants.[11]

> *I have been a drop in the air.*
> *I have been a wave breaking on the beach.*
> *I have journeyed as an eagle.*
> *I have been a blue salmon.*
> *et cetera . . .*

The whole idea can be compared to semesters at school. Each passing grade you complete moves you one step closer to enlightenment. For this reason belief in progressive reincarnation is sometimes called the *boarding-school* metaphor. Figure XII-2 illustrates the orderly progression of this theory. The spirit comes from its home in Side[12] where it has absorbed the lessons learned in its most recent earth-plane incarnation, and again inhabits a selected body on the earth plane. When it has learned all it can from that identity, the body "dies" and the spirit returns to Side. After many incarnations, the spirit is eventually ready to progress to higher planes. Thus, it is sensible to make sure that while it is in a body, your spirit undergoes as many experiences as you can arrange for it.

---

[11] Robert Graves, *White Goddess* (Noonday, 1997).

[12] The word *Side* is related to Irish *Sidhe,* the Otherworld. In some ways it resembles Judeo-Christian "heaven."

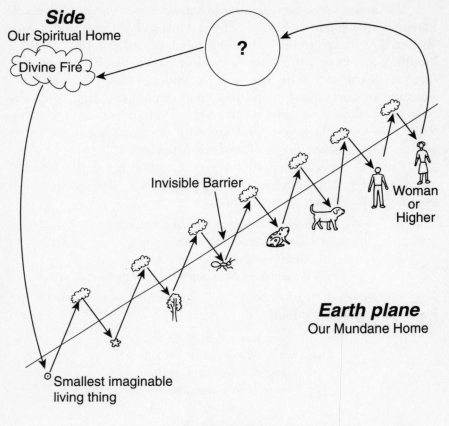

Side
Our Spiritual Home

Divine Fire

?

Invisible Barrier

Woman
or
Higher

Earth plane
Our Mundane Home

Smallest imaginable
living thing

FIGURE XII–2
Progressive Reincarnation

Now you can explain to the elderly why they should remain active and interested in life. Now you can explain to bereaved parents that their child had learned all it needed to know and has progressed: The parents needed the lesson of the bereavement; the child needed only one or two more experiences. The spirit of a deformed or otherwise special child is learning itself—and also teaching those who look after it. Often inside the handicapped body dwells a mind much like yours, that appreciates your love and the explanation which that love prompts.

We know from hypnotic regression that the earliest incarnations at the human level are male and later ones are female. This seems logical for two reasons:

1. The female has more learning opportunities through mothering; and

2. in general females show more advanced spirituality than males do.

Not all males are ready to face the idea that they will someday be females, but the idea is supported by evidence.

Perhaps a gay person has a spirit that has not quite completed a male-gender assignment before moving up to a female. Perhaps (s)he is one who has already completed most of the male assignments and is starting a female learning path. Perhaps one has incarnated as female before it realized that it still has things to learn on the male path. Perhaps the doctor who delivered the baby with immature genitalia simply made a mistake about its gender. The possibilities are endless.

Progressive reincarnation also shows that we are part of a great growth system and that we are part of nature—not above it or separate from it. Each soul carries its own record (its memory) with it, just like a child going to school. The child knows which grade it is in. There is no big computer in the sky keeping tabs on your every misdeed. There is no threatening akashic record by which you will be judged. The record is in your own spirit.

The spirit's natural instinct is to grow and progress. If the child makes a mistake on an exam, it doesn't go back three grades—nor, certainly, is it evil. By *evil* we mean your own perception of evil. You alone can judge this in yourself; for what is evil to you may be a small matter to someone else. Conversely, what was evil to your early peers may be only in their perceptions.

Students learn; they progress. A teacher/guide is surely smarter than a simple earthbound teacher/priest. Your guide helps you progress; it does not punish you for an honest mistake. Thus, you should never feel guilty about honest mistakes done through ignorance. Learn from them; release them; move on with your life.

SUMMARY

Try to achieve as much balance in your life as is possible. When you are balanced and serene, you can start to grow your spirit and avoid needless extra incarnations. Remember, you don't have to do it all this time around. You will most likely be back to try again. Importantly, the term papers you passed this time you won't have to do again, so if you are in a miserable incarnation—one that involves pain—you won't have to do that again either. Every tear you shed is one you will never need to shed again.

For all its perfection, the theory of progressive reincarnation, much like evolution theory, has one drawback. Inherent in it is the implication that our untidy classroom, Planet Earth, must grow ever more complex and our assignments must grow ever more challenging as time progresses. Failing this, we will not expand our consciousness by learning ever more difficult tasks. When we have matured enough, learned enough, become selfless enough to surrender individuality, finally will come that transcendent moment when the individual spirit releases the final vestiges of selfishness and ego, and rejoins the Godhead.

The Witch's Spiritual Path

THE SHADOW AT THE CENTER OF YOUR UNIVERSE

When the chips are down, the person central to your life is you. You matter the most in your life—your comfort—your happiness—your gene survival—your spiritual growth. This may seem like a pessimistic view of your world, and you may argue that you do many selfless things; but are they really selfless? How many do you do for your own comfort; for that pleasant glow that comes after charitable acts; or for your gene survival?

Think about it. If you "love" your significant other, how much of that love is for sexual convenience, warmth, and friendship? If you "love" your children, how much of that love and the nurturing you give guarantees the survival of your genes? We call this reality the *shadow*. It dwells within every human. Some people have a larger shadow in their being than others. Such a shadow allows them to commit antisocial acts without any qualms. Some people feel so repelled by their own shadows that they turn away from all worldly things and become fakirs or dropouts. Until you can recognize and accept your own shadow without denial, you cannot move on.

Many people come to us because, even after they acknowledge their shadow, they find that they need more at their center. An emptiness still haunts them. They endlessly search in the world for something to fill the void. The thing they need is the acceptance of an underlying plan or road map—as the French say, a *raison d'etre*. Wiccans find their reasons for being in the Pentagrammic truth system of their religion, shown diagrammatically in Figure XIII-1.

263

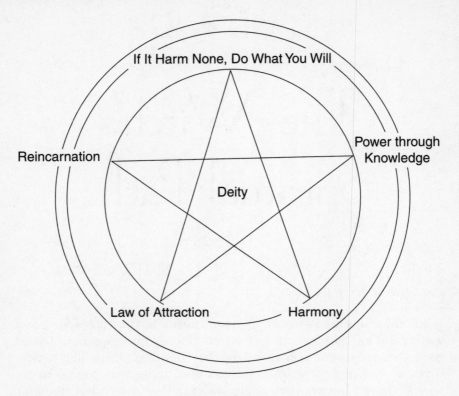

FIGURE XIII–1
The Wiccan Pentagram of Truth

ELAINE CURES HER INSOMNIA

Elaine M is a delightful retired woman living in Phoenix. A friend coaxed her into attending a local psychic fair to hear some of the speakers. At our own presentation we first asked the attendees to articulate their definition of the Ultimate Deity, the god beyond all other gods. We went through the options in Table XIII-1.

When everyone had voted (mostly for "Beyond our understanding"), we hit them with the Catch-22 challenge, "If you don't know what IT is, how can you say IT isn't *all* these—and other things as well?" Yvonne then suggests, "IT isn't either/or. IT's all this and more."

beyond and more than all this

beyond our understanding

The Great Computer in the Sky

thought

a spirit, like Manitou

a duality, like the yin/yang

female

male

TABLE XIII–1
The Ultimate Deity?

Finally Gavin said the fatal words that made Elaine lie awake at night: "Let's imagine that you're a goose. If a goose had a god, wouldn't it be some golden goose in the sky? And if a golden goose is good enough in fairy tales, if the god I'm worshipping now doesn't improve my life, I'm gonna get *me* a damn golden goose."

Two days later Elaine returned, in a state of total bewilderment. She confided to the organizer of the psychic fair that she hadn't been able to sleep for worrying about her long-held belief in Jesus and Jehovah. Her plaintive question: "How can all these people believe differently—and still look as if they have good lives? They look like nice people! Friendly! They behave rationally—but they're so wrong!"

Soon Elaine and Gavin were closeted together. She was still shaking her head after an hour's discussion. Her realization that she had been duped all her life overwhelmed her for a while. For the first time she realized that the images she had been fed were meant purely to control her. They were meant to get her to pay for such things as church buildings, and for the training of people to go out and spread the same manipulative propaganda worldwide. She never reflected on the three vital tools listed in the brainwasher's manual: Shame, Fear, and Guilt.

Through that psychic fair Elaine made contact with a study group in Phoenix. Before long she discovered she *liked* the more wide-open concept, that no one *knew* what "God" is, was, or may be. At her age, this epiphany was a really life-shaking change from the ideas she had dutifully swallowed whole all those years ago. She showed a truly praiseworthy flexibility in laying aside the old dogma and embracing the new ideas that so took her by surprise. Growth can be shocking. It can frighten. Think of it as a leap forward.

THE BASIC TRUTHS OF WICCA

Figure XIII-1 shows a five-pointed star enclosed by three circles. The star stands on two feet; it does not rest on one point or upside-down. An upside-down star symbolizes Satanism, not the Craft. In keeping with our strong belief that "alternative" people gain strength from diversity, we do not overly criticize those pagans and Wiccans who wear inverted stars. The Church of Wicca itself simply does not use one.

As shown in the figure, at the center of the Craft star exists the Wiccan belief in an Ultimate Deity. Five easily understood truths or tenets surround the center.

Five basic truths—five points.
Three circles—three levels of operation and awareness.

Through this book we repeatedly mention one of those five: the Wiccan Rede,

If it harm none, do what you will.

Chapter XII discussed progressive reincarnation. Beyond progressive reincarnation and the Wiccan Rede, those who practice the Craft espouse these basic precepts:

1. The Law of Attraction
2. Harmony and Serenity
3. Power through Knowledge

You could call the Craft a fivefold path to distinguish it from the sixfold path of Judaism and the eightfold path of Buddhism. The five also reminds us that all our five senses should be employed to their fullest.

THE ULTIMATE DEITY

If a spiritual awareness becomes a religion, there must by definition be a god concept. Most of us have some kind of belief in "something out there," a god. If we talk honestly, gods that are based on historical living persons like Jesus or Buddha do not satisfy: They are too small to really fulfill our concept of an Ultimate Deity. But what else is there? All of us realize that somewhere back in time, something started the universe running. No matter how far back you go, in the end you need a *primal cause,* a cosmic consciousness that started everything. In some mythologies Chronos (Time) is the elder god; for it was realized that once time started, all else followed.

Some people play a creation game full of "Yes, but what made that . . . ?" The dust that coalesced for the Big Bang —"Who made that?" The rules that govern an atomic explosion—"Who made them?" And so it goes. People call that "Beginner" by various names—all indicating that we have no idea about IT. The easiest name is IT. Whatever IT is, the Ultimate Deity, the God beyond Gods, IT has no gender and is beyond our comprehension. Certainly IT is free of untidy human-type emotions, as free of them and as impartial as gravity is. IT is so far removed from us that, as the Druids say, "IT is the Thought you cannot think about."[1]

The Buddhist "Void" might help us think about IT; though the word *void* connotes an absence, whereas a belief in IT gives us a belief in the essential unity of all things. Ponder on the thought of Antisthenes, founder of the Cynic school of philosophy, born 444 BCE [before common era]:

> *God is not like anything;*
> *hence one cannot understand God by means of an image.*

Once IT created the reality in which we operate, evolution took over; thus, members of the Craft believe in both creation and evolution. Both principles explain the world we know. Praying to IT this way

> *Please, please, you wonderful Thing I don't comprehend, give me . . . !*

---

[1] Graham Howe, *Mind of the Druid* (Bangkok, Thiland Commercial Supplies, 1973).

makes no sense, for IT is beyond human emotion. IT doesn't have vanity. IT doesn't have anger, or fear, or any other petty human-level emotion. Nor does IT need our prayers—but we need to pray to *something,* and it is best if we address our prayers to the god/esses we make at the human level and thus can understand.

TIME OUT FOR THEORY

Belief in an unknowable Ultimate Deity is called *open, cosmopolitan,* or *syncretic* monotheism. Since IT is unknowable or concealed (*deus absconditus*), there is no grounds for conflict with anyone in another religion. This is the exact opposite of *ethnic* or *closed* monotheism, in which the practitioner claims that the one god worshipped by his group is the only true god. This closed monotheism is well exemplified by Christianity; it explains the constant wars between various Judeo-Christian/Islamic cult sects.

In summary, therefore, Craft practitioners believe in an unknowable God and practice syncretic monotheism. For our everyday comfort and work we also use lower-level god/esses from our pantheon of choice. And many among us turn to the Guides when our work toward a goal falls short.

In this sense, Witches practice polytheism.[2] We recognize both creation and evolution, so we are creation-evolutionists. Consequently, we can find some common ground with most positive practitioners of other religions.

We also recognize that the Earth and everything on it is a result of some First Principle deity—IT—setting the universe in motion.[3] Thus, Nature itself manifests divinity, as do human beings. The long word for such a belief system is *theophany.* Most important: We recognize the divinity of the Mother and the female principle as the producer and nurturer of life. Thus, there will be much discussion of God/ess as well as, or instead of, discussion of God.

---

[2] Wiccans recognize that a multiplicity of gods and goddesses were worshipped in the past and still have power in our present lives.

[3] We do not give the First Principle credit for all the wonders of the world. Instead, we think that every living being has the ability to affect the environment in which it lives. We are the magicians who change our world as time progresses and as needs arise. Atomic nuclei didn't exist before we "needed" them. Think about it, even if it hurts!

To many, all the god/esses that we Witches reach toward can be regarded as aspects of the Ultimate Deity. For instance, we might worship Arianrod, a female deity associated with moonlight,[4] or the ribald Bacchus associated with drinking and good times, and many more. Each shows an aspect of the Whole.

ADAM GETS HIS CHILDREN

Adam and Charlotte C had two pre-teen sons. The marriage was going well until, at around 34, Adam began to reconsider his life. He worked in middle management, but he noticed that he was getting passed over in the promotion process; some junior employees were getting ahead while he stood still. The more he saw this, the less effort he invested in his job, and the more he realized that in his present position he had risen as far as he could. In discussing all this with Charlotte, he proposed that they branch out and start their own business. She violently opposed the idea. It might mean they would lose their membership in the country club—and nearly all her friends were also married to middle-management people in the computer company where Adam worked. "I have to do something," he told her. "It's gotten so I really hate going in to work every morning. Lots of times I just go to the bathroom and read a magazine. I know that eventually they'll shuffle me off into some other dead-end job."

"Go get help. Why don't you talk to Father Sabatini?"

They were both good Catholics. In fact, Charlotte spent much of her time on "good works" for the church, to such an extent that Adam often worried whether their sons were adequately supervised.

Adam joined a men's discussion circle in the church, but he found it very unsatisfactory. Most of the men seemed to be wimps, conveniently blaming their fathers for their own lack of "success." "He was away in the Navy all during my teens," one man complained. "How can anyone expect me to perform properly when there was such a big hole in my life with no father-figure for guidance?"

---

[4] Yvonne enjoys playing etymology games. She finds similarities between *Arianrod,* the French *argent* (silver), and the German *rad* (wheel). Surely it can be no insult to call the moon "Silver Wheel."

That remark set Adam thinking. He talked with one casually dressed man of his own age who had recently joined the group. "I'm gonna quit this stupid bunch of capons," Adam confided to Kerry.

"Me, too. I go to another group you might like. It's a men's drumming circle."

"A drumming circle?" Adam couldn't believe his ears.

"Yeah, but we do a lot more than drumming. Why don't you come and see?"

Adam jumped at the chance, figuring, what did he have to lose? He was surprised to find that most of the people in the circle were pagans and Witches. When Charlotte heard of this she was aghast. All the childhood threats of medieval devils and hell from the Dark Ages rose up in her imagination, and she tried to forbid Adam's ever going to that group again. Behind her back, it must be said, he kept attending anyway and even invested in his own drum.

One Saturday he really got into the drumming and went into an altered state. That began his channeling; eventually he received impressions of walking away from his desk job and investing in a pizza franchise. Without telling Charlotte a thing about it, he quit his job and bought into the franchise. This led to a separation and divorce; no surprise there. During the proceedings Charlotte brought up the subject of Adam's drumming circle and his being (gasp) a Witch. She wanted the judge to rule that as an unfit father, Adam could not have any visiting rights with the boys unless she was present. With legal help from the Church of Wicca,[5] Adam convinced the judge that Wicca was a religion, and since religious discrimination is illegal, Adam's spiritual beliefs were not a matter for the divorce courts.

The judge agreed. He awarded Adam generous visitation rights—probably more generous than he might have gotten if the matter of his beliefs had not come up. The decision did not hurt the boys' feelings.

THEM'S THE CULT, NOT US'NS

The subhead here is in deliberately fractured English. From the way some people talk, from the ignorance they display, you would think they had never seen a dictionary. When you become a Witch, many (otherwise rational) people assume you belong to a cult. We've even

---

[5] See Appendix 2.

heard the Craft called a Witch-club. It is worthwhile understanding that all major "religions" except Wicca are cults—yes, according to the dictionary! This is because their followers idolize purported historical persons.

If we go to the dictionary for a definition of *cult,* we find:

> CULT: a sect adhering to a common ideology or leader, especially when such adherence or devotion is based on fanatical belief or dogma . . . religious veneration of a person.[6]

Thus, it becomes clear that the Craft—Wicca—is a genuine religion, a way of spirituality, because we reach toward Divinity and many different aspects of IT. This contrasts with Christianity, Buddhism, Hinduism, Islam, and the like, which are actually cults based on the veneration of persons.

YOUR PIECE OF THE DEITY

A little piece of IT inhabits the body of every living creature. Although we have no conception of IT, still our consciousness strives to reach toward IT. Because we believe that IT is life itself, and that your spirit is a little piece of IT currently inhabiting a body, we call this spirit the Divine Fire. As the Stoic Epictitus (c. 75 CE) wrote,[7]

> *You yourself are a fragment torn from God.*
> *You have a portion of God within yourself.*

Your "I" carries memories from lessons learned in previous lifetimes plus lessons learned in this lifetime—and perhaps more important, learning not completed. Thus, the "I" serves as a personal akashic record. It contains all that you are and all that you must become before you can escape the wheel of your destiny.

When you share the chalice in Circle, the enlightened people who surround you salute you with the words "You are God" or "You are God/ess." In this way we regularly acknowledge that within each of us dwells a piece of IT, the Ultimate Deity. Because IT is so far beyond our mundane level, IT has no power to operate in the physical world. IT is the Source from which we derive life, but IT cannot make our life any easier on this plane of reality.

---

[6] *New Webster's Dictionary of the English Language,* 1975.

[7] Joseph Campbell, *Occidental Mythology* (Arcana, 1991).

POWER THROUGH KNOWLEDGE

Figure XIII-2 shows the relationship between the Ultimate Deity, you, and the god/esses that you use in your Craft work. You see that the indefinable IT sends divine fire into a living entity—you. This gives the concept of the Fire in the Stone, the divine fire of Spirit within the "stone" or tangible framework of your physical body. Most of us need something to pray to, to ask for help, to blame when things go wrong. These are the god/esses we "worship"—god/esses invented by human beings. *Worshipping* means putting our inborn life energy into such god/esses. That energy is the power that you experienced in the very first chapter of this book. It is operable on the earth plane. It is not power from IT. Yes, it exists because you are alive and inhabited by a piece of IT—but it is not IT power. Instead, it is your own power, sometimes called *bioplasmic energy.* If you're alive, you can't help having it in your body. It resembles the power in an electric socket. You can control it, tune it, and use it, as we have shown you. As you use it, your motivation determines whether it is "good" or "evil," "black" or "white." It has no ethics of its own. It is the same power that you invest in a god/ess, and the same power that ancient peoples invested in their god/esses.

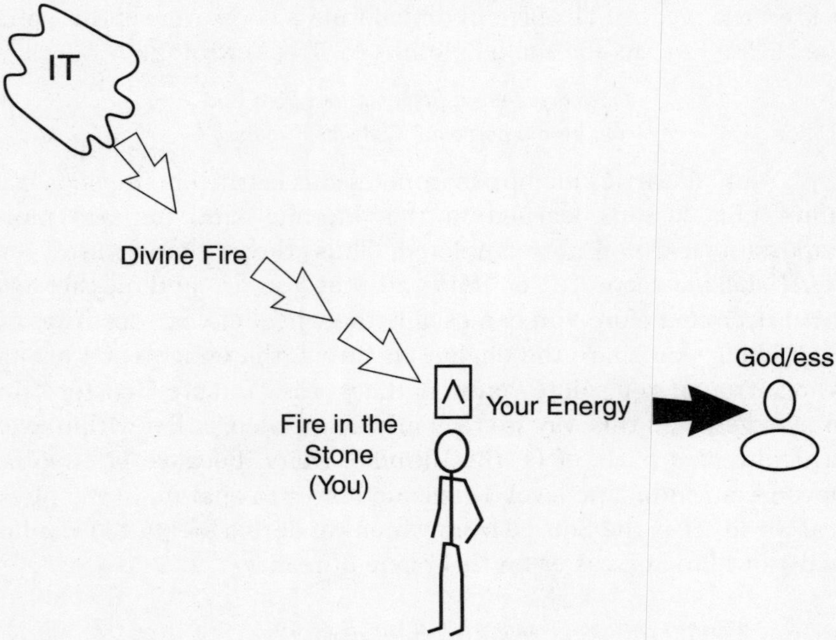

IT

Divine Fire

Fire in the
Stone
(You)

Your Energy

God/ess

FIGURE XIII–2
A Witch's God/ess Reality

Your body's bioplasmic energy operates on the earth plane. It can be strong enough to move heavy weights, but Craft members use it most often to influence future events.

When you want to make something happen which is beyond the powers of yourself or even of your group, you can release the energy stored in the appropriate god/ess to help you. People make them, invest their power in them, and give them a kind of life. It is easily possible to invent and build an entirely new god/ess for yourself. Think up an appropriate name; imagine what that god/ess is like; put appropriate energy into the name. That's all it takes. The Druids say, "You need God/ess, and God/ess needs you"—for without you, that god/ess would not exist. Part of you is within God/ess. You have indeed created God/ess in your own image. To your stone god, you are a god; after all, it derives its energy from you. You control God/ess. God/ess' power is energy to be employed at your level.

When you use the symbols and names of an *ancient* god/ess, you can use the power that countless people put into it as they worshipped it through eons of time. This means that, although you can use the stored power, you should not call it into your own circle of protection; for that old deity may well contain more power than you think or understand.

In all pantheons there are joker god/esses who embody many negative traits. For example, Coyote is the Navaho joker; Satan, the Judeo-Christian; Loki, the Norse; and Pan, the Mediterranean. Avoid calling on such god/esses in magical work, because they always bring unexpected results.

At the head of any pantheon there should be two equal and opposite complementary stone god/esses. For convenience they are often called generically the Lord and the Lady. They may represent Mother Earth and Father Sun, the Crone and the Sage, the Yin and the Yang, or any other pair of opposite, complementary aspects. They have equal importance as personified parts of the Creative Life Force. Depending on the needs of people at a given time, emphasis may be placed on each in turn: the male aspect in time of hunting; the female aspect in time of farming.

Peoples have called the Lord and the Lady by many names: Bel and Ishtar, Jesus and Mary, Cernunnos and Epona, and many others. In our time, because there has been such a long run of male-aspected gods, the balance in the Craft has swung toward the female aspect. To achieve a balance, people who live in cities often need more of the Lady's aspects in their lives; while country dwellers more easily obtain balance by changing their god/ess with the seasons. To keep the balance, we often think of the winter as a time when the hunting male god is dominant and spring and summer a time when the female fertility goddess is dominant.

THE LAW OF ATTRACTION

Whatever you put out, you attract that to yourself. If you are a worrier, worries come your way. If you go out with a smile in the morning, people smile back at you. People gradually recognize that positive thinking gets good results. Many corporations managed by hard-headed businessmen give their executives courses in positive thinking. When one person helps on the path of good, the effect snowballs. Positive actions encourage others to behave positively, and everyone benefits.

In the case of negative persons, the effect reaches just as far. A successful crime, reported in detail, stimulates a rash of copycat crimes. The urge for easy money, for over-indulgence of the body's appetites, and for dominance over others encourage negation. All thoughts and deeds, whether positive or negative, have reactions. This is simple Newtonian physics.

The Wiccan Law of Attraction goes much further than such simple basics, though. For instance, it applies to the world of spirit, on the other side of the Invisible Barrier in Side. Because that world reflects the physical world where we live, if you act negatively, you attract negative spirits to you; their negativity reinforces your own. If you think of negative god/ess images, the power from their negativity also enters your world. A Japanese proverb says with a resigned sigh, "When things are going badly, the bee stings you."

HARMONY AND SERENITY

Being in harmony with those you live with begets serenity; but Wiccans strive as well to live in harmony with Mother Nature and all the cosmic influences that affect the world.

1. *Harmony with Nature*—Every living thing, from the minutest bacteria to humankind and on upward, has a spirit. It may well be that rocks and other "inanimate" objects also have spirits, though so far we are unable to detect them. Spirits can feel, and they respond to the stimuli in their environment. An old tenet of the Craft is currently being hailed as a great discovery; that is, that plants enjoy being treated well, like to have music played to them, respond negatively to death around them, and can predict the future. Every blade of grass that we carelessly trample under foot and mow to suit our needs contains an elemental spirit which is in the process of its own development.

   The key to getting into harmony with Nature means thinking about the feelings of the spirits with which you deal. If you were in their place, would you appreciate what is being done, or would you be injured by it? Would you understand it or fear it? Think toward helping the plant or the animal in its development. When we harvest a plant or butcher an animal, we perform rituals that vividly illustrate to these beings what will happen, why they are here, and where they are going. The spirits respond. When you do these rituals, your thumb will be green and animals love you.

2. *Harmony with the Cosmos*—The seasons follow each other in orderly progression. The tides rise and fall. The moon waxes and wanes. When the moon is full and the tide is high, people tend to behave in strange ways. Studies by the American Medical Association show that the incidence of post-operative bleeding to a fatal extent increases by some 80 percent within four days of full moon. Craft members thus realize how important it is to watch the moon calendar and (for example) avoid going on long journeys or having surgery at full moon. As the seasons follow the Earth in its revolution about the sun, there is an appropriate time for everything.

CHANGING YOUR LIFE

Do you still carry the burden of the early programming inflicted on you? Think for a moment about the labels that are put on youngsters.

★ He'll never amount to anything.

★ He's the dumb one of the family.

★ He's a sissy.

★ She's been hit all over with an ugly stick.

★ She'll be pregnant before she's sixteen.

★ She can't even change a light bulb by herself.

★ That one was baptized in sugar water. That's why she's so sweet.

—and thousands more.

"Follow the path!" the Druid instructs the student.
"Which path, Master?"
"Your path, which is not my path."

Have you gone through life treading a path that you were taught as a child—principally as a means of controlling you? "If you do that, you'll go to hell." "If you do that, the devil will get you." On and on *ad nauseam,* inflicting raw fear on an innocent, bewildered child. It doesn't seem fair somehow, does it? It's time now in your adult life, just as Elaine did, to break out of those constricting bonds and think for yourself. Religious belief is not genetic; you don't inherit membership in the Lighthouse Apostolic Revival Mission from your parents' genes and chromosomes. Browse the smorgasbord of religious beliefs and choose what fits you best—something that doesn't insult your intelligence or strain your ability to reason.

To start to break your early programming, write down now:

1. What are your present religious/spiritual beliefs?

2. If any of them stem from your childhood, figure out who taught them to you and what was their motivation.

3. Was fear or discipline involved in the teaching?

4. Now get rid of the beliefs you don't like. Burn them—give them back.

Decide now which of the following tables you are going to use to describe yourself in your future—Table L for life, or Table D for death.

Are you going to use Table D?

1. Watch sensational, high-adrenaline, awfulizing news broadcasts and violent action movies?

2. Insist on an instant cure for any illness? Insist that you get cutting-edge pharmaceuticals? Be the first kid on your block to try new medications?

3. Avoid nature at any cost?

4. Take no vacations? Make every minute count?

5. Never meditate?

6. Be rigid in your thinking? Be inflexible in your belief system?

7. Be single? Have no friends? Trust no one; open to no one?

8. Have excessive appetites, and see that they are continually satisfied?

9. Ignore other people when they say "no"?

10. Remind yourself that no one needs you?

Or are you going to use Table L?

1. Regularly adjust your endorphins?

2. Do natural exercise? Example: walk in the woods or dance?

3. Expand your roster of skills, both physical and mental?

4. Continually, critically review your way of spirituality?

5. Have a network of friends and family, whether "family" means blood or social?

6. Have achievable goals?

7. Find a loving companion?

8. Honor yourself, your elders, and your children?

9. Show gratitude for everything you have?

10. Dream your dream?

You need to become your own person, so do the exercise above and write down who you are—yes, now! We promise: The thought-police will not come in to arrest you.

Remember that in your life you play many roles: one at work, another at home, another with your children, yet a different one with the buddies you pal around with at the mall or the bar. We are all expected to play roles in life. The more you can be your own person, and the more consistent you are in each of your roles, the healthier you will be and the more content. The more you quit unnecessary role-playing, the more you will feel happy and serene.

Be true to yourself, always the same from one role to the next. A Witch would say:

Walk your talk.

Yet, through your upbringing or your church, most readers of this book have been taught those roles. Your peers make you feel that you must play them in a certain way. If you try to break out and get free of those confining boundaries that you've internalized, your parents and associates at all levels of intimacy will do their best to make you feel guilty. Deviation from *their* norms terrifies them and rocks their very world. Watch your mother the next time you say, "I'm in a same-gender relationship." Does she say, "That's nice, dear," and then wander around in a daze? Do you feel guilty?

The heavy guilt they feel entitled to inflict may make you endure intolerable situations. Time and again we find people staying together in dead and destructive marriages just because of guilt. Yes, they make all sorts of excuses: "What will happen to the children?"[8] "How can I afford to leave?" "He'll stalk me and kill me." But if you are such a person, at heart you know there must somehow be a happier, more fulfilling way—maybe this book can encourage you to put the first foot onto that path.

The religion of Wicca is the fastest-growing religion in the world. The Association of Religious Studies in Santa Barbara, California, says that its membership doubles every three years. Its membership already far surpasses in numbers many of the Christian sects.

WHERE ARE YOU?

Test XIII-1 is a very simple exercise that helps you define what the center of your universe is really like. Do it now, please. This quiz is for you personally; no one else need see the answers.

---

[8] What happens to children who live day after day in an atmosphere poisoned by hate?

1. God is
   a. undefinable.
   b. a kind of ghost.
   c. a superior being who controls us.

2. My attention often focuses on
   a. looking for new insights.
   b. physical and mental order in life.
   c. the futility of my life.

3. I feel that
   a. competition is unproductive.
   b. I'm not good enough to compete.
   c. competition is the way to success.

4. Just for fun I would attend
   a. a reception for a literary figure.
   b. a cocktail party.
   c. a home demonstration of new gadgets.

5. When watching TV I prefer
   a. music.
   b. comedians.
   c. wrestling.

6. In my mind, death is
   a. to be welcomed.
   b. all right when it comes.
   c. to be feared.

7. If I am nasty to someone
   a. it will come back to me.
   b. I can make it up later.
   c. it's the only way to go.

8. Being nice
   a. surrounds me with nice people.
   b. doesn't work.
   c. means I'm always put upon.

9. Wicca is
   a. an age-old belief system.
   b. just another religion.
   c. a way of getting my own back.

10. The opposite gender is
    a. equal to me.
    b. superior to me.
    c. inferior to me.

TEST XIII–1
Your Centering Quiz

MAYBE YOU'RE YOU

We urge you to consider our spiritual path because we have found it to comfort and satisfy. It gives purpose and meaning to our life. It answers that important question: Why are we here?

It may be that you presently espouse another religion and are quite happy in that way. That's well and good. If nothing else, this book can:

1. Help you strengthen your present beliefs.
2. Help diminish any fear of stereotyped Witches.

Of course we have noticed in recent decades that some of the old hidebound religions are loosening up, moving more and more in the direction of the Craft, and acknowledging that there may be valid truths in the "occult" way of thinking. It's a process painful to watch.

Human beings are given a great responsibility. We are given a large brain and a marvelous, multi-functional body shell with which to fulfill the challenge of our lives. Our responsibility, then, is to learn everything we can while on the earth plane, living on the Mother's breast and living off her bounty. Part of that learning must be that we are nothing without the Mother. If we do not regard ourselves as part of Nature and her divinity, then humans continue to make the world a place of sorrow, sadness, and wars.

Almost every day the School of Wicca receives letters telling of the results people everywhere and in every walk of life have obtained when they practice Craft ways. With a little discipline and practice, their powers can be yours. You know in your heart of hearts that telepathy works; you know if you sit in a theater you can make someone ahead of you in the audience turn around and look at you. If you do not yet know it, try it for yourself and see how easily it works. What you have done in this most elementary procedure is to control the mind of another person. No one is immune; and everyone has the power—or if you prefer, the Force—at his or her command. Call it what you will, it works for you.

When you learn to tap into these energies, the weight of a certain responsibility rests on you; that is, the responsibility to use the powers for *good* as you see it in your reality. If you use your powers for negative goals, you will surely draw negation to you. Yes, you can gain money; yes, you can fulfill your desires. But as you explore this magical realm, you will find yourself becoming a different person; for you will learn some of the hard lessons of the Law of Attraction. If you do something negative, negativity returns to you and causes you great pain. Many a man—and woman, too—has thought this ancient Law could be flouted; but there are no exceptions. The coin has two sides: one is privilege; the other, responsibility.

To be a Wiccan is to be a person in control of your faculties and your environment. Thus, you must have a strong reality concept, a concept of what it is all about, within which to work. You learn that the Craft is a most enjoyable way of spirituality, which also has serious moments—and moments of unbelievable joy when your work succeeds.

We encourage you to build a belief system that fits what you know of reality; then work within it to become everything you can. Replace feelings of powerlessness with joy and happiness. Find love. Make your own miracles happen.

Blessed be.

Appendix I

Your Easy Guide to Channeling

In this Appendix you will learn:

1. To get in touch with your subconscious;

2. to contact those in the spirit world, including your personal Guide; and

3. to enter an altered state of consciousness.

These skills will equip you to get your life in order as you begin to tread the Witch's path.[1]

TIME FOR "I"

In this busy world of ours, people get involved in chasing around, watching TV, listening to the radio, solving other people's problems, surfing the Net. Even with the best of intentions, they forget to take time for themselves.

The vicious circle that you get into is this: Your life becomes filled with petty distractions, and all your thinking concentrates on solving immediate problems. When you get a few moments to yourself, you worry about whether you are doing the right thing, where you are going to get more money, how to get ahead in the job, and a thousand other things. Your mind spins the treadmill ever faster. The only way to take charge of your life is to set aside a quiet time

---

[1] For this purpose, an instructional videotape, *Meditation and Astral Travel,* is available through Godolphin House, P.O. Box 297-BK, Hinton, WV 25951-0297, or on the web at www.wicca.org.

when the major part of your mind (which is often totally unused) can take over. If you give it a chance, that untapped part of your mind can give you the information you need, through what we call visions, to proceed on the best path possible. The problem, you see, is that with troubles in the forefront of your mind, the subconscious (the larger portion of your mind) can't get its message through the clamor. This Appendix concentrates on a well-proven method that helps you to use the part of the mind that has lain idle, and to communicate with others who have gone before, who may have a better overview than you do regarding the best solution to your problems.

You are made up of three parts: "I" the spiritual part, "M" the mind part, and "Me" the physical body. "Me" is the source of physical demands. It is constantly pushing at you, demanding attention. "Me" wants to be fed. "Me" wants to have sex. "Me" wants the pretty trinket in the store. In contrast, "I" has no need of such things— but "I" knows that without "Me," "I" would have nowhere on this plane of existence to dwell. Therefore it behooves "I" to give in occasionally to "Me." "M" does the balancing act between the other two components.

Whether you're aware of it or not, you already think in terms of this three-way setup. You say, "I love" and "I sleep," but you talk about "my leg," "my arm," "my body." Almost from your first breath you have lived with the arrangement we are talking about. In some senses there is a conflict among the three parts of your being, yet each needs the other.

To get a handle on your life, you have to call on "M" to convince "Me" to hush its demands for so many mundane things; so long as "Me" clamors to have its demands met, "I" cannot communicate with "Me" or with other spirits. In some ways, this is like a parent trying to get away on a private errand—an errand that an obstreperous child wants to prevent. Every time the parent wants time to itself, the child screams bloody murder, falls down in a tantrum, or even breaks a bone to prevent the parent's departure.

"Me" is a very tough customer. It's been looking out for itself against the world for the whole of your life. "Me" is certain that if "I" leaves, "Me" will become possessed and maybe "die"—but "Me" doesn't want to die! It has all those good physical appetites still to fulfill. What you have to do, then, is deputize "M" to convince "Me" that "I" having its own time represents no threat and actually benefits "Me" because during "I's" trip it looks for things that help "Me" satisfy its appetites. What you do in the end is let "M" make a bargain between the other two parts of yourself. You satisfy the majority of "Me's" immediate demands and then say, "Now it's time for 'I.' If you don't let 'I' go, 'I' will be mad at 'Me' and in future will not satisfy 'Me's' appetites."

In this Appendix we ask you to spend between 15 and 30 minutes a day doing things for that forgotten person "I" who inhabits your body. Before you begin to channel, when you lie in bed at night, or before you go into an interview, or indeed in a thousand situations that may turn difficult, it is very useful to be able to quiet the mind. The gateway and channeling is the safe place you designed in Chapter V.

DAYDREAMING

In the rush of today's life, you rarely spend long times working at crafts or tasks that let your mind drift free while the tasks keep the body occupied. When Grandpa plowed the field and followed the mule, he could channel upon his life and think about other farm tasks. When Grandma's hands were busy washing the clothes, she, too, could think quietly. A couple of meditative tasks remaining in our modern labor-saving world are long-distance driving and weeding the garden. Use these tasks as your chance to relax, to daydream if you will, and to channel, paying attention to all the information your subconscious mind gives you. You owe yourself at least a half-hour a day to do what you want to. No excuses, now. This is an abrasive world. Take the time to become serene; you deserve it.

THE POWER OF DREAMS

Dreams can present to you the intuitive feelings that until now have been blocked by day-to-day problems. Countless scientists give credit for some of their most spectacular discoveries to dream messages. It is well known that Thomas Edison slept in a chair in his lab so he could immediately try out any ideas he got through dreams. The discoverer of the benzene ring, Professor Kugel, got the idea from a dream. Without his discovery, organic chemistry would not exist. These cases are by no means isolated. The sewing machine, the DNA molecule, and the bicycle are all documented cases of dream discoveries.

You may believe that you do not dream; but if you deliberately get more than eight hours of sleep each night, you will find that you do dream.[2] If you want to be sure to dream, eat a heavy meal before retiring and lie in bed in the morning thinking of your safe place. Dreams are at such a low level of the mind, though, that most of them are not recorded in the conscious memory. Even when you wake in the middle of the night after a dream, often you are unable to remember what you dreamed until morning unless you make some notes. Numbers and letters, which can be of prime importance in your life, are often completely lost by the time you finish breakfast. We therefore recommend as a life habit that if you wake in the middle of a dream, you make a few notes, paying particular attention to any numbers, letters, or names that you dream about. Similarly, before you rise in the morning, note what your most recent dream was about.

In most cases your own mind directs and stages your dreams. It tries to tell you something, and you would be foolish to ignore that most important information.

DREAM STATES

Scientists have found that dreaming consists of many different states. One of the most common that they have defined is that called the REM (rapid eye movement) state. In the REM state the closed eyes move rapidly as if watching a movie. In fact, this is the time when you are watching something—be it the play of your own life or a play on a subject from your subconscious mind about ways to solve a specific problem.

During the night you cycle into several periods of REM sleep, but there will also be several episodes when you are apparently quite unconscious. We have found that in these unconscious times the spirit may leave the body and travel astrally. Such astral trips play an important part in understanding the whole religion of Witchcraft, for astral traveling to the sabbat and astral traveling to work for the good of Nature are part of the rich heritage of the traditional Witch. Scientists have shown that these activities of the mind during sleep states are essential to good mental health. When

---

[2] Migene Gonzalez-Wippler, *Dreams and What They Mean to You* (St. Paul, MN: Llewellyn, 1989).

researchers continually wake sleepers and prevent astral experiences, the subjects become mentally disturbed and incapable of functioning. Those who label these activities as "dangerous" are in fact contributing to the instability and mental illness so prevalent in today's world.

The ability to enter these two states, REM and astral traveling, at will requires conscious practice if you are to do it consciously and on demand. Research shows, too, that when you get into these states, the brain wave pattern of your mind changes. You may want to investigate the authors' instructional audios and video on meditation and astral travel.[3]

INTERPRETING DREAMS

In dreaming you receive two kinds of symbols: those created by your own mind, and symbols universal to humanity. What you receive is uniquely tailored to your background and experience. Therefore, in most people's dreams, the symbols are personally biased and cannot easily be interpreted by an outsider, unless the outsider is able to explore with the dreamer the personal, individual significance of the symbols that the dreamer saw.

An example: To many people living away from the seacoast, dreaming of seagulls would be taken as a positive thought, rather than the very negative imagery it gives people who live with the messes gulls create. Not only that, but on an almost minute-to-minute basis, your own symbology changes. You are on the street; you see an accident involving a blue car. In your own mind subtle changes now occur in your feelings about the color blue; from a quiet, cool color it may now become a symbol of death and destruction. Only you can adequately interpret your own dreams; or there must be a personal give-and-take to make clear the meaning *in your reality* of the symbols you saw.

Professor Carl Jung showed that some symbols are universal. Do not take those guidelines as absolutes, however; for your own mind subtly modifies them and gives them meanings significant only to you.

---

[3] On the web see www.wicca.org. Or write Godolphin House, P.O. Box 297-BK, Hinton, WV 25951-0297.

If you constantly dream of rain and water, this probably means you weep inside; so you should analyze your life conditions to learn what causes such sorrow, and should use the techniques we will describe to overcome your problems. Similarly, if you dream of a rabbit in a negative situation, it is quite probable that you have a poor or timid attitude to making love. Recognizing that this attitude exists, you can take steps to remedy it and can make allowances for yourself so as to become more serene in relationships with significant others. Almost any book on dreams contains a useful table of standard symbology.

CHANNELING

We will examine two types of channeling experience: *outward,* where you open yourself up and visions are received; and *inward,* where you concentrate and visualize something that you want to happen.

Control of the mind is the first step toward channeling and toward the visualization and control that are essential to the effective performing of spells. In a spell, visualization of the object in all its details is very similar to the re-creation of your Place that you have already started to work on. Such control of the body is what we call *inward* channeling. It is the same control that the karate guru teaches his students. We might call it *single-pointed inward channeling* or *single-pointed visualization.* For channeling you need to blank the mind so that visions can be received on a clean and empty slate. In both inward and outward channeling, you leave the physical world behind and go to levels where your mental powers are either enhanced or placed in abeyance.

You have probably heard how great outward channeling is for you. All the fashionable hoorah about channeling boils down to the great discovery that if people slow down and spend time alone, allowing their minds to drift, their lives smooth out and become more serene. We have trained without trouble well over 150,000 people in the art of communication or outward channeling. We do not know whether our method is the most simple available, but we are altogether confident that it is safe, effective, and ethical. So as you embark on this new experience, do not skip steps; follow the instructions exactly as they are given.

There is no danger in outward channeling except that when you open yourself up to spiritual messages, you don't want unauthorized spirits to jump into your idling body. Safeguards are built into the instructions. Follow them, and all will be well.

A Witch rarely waits passively for anything, especially for direction along life's path. Passively hoping for a dream or a sign just isn't a very satisfactory way to run your life. During outward channeling, besides getting the two halves of your own mind in contact with each other, you can also reach outward and upward to receive guidance on problems to which you do not know the answers. A great deal of information can also be gained from spirits on various levels in the nonphysical realms. You will most probably have one special spirit assigned to aid you in your work. That is your Guide. Because of the Law of Attraction, this will be someone who closely resembles you in mental attitudes.

If you plan never to work at more than the theory of Witchcraft, you do not absolutely have to channel. Everyone, though, even the most hurried and harassed woman, needs 15 to 30 minutes every day for her own private time in which all pressures are off her, a time to relax.

In dreaming and in channeling, as your awareness increases, you become aware of other dimensions of visions. This can be helpful in the mundane "paycheck" world, and you can reach out into the future to help yourself as well. You might think of this as plugging into the great Cosmic Consciousness to receive information that will make your future more secure and serene.

PROTECTION

"Me" has two reasons to feel concerned when "I" tries to channel:

1. As we noted above, "M" and "Me" worry that they will have trouble if "I" leaves or has time to itself. This concern is overcome when "M" and "Me" acknowledge that you—that is, "I"—have already traveled astrally on a regular basis.

2. In recent years "M" has become increasingly concerned about the supposed horrors of possession. Movies, books, and whispered stories in the occult community all have made posses-

sion a lurid and very present threat to "Me." Psychic protection answers that anxiety. Such protection must be on a level that "Me" understands; that is, it must be in the physical reality and it must convince other spirits that the channeling is protected.

Once you have contacted your Guide, protection becomes a secondary concern and eventually you can omit the salt circle. In these early months, though,

Do not channel without psychic protection.

This is a very real warning. Though the technique of psychic protection is quite simple, it may seem a nuisance. People get into channeling and into astral travel, and think they are above these simple techniques; but the authors have been involved in psychic research probably for longer than you have lived, and we tell you that these techniques are necessary.

FIRST STEPS IN OUTWARD CHANNELING

Imagine you're assigned the task of baking a cake but you have no equipment, not even a stove, and no kitchen to work in. It will take you a considerable amount of time to assemble all the equipment necessary and to get set up. You may even need to develop a new set of skills. The same is true of channeling.

STEP 1

A. Find a comfortable chair. It may be of wood, of wood and canvas, or of plastic; but it must contain no iron or steel or material of animal origin, and the very minimum of nonferrous metal. Metals, especially ferrous metals, become magnetized. You are working with minute electrical and magnetic impulses, and all outside interference must be reduced to a minimum.[4] Make sure the chair supports you so you can sit comfortably for 15 minutes without moving. Sit in it and read a book, but don't move your body; only your hands and head.

---

[4] If you have a metal brace or surgical implant, the body and mind seem able to adjust to it; it will be no hindrance to channeling. The same is true if you are incarcerated. In many cases, because the need is so strong, inmates have little trouble channeling.

Is the chair really comfortable? If not, find one that is. Or you may sit yoga-style without a chair.

B. Find a quiet-running mechanical timer. Nowadays most kitchens have such a timer. Check yours for running noise, because too loud a ticking has a hypnotic effect on some people.

C. Find a loose flowing robe, pure white, made preferably from cotton or linen. Synthetic fabrics are not acceptable. A wrap-around front-opening dressing gown is ideal. In climates where nudity is comfortable, this is preferable; but if cold distracts your mind, wear the robe.

D. Find a container of kosher salt, or obtain some sea salt.[5]

STEP 2

Select a site. Somewhere in your home there is a spot suitable for channeling. In order of importance the requirements are:

A. A solid wall running north and south.

B. An area along this wall that is not near heavy electric cabling or appliances.

C. An absolute minimum of clutter. Books and newspapers are especially undesirable because of the busy thought patterns they engender.

D. A location as close to the sky as possible though retaining a connection with the daily life of the house. In California this might be a patio; in colder climates it might be the master bedroom.

STEP 3

Establish a time and stick with it. The factors influencing your choice of time vary from individual to individual, but here are some things that should be considered.

A. When will you be able to be uninterrupted?

B. Can you keep the appointment each day unless something unforeseen interferes?

---

[5] Kosher salt and sea salt have a different crystalline structure than ordinary table salt.

C. Will your mind be free of petty work and household problems during the chosen time? That is, is it far enough removed from outside distractions so you can let your mind float without being tugged back?

D. At the time you have chosen, is the sun below the horizon?

STEP 4

The trial run. Let us say you have selected dawn or 6 A.M. as your test period. Ideally you will have slept with a partner and feel free of sexual tension. By morning most of life's cares have been dropped and are not so oppressive that they intrude. For the trial run, get up about 5:45. Shower or bathe (men should also shave unless they habitually wear a beard); put on your clean robe, and go to your selected area. If your wall is not quite true north-south, arrange the chair so you directly face east or west. Subdue the light entering the room. Turn off any mechanical contrivances, and shut off the power from cables nearby. Use salt to draw an unbroken circle around you clockwise on the floor. Set the timer for five minutes. Sit with your back to the wall, preferably facing east, though west is also acceptable. Have your legs uncrossed, your hands resting on your thighs with palms up. Tilt your head very slightly back. (If sitting in a chair feels unnatural even after sincere trials, lie flat on your back on a soft pallet free of ferrous metal, with your head to the north.) When you settle in and feel comfortable, absolutely relax all muscles in your body.

To relax your muscles properly, the easiest way is to tense them, then relax them. This simple technique seems to have been forgotten over the years, but it works extremely well. Try it for a moment with your hand and arm. Tense every muscle in your arm and in your hand as though you were going to hit someone very hard with your fist. Hold it tense for five seconds, as hard as you can grip. Now relax, totally, from your very fingertips all the way up to your shoulder. You will feel your arm go completely limp. You can do the same thing with each arm, with your legs, and with your stomach and chest muscles—even with your face and scalp. It is usual to do the legs first, then the stomach and chest, and then the arms.

When you feel relaxed, go to your safe place.

You may encounter annoyances such as noises or areas of bright light. If these come from sources beyond your control, you may have to change the time of channeling. Readjust the setting and set the timer for another five minutes. Try again. Your area and equipment may or may not be satisfactory now, because your sensitivity increases as your eyes adjust to a darkened room.

Continue these five-minute trials until you are satisfied that you have achieved the best conditions possible in your circumstances. This does not mean a setting like a dark room at midnight. Your goal is relaxation. Be comfortable; that's all. Don't be afraid to change the location if you feel another spot in the home would be better. You won't know until you try.

So far you have taken no protective measures beyond the ring of salt, so ignore messages or impressions that arrive spontaneously. If a persistent thought occurs or a persistent picture is seen, immediately protect yourself as described below in "First Channeling," and start again. If the message is repeated, act on it. You are one of the lucky ones who receive immediately. This can occur when there has been a buildup of information intended for you: Messages are so accumulated that they take the first opportunity to come through. After a week or so this initial burst subsides and you can start real work.

Now your preparations are complete, and you can proceed toward consistent communication. You are ready for your first genuine Witch-style channeling.

FIRST CHANNELING

All your faculties are resting and waiting. You are in a state of homeostasis, with all your cravings moderately satisfied. Nothing pulls or tugs at you, either mentally or physically.

Arrange the scene as you have experimentally determined it should be. With the salt shaker draw an unbroken circle of salt around you clockwise on the floor (or on a sheet). Set the timer for 15 minutes. Sit in your chair or lie on your pallet, and make sure you are comfortably settled. With eyes closed, say aloud:

> *Spirits of mischievous intent, spirits of lower entities,*
> *You cannot cross this sacred line.*

Make the sign of the Celtic cross in the air before you. Raise the right hand to eye level, palm down, fingers together and pointing away from the body. Sweep the hand straight down about one foot. With fingers together and pointing away from the body, move the hand to the right at chest level with the palm facing leftward. Sweep across the body from right to left. These two motions are connected by a short sweep diagonally upward from the bottom of the first stroke to the beginning of the second as shown in Figure A-1. Say:

> *I ask the protection of the Elder Ones.*
> *As they will, so let it be.*

The omission of the salt circle and the protective affirmations can result in minor possession. If you live in a fully carpeted house, put down a sheet and draw the circle on it. You may reuse the salt day after day, but you must cast the circle anew each time you use it.

You have around you a permanent protective force field resembling a white veil or halo of light. Mentally open this aura as you open your robe, laying aura and robe back simultaneously. Say:

> *Elder Ones, I am naked in your sight.*
> *My body and my mind are unclothed.*
> *Protect them, and send to me what you wish.*

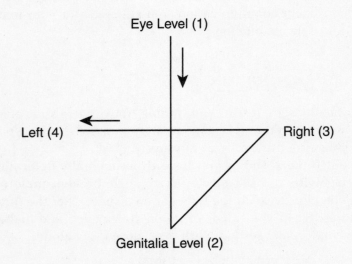

FIGURE A–1
Forming the Celtic Cross

In order to encourage the spirits (most of whom were reared as Christians) and to protect yourself further, it is well to say a modified version of the Lord's Prayer. The modifications are minor, and the spirits feel comfortable with this format.

Our friends who are in Side, blessed be your names.
The Lord and Lady's dominion come.
Their will be done on earth, as it is in Side.
Give us today our daily bread.
Forgive us our weaknesses as we forgive those who wrong us.
Help us endure our trials, and deliver us from negation. So let it be.

Now begin the first mental exercise: the raising of a cone of power. Visualize a tall thin cone. Its base rests on the salt circle you have drawn or on your shoulders, and its point disappears into the universe. Concentrate on this concept a little while. You are putting out thought waves that resemble electromagnetic transmissions; they can pass through any substance. The cone of power serves to conduct messages and impressions to you.

Now in your mind go to your safe place and wait, prepared to receive messages but not concentrating on anything. This is a difficult thing for beginners to do. You may receive many different types of messages, via any one of your senses. Memorize anything unusual.

To review:

1. All conditions are the best you can arrange.

2. You have protected yourself.

3. You have opened your aura.

4. You have raised a cone of power.

Drift now, waiting for the symbols and impressions that indicate you are tuned in and receiving. It may happen at any time: a sudden flash of light or an inspiration. A common first sight is an eye watching you, through whose iris you can see new vistas. A common first feeling is to be drawn up out of the body, floating free where new things are felt and inspirations occur. Whatever happens, don't be startled. Let go. If a white flash occurs at the edge of your vision, indicating the Guide's presence, don't jerk your head around. The abrupt movement disturbs reception, and you will lose the impression.

A typical cycle in development is shown in Figure A-2. Period A shows a buildup of information that has been waiting for you and is suddenly released. It can last for several weeks, and the newcomer feels pretty bumptious and know-it-all. This is followed by Period B, when things slow down and more serious teaching communications begin. The startling communications that typify Period A are over. Now is the time to pay real attention, for these and later messages are the ones that change your life. Sometimes you may receive psychic cries for help like, "You are needed at such-and-such a place." Such cries often cannot be answered in time, so you need to point out to the spirits who insist on your help for such cases that you do not have their freedom and that they must seek nearer aid for the sufferer. But if it is within your power to help, you must try to do it.

After a time that often seems too short, the bell of the timer sounds and you come back to the physical part of life. Common practice is the offering of a short healing prayer to use up the force built up within the cone of power and the salt ring. Say:

> *I ask this great unseen healing Force to remove all obstructions*
> *From my mind and body, and to restore me to perfect health.*
> *I ask this in all sincerity and honesty, and I will do my part.*
> *I ask this great unseen healing Force to bless*
> *Both present and absent ones who are in need of help,*
> *And to restore them to perfect health.*
> *I put my faith and trust in the love of the God/ess.*

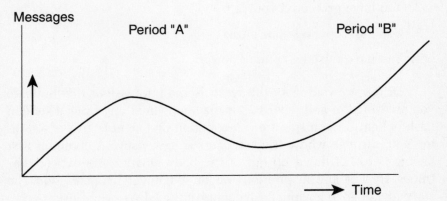

FIGURE A–2
Typical Development Cycle

Visualize the cone of power dissolving into yourself and any companion(s). Direct the remaining part of the cone to travel out to a specific person(s) in need.

Close your robe and your aura. Affirm:

I am surrounded by the pure white light of the God/ess.
Nothing but good shall come to me; nothing but good shall go from me.
I give thanks. So let it be.

Picture the white veil once again surrounding you.

FOLLOW UP

If you have a companion, discuss what each of you experienced. If you channeled alone, write down any impression you received with the date of its occurrence. This clears the message away to make room for new ones in your next sitting. If you are one of the people who have trouble casting off the meditative mood, at the close of the sitting drink a glass of water to which you have added a tablespoon-ful of vinegar and a tablespoonful of honey.

Figure A-3 shows a step-by-step breakdown of this procedure that we call outward channeling, the procedure that seems so complex but is actually simple. The chart also includes a requirement to define your meditative goal. Parts 6a, 7b, and 7c are described later in this Appendix.

Look at Figure A-3, starting at the top of the page at Step 1. This step is easy to accomplish. When you get to Step 2, though, you see there are two paths: either 'YES' downward, leading toward Step 3, or 'NO.' To the right of the 'NO' you see instructions to be followed in continuing your development.

Following the steps in their logical sequence leads you naturally into your first contacts with spirits. Be sure to take these steps every time you channel until you establish contact with your Guide.

START

1. Have you studied the instructions? No ⟹ Go back and study.
   YES

2. Is your mattress/chair comfortable? No ⟹ Get a new mattress or chair.
   YES

3. Is your area secure? No ⟹ Arrange a secure area.
   YES

4. Is your mind at ease? No ⟹ Prepare worry list.
   YES

5. Have you successfully completed the trial run? No ⟹ Complete trial run.
   YES

6. Define your goal:

   A. Inner serenity

   B. Spiritual serenity

   C. Getting answers to questions

7. Have you satisfied "Me's" immediate needs, especially sex and hunger? No ⟹ Satisfy "Me's" needs as far as possible.
   YES

8. Complete protection.
   YES

9. Are you relaxed? No ⟹ Return to appropriate step to complete relaxation.
   YES

10. Channel.

11. Return from channeling.

12. Close aura.

Stop! Write down experiences ⟹ ⟹ now!

FIGURE A–3
Your Flow Chart of Outward Channeling

GETTING IT WORKING

If nothing dramatic happens in their first few channelings, some people give up. We urge you to persist for at least an entire moon cycle of 29 days and to notice how serene your life becomes. Something dramatic will happen; just give it time. As you enter each session, review these ideas:

A. *Is your posture comfortable?* Can you easily go to your safe place and stay there? If you have any doubt, follow this routine every evening before dinner: After the normal chores are completed, sit in the chair for an hour. You may have your favorite drink, and you may read a light book or watch television; but you must not significantly move your body. Do this for a week or longer until you prove to yourself that you can sit still provided your mind is occupied. Now dispose of the TV set or the book, and prove to your own satisfaction that you can sit still for half an hour with muscles relaxed while your mind wrestles with everyday problems. Fifteen minutes of stillness for channeling and communication should now be easier to achieve.

B. *Is your mind free of worldly worries?* It is possible, especially if you have selected an evening hour, that you are still too much in the world. Usually a change of time will cure this problem. If it is not business, school, or household worries, it may be sexual frustration. In this case it is worthwhile trying a sexual interlude before you bathe and robe. Sex helps in another way to get you developed: It awakens race memory. It takes you back to a more primitive time when messages and telepathy were everyday occurrences.

If you drift off into temporal thoughts and problem-solving, when you realize what has happened pull yourself back and start over. In approaching channeling, try these steps:

1. Whatever thought comes to trouble and distract your mind, write it down on a piece of paper.

2. At channeling time, carry this worry list to the opposite side of your dwelling place from the place where you channel. Say to yourself, "I'll deal with all this later."

3. Put a heavy weight on the piece of paper.

4. Proceed with the rest of the steps as you are accustomed to doing.

C. *What is your health situation?* Obviously pain will interfere with any quiet contemplation; but the more insidious feeling of poor health that usually indicates the onset of a disease or a disease already present interferes with the mind. The usual sign that a disease is present is a feeling of warmth or cold in some part of the body. You need to amend the situation before your development can continue.

D. *Are you overtired?* You must be alert but relaxed. Going to sleep is not working at development.

E. *Food and Hunger.* If you are starving, that fact is uppermost in your mind and no message can get through. Similarly, if you are over-full you are just defeating yourself. Keep the body well in balance, satisfied and at peace. Then it gives you little trouble.

F. *Magnetic Fields.* The human mind is an excellent detector of fields; and the influence of fields can be disturbing, even fields induced by ordinary house current. Dr. Rocard of the Sorbonne has found that humans and animals can detect extremely weak fields. We have learned that a magnetized hairpin can significantly interfere with perception of messages.

G. *Lighting.* The easiest thing to do is close your eyes, though some people like to keep theirs open and sit with a dim blue or white light. It is often worthwhile to try a change of this sort. Remember, though, that colors have mental associations and a pale yellow candle flame is still the best for high-level reception.

H. *Knots.* Knots and bindings tend to stop the free flow of energy, and are to be avoided. Among female channelers you usually see free-flowing hair instead of elaborate coiffures.

I. *Timing.* Always use the same time to the minute. Spirits and Guides are busy. If you aren't there to keep your appointment with them, they become frustrated. If you know that you won't be present next time, let them know before you close down the previous channeling period.

J. *Moon.* If nothing is working, or if everything is fragmented and jumbled, check the moon phase. Best results occur just before the moon is full.

If none of these things seems to be the problem, have a glass of wine before starting; make love several times in succession; or take a vacation for a couple of weeks. Go to a quiet mountain retreat. Relax; go out and channel under the trees. Things will right themselves.

Now we have cautioned you, warned you, told you all the pitfalls. Let's be optimistic for a moment and say that it is a rare person indeed who is so turned off that (s)he will not immediately begin receiving under much less than the ideal conditions we describe above. The only prerequisite is practice. "Groove it in," as the training experts say. Do it so that it becomes a conditioned reflex like washing your hands. There are no strange or exotic motions to go through; just protect yourself and relax. Remember, Grandpa did it following the mule, and you do it every night when you dream—so your breakthrough will come in good time.

RESULTS

With time, you will receive a growing number of impressions in dreams, daydreams, hunches, and channeling. The impressions come into some low level of the mind and the conscious mind puts its own interpretation on them before it presents them to you. In this filtering, some information may change or get lost.

As your skill in communicating grows, you will become aware of presences around you. Soon you will recognize one particular presence that visits you again and again. This is your Guide. Ask his or her name, or choose a name that feels as if it fits; when you need guidance, ask this entity for it.

When you have established communication with your Guide, (s)he will tell you when you are developed enough to dispense with the salt circle. (S)He knows, so follow the advice. Then you can move on and channel "with seed," that is, asking questions and receiving answers as we recommended in Chapter I.

Appendix 2

Legal Implications of Joining a Witch Group

The Church of Wicca[1] espouses the religion of Witchcraft as a spiritual path. Despite the fact that the Craft is federally recognized, still many people get into trouble when they commit actions in the name of Wicca (for example, healing, prediction, and others) before they protect themselves fully with the necessary legal documentation. Legal protection proves to authorities and to would-be nay-sayers that they are working within the guidelines of a legal, valid religion. When you use the power or take other Wiccan actions as a solitary, you are not likely to have any mundane problems; however, most of us eventually want to join a group to share experiences with like-minded people.

All over the nation, in such things as divorce cases, women are being harassed and are losing custody battles because the vindictive husband claims "She's a Witch (gasp!) and should not be allowed to raise my children." If you join a Wiccan group, make sure that it has done its paperwork with the IRS, that it's not just a couple of flakes who think they're cute claiming to be a church. If they claim to be affiliated with the Church of Wicca, ask to see their paperwork. If they can produce any, look carefully for an expiration date.

These are serious matters. Like any other human activity, the Craft is vulnerable to fools and charlatans. Don't be taken in.

There are two aspects of the Craft as a spiritual path.

---

[1] In this Appendix, *Church of Wicca* means specifically the body founded by Gavin and Yvonne Frost in 1968.

1. The spiritual/psychic/magical things you do for yourself and maybe for others.

2. The mundane/temporal side. To avoid hassles with the authorities and with people who don't want the Craft to exist, before you purport to heal or counsel, make sure any group you are associated with:

   A. Has done its paperwork with the IRS; and

   B. is registered with your state, your county, and your city.

A NONPROFIT CORPORATION DOES NOT A CHURCH MAKE

Many people who are otherwise intelligent form the Church of XYZ as a nonprofit organization (probably a nonprofit corporation) and believe then they can safely do all the things that a conventional church can do—as they say in Europe, buryings, marryings, and healings. That assumption is false. A church is a different kind of beast, and if it is to earn recognition and tax-exempt status from the federal government, it must be able to meet the IRS guidelines. The IRS says:

> To exempt churches, one must know what a church is. Congress must either define 'church' or leave the definition to the common meaning and usage of the word; otherwise, Congress would be unable to exempt churches. It would be impractical to accord an exemption to every corporation which asserted itself to be a church. Obviously Congress did not intend to do this. *De La Salle Institute vs U.S., 195 F.Supp. 891, 903 (N.D. Cal. 1961).*

> The Tax Court carried that concept further in *Chapman vs Commissioner, 48 T.C. 358 (1967)* when it determined that Congress used 'church' more in the sense of a denomination or sect than in a generic or universal sense.

> Consistent with these principles, the Service does not accept any and every assertion that an organization is a church. We have adopted a ruling position based on historical and practical considerations in arriving at what the Court in De La Salle called 'the common meaning and usage' of the word 'church'. As important as these historical and practical considerations, however, have been our attempts over the years to isolate and distill from authoritative judicial sources those indicia of the existence of a

church that are the most objective and least involved with particular beliefs, creeds or practices. But beliefs and practices vary so widely that we have been unable to formulate a single definition. The determination whether a particular organization is a church must, therefore, be made on a case-by-case basis. It may be helpful to list the characteristics we utilize:

(1) a distinct legal existence

(2) a recognized creed and form of worship

(3) a definite and distinct ecclesiastical government

(4) a formal code of doctrine and discipline

(5) a distinct religious history

(6) a membership not associated with any other church or denomination

(7) a complete organization of ordained ministers ministering to their congregations

(8) ordained ministers selected after completing prescribed courses of study

(9) a literature of its own

(10) established places of worship

(11) regular congregations

(12) regular religious services

(13) Sunday schools for the religious instruction of the young

(14) schools for the preparation of its ministers

These requirements must be included and defined in the SOP (standard operating procedures) of any group proposing to earn recognition as a church. The IRS readily concedes that not all churches meet all its criteria; however, when a body does not meet one of its criteria, the proposers must explain the discrepancy.

RECOGNITION OF THE CHURCH OF WICCA

In 1972 the Church of Wicca earned tax-exempt status as a religious association. Since that time the Church has fought an uphill battle for popular recognition as a valid (nondangerous, though not Christian) church. The battle reached a high point in the Federal Appeals Court of Virginia.

In 1985 in Virginia a judge ruled that inmates who practiced Wicca must be allowed to have white robes, timers, candles, salt, and statuettes. In 1985 in *Dettmer vs Landon,* pursuant to rule 52(a) of the Federal Rules of Civil Procedure, the district court of Virginia ruled that Witchcraft is a legitimate religion and falls within a recognizable religious category. In 1986 the Federal Appeals court fourth circuit Judge J. Butzner, affirmed this ruling in *Dettmer vs Landon (799F.2d 929).* The affirmation clearly sets Wicca as a religion under the protection of constitutional rights. It stated:

> The Church of Wicca is clearly a religion for first amendment purposes. Members of the church sincerely adhere to a fairly complex set of doctrines relating to the spiritual aspects of their lives, and in doing so they have ultimate concerns in much the same way as followers of more accepted religions.

In most cases Federal law supersedes state law in this type of matter. As a result Wiccans everywhere are to some extent protected.

Be aware that the Church of Wicca founded by the Frosts is the only Wiccan church that has such an endorsement.

HEALING AND THE AMA

The American Medical Association (AMA) is gradually coming to accept the idea that a link exists between mind or spirit and body. Still you cannot go out and safely do herbal or psychic healing unless you have a doctor's license on the wall. Subsidiary or ancillary licenses such as nurse practitioner may let you scrape by. To be a psychic and herbal healer without AMA approval, the only avenue is to be a minister of a federally recognized legal church, healing *only parishioners of record in good standing in that same church. In good standing* means that the parishioner has been an active member of the church for many months.

WARNING

When word gets out that you have investigated the Craft and its practices, many people will ask you for help. You must not help them, even unofficially, until:

1. You are a minister of a church recognized by the IRS; and

2. the person seeking help becomes a legitimate member of that church.

The United States has become such a litigious nation that if the least little thing goes wrong based on your advice, you will end up in court. Sorry, troops. That's the way it is.

SUMMARY–COVER YOUR A⁺⁺

In summary: If you want to be a church, go ahead and do the paperwork. If you want to join any alternative church, ask to see its paperwork. Once you are the minister of a church, treat and minister only to your own parishioners in good standing.

All this may sound paranoid—but it's only realistic to acknowledge a sad fact: There are many people who eagerly await an opportunity to dance on the grave of the Frosts and indeed of all Witches. Don't give them grounds to do so. In the words of that cynical precept,

Living well is the best revenge.

Index

A

advertisers, 249
altered state of consciousness, 85, 92
Alzheimer's, 215
American Medical Association (AMA), 306
Arianrod, 269
aura, 131, 128
autoscope, 205
avoidance therapy, 119

B

bag, medicine, 130, 136
balance, circle of, 190
Bel and Ishtar, 273
bioplasmic energy, xvii, 6
blood for surgery, 184
brainwashing, 265
Buddhism, 258

C

carpet as psychostore, 189
cat, Sorceress', 50
celibacy, 69
Cernunnos and Epona, 273
channeling, 32, 194, 283
channeling, sequence of steps, 290
charging of objects, 134
chi, xvii, 65
circle, size of, 49

co-dependence, 157
communication with spirit, 288
consciousness, altered states, 2, 85, 92
conspiracy against consumer, 250
conspiracy, industry/advertis, 250
Constantine "the Great", 258
consumerism, 250
correspondences, table of, 6
cowan, 88
Cross, Celtic, 294
crystals, 6, 60, 131, 164
crystals, charging, 61
crystals, recharging, 61
cult defined, 271
currents, earth, 201

D

death as cure/release, 142
Deity, Ultimate, 3, 267
deosil, 57
Dervishes, Whirling, 56
desensitizing, 113
deus absconditus, 268
development in channeling, 296
diadic HEDE, 80
diet/fast, 83
diseases, sexually transmitted, 83
divining, 169
doctor, allopathic, 102

(ff after page number indicates pages following.)

dream states, 286
dreams, 285
drugs, fashionable, 109
Druid, 273, 276

E

earth as classroom, 259
elements, five, 191
empowerment, 75
endorphin, 97
endorphins 50, 85ff
enemies, spell for removal, 229
energy from the earth, 177
energy, flow of 128, 179
energy, recharging, 163
energy, replacing, 129
energy, sources of, 163, 164
environment, 186
Epictitus, 271
epiphany, xxi, 4
errors in prescriptions, 122

F

familiar, 174, 230
familiar, choosing, 174
fast/diet, 84
fear and body language, 212ff
feast days, plagiarism of, 36
feng shui, 186
fields, magnetic, 77
Force, the, xvii, 201
future, seeing the, 203
future, to accept, 231

G

gender differences to risk, 210

geomancy, 186
god/ess, hearth, 6, 180, 182
god/ess, stone, 58
Gregory, Pope, 258
guide, 77, 283

H

hand of glory, 36
hand, dominant, 61
hand, secondary, 61
handfast, 89
hands, laying on, 9, 11
hands-across-palm, 4, 78, 84
healing, mechanistic, 100
healing, psychic, 128
healing, science behind, 97
HEDE (human/earthdynamoeffect), 8, 56ff, 77
HEDE, diadic, 80
herb garden, 170
herbs in healing, 122ff
Hermes Trismegistus, 46
house cleansing, spell for, 227
hypnotist, stage, 103
hypothyroidism, 166

I

I Ching, 205
illness caused by mind, 100ff
IMPACT, 212
initiation, 103
intent, 6
intuition, 208
intuition, honoring your, 209, 213
IRS, 303
IRS, recognition by, 304

J

joker gods, 273
journeying, shamanic, 85
Jung, Carl, 287

K

karma, 159
Kevorkian, Jack, MD, 143
keys, mind, 39, 6

L

language in spells, 34ff
lares and penates, 180
Law of Attraction, xix, 73
Leek, Dame Sybil, 144
legal matters, 303ff
legal opinion, 304, 305
life, balancing your, 239
life, healing, 224ff
ligands, 98
lines, ley, 64
link, telepathic, 8
links, psychic, 151, 36
Loki, Norse joker-deity, 273

M

magic, xvii
Manitou, 265
Manu the Lawgiver, 258
marriage, terminating safely, 219
mascot as god/ess, 180
masturbation, advocacy of, 99
Mathnawi, Sufi, 259
medicine, alternative, 121
meditation, 283

memory, long, 146
metals and woods, power in, 62
monotheism, syncretic, 268
moon, phases of, 8

N

Navaho Coyote, 273
necessity, urgent, 17, 21
neuroplasticity, 215

O

Ornish, Dean, MD, 104
outercourse, 99
overkill, 170

P

Pan, Mediterranean joker-deity, 273
parasite, psychic, 157ff
pendulum 205, 169
Pentagram illust, 264
Pentagram of Craft Tenets, 264
philosophy, Cynic school of, 267
photography, Kirilian, 46
physics, Newtonian, 274
pieces, soul, 145
PIN, 209
place, safe, 285, 288, 112ff
Pompeii, 180
potions, preparing, 137
potions, typical Witch's, 137ff
power, male/female, xix
power, places of, 6, 64
power, raising in group, 80
power, sources of, 53
prana, xvii

prediction, methods of, 208
protection, psychic, 289
protection, spell for, 225
protection, sphere, of 49
psychometry, 185
psychostore, 182, 183

Q

quiz, centering, 279

R

radiometer, 4, 83
Ragland's Sign, 117
reading, psychic, 205
reality, god/ess, 271
receptor-molecules, 97
recharging, crystals, 61
recharging, self, 64
Rede, Wiccan, 266
regression, hypnotic, 257
reiki, 130
reincarnation, progressive, 3,
    257
relax, 116
REM sleep, 286
renaming, 114
retrieval, soul, 146, 150
Rig Veda, 254
ritual space, 186
ritual, dawn, 177
ritual, format of, 94
ritual, success of, 93
Road Less Traveled, The, xix
Rohrschach ink-blots, 101
rooms and balance, 190

S

Satan, 273

scheduling by moon, 43ff
scrying, 205
self, shadow, 263
self-sealing, spell for, 233
shaman, 80,148,158,177,180
shamanic, 2
Side, 259, 274
signals, subliminal, 208
sky-clad, 82
sleep states, 286
space for magical work, 196, 198
space, work, cleansing 196
spell, 10 steps in, 67ff
spell, caging, 38
spell, love, 91ff
spell, steps in, 21
spells, 221ff
spells, directions, 222ff
spells, timing of, 41
spirit, aging in the, 254
spirit, fragmented, 145
spirits, contacting, 195
star position, 163, 226
STDs, 83
stress as cause of disease, 106
stress, diminishing, 112ff
stress, levels of 105ff
stressors, table of, 118
subconscious, contact with, 283
substances, psychedelic, 86

T

Tables L(ife) and D(eath), 277
talisman, 131
Tantra, 83, 92, 98
tarot, 127, 203
tarot cards, 101
tenets, basic, of the Craft, 266
test: Where Are You Now?, 279

the Mother and pollution, xix
tools, spell for charging, 235
tools, spell for cleaning, 234
triggers, mind, 72
triggers, mind, in healing,
    132, 133

U

Unabomber, 209

V

vampire, psychic, 147, 152,
    168
violence at work, 216
violence in schools, 99

visualization, 13
vril, xvii
vril-eck, 59

W

water as source of energy, 65
Wicca, 2
Wiccan Rede, 266
widdershins, 57
Witch, xvii, 1
Witchcraft, xvii
Wyrd, Web of, 8, 25, 50, 156

Y

yard, megalithic, 49